50 MYTHS and LIES

That Threaten America's Public Schools

The Real Crisis in Education

To
Judith
Thanks for all you do for
all our kids—

David Berliner
Oct 2014

50 MYTHS and LIES
That Threaten America's Public Schools
The Real Crisis in Education

DAVID C. BERLINER
GENE V GLASS

Jesus Cisneros ✦ Victor H. Diaz ✦ Lenay Dunn
Erica Nicole Griffin ✦ Jarrod Hanson ✦ Jessica Holloway-Libell
Jamie Patrice Joanou ✦ Rucheeta Kulkarni
Rebecca Lish ✦ Bonnie Streff Mazza ✦ David E. Meens
Noelle A. Paufler ✦ Ryan Pfleger ✦ Jennifer D. Shea
Monica L. Stigler ✦ Sylvia Symonds ✦ Melinda Hollis Thomas
Amelia Marcetti Topper ✦ Kathryn Wiley

Teachers College, Columbia University
New York and London

Published by Teachers College Press, 1234 Amsterdam Avenue, New York, NY 10027

Library of Congress Cataloging-in-Publication Data

50 myths and lies that threaten America's public schools: The real crisis in education / [19 authors]; edited by David C. Berliner, Gene V Glass.
  p. cm.
  Includes bibliographical references and index.
  ISBN 978-0-8077-5524-2 (pbk.)—ISBN 978-0-8077-7281-2 (ebook)
  1. Education—United States. 2. Educational change—United States. 3. Public schools—United States. I. Berliner, David C., editor of compilation. II. Glass, Gene V, 1940– editor of compilation. III. Title: Fifty myths and lies that threaten America's public schools.
  LA217.2.A15 2014
  370.973—dc23

                                                              2013047389

ISBN 978-0-8077-5524-2 (paper)
eISBN 978-0-8077-7281-2 (ebook)

Printed on acid-free paper
Manufactured in the United States of America

21 20 19 18 17 16 15 14   8 7 6 5 4 3 2

To our nation's teachers, often underpaid and underappreciated, expected to reach unattainable goals with inadequate tools, who still have managed to make our public schools the path to self-fulfillment for generations of Americans

To the educators in our immediate families:

Dixie L. Axt	Jean A. Hollis
Brett A. Berliner	Diane Huntley
Zoe Berliner	Ron Huntley
Laura Braidi	Petra Lish
Dr. Jon Bruschke	Chelsi Lish
Ursula Casanova	Christine Louthain
Ruben and Julia Castillo	Alvin Marcetti
Shawna Crist	Larry Meens
Becca Childress	James P. Shea
Ariel Diaz	Sharon Stowers
Mary Ellen Scully Dunn	Dr. Adam Symonds
Karen Fricke	Michelle Thompson
David Fricke	Geraldine Topper
Sandra Rubin Glass	Kevin Topper
Myrtice Griffin	Lynda Topper
Gregory P. Hollis	Denise Wilson

Educational reform is a euphemism
for the destruction of public education.
—Noam Chomsky

Facts do not cease to exist because they are ignored.
—Aldous Huxley

Contents

Preface

In 1996, one of us (DCB) published a book with Bruce Biddle entitled *The Manufactured Crisis: Myths, Fraud, and the Attack on America's Public Schools.* Whether Berliner and Biddle were first to use the phrase "manufactured crisis" is unclear, but what is less debatable is that the phrase has entered popular parlance as a woeful commentary on our over-politicized times. The 1996 text focused on the false narrative being constructed by certain political interests of that day. By the 1990s, public education was feeling the full impact of the Reagan commissioned *A Nation at Risk* (1983). That narrative spoke of a rising tide of mediocrity and held that America's public schools were failing to teach our children; that student achievement in America was inferior to that in other countries; that Japan was about to bury our economy. At the time, Japan was beginning to dominate the automobile market, but that had to do with short-sighted industry executives who failed to take seriously America's desire for fuel efficient cars. Reagan had received *A Nation at Risk* from his blue-ribbon commission at a press conference in the White House rose garden, and he thanked the commission for their strong stand in favor of vouchers and abstinence education—neither of which is mentioned in the report. But that is a story for another book.

In 1996, we only vaguely sensed the beginnings of an organized movement to destroy public education. What appeared to be an uncoordinated attack by many on the public schools has been revealed, 18 years later, to be an all-out attack on public schools that is both well coordinated and very well funded. We hope the public will heed our current message, namely, that something nasty, unlovely, and undemocratic, this way comes.

A war is raging for the hearts and minds of Americans. At stake is the nearly 200-year-old institution of the nation's public school system —the institution that, more than any other, is responsible for the evolution and preservation of the oldest, most successful constitutional democracy in the world. Opposed in this war are two formidable combatants. On one side are the forces of corporate America seeking to gain a share of the billions of dollars expended annually in support of K–12 education. Enlisted in their cause are the American Legislative

Exchange Council, hundreds of conservative politicians, and a network of Right-wing think tanks. On the opposing side stand thousands of academic scholars, scholars-in-training in our universities, and practicing teachers. We stand unapologetically with the latter groups.

We, the authors of this text, span three generations. The Associates are young enough to be the grandchildren of the first two authors. In total, hundreds of years of experience with the nation's public schools, as researchers, teachers, trainers of teachers, parents of students, and students ourselves, are brought to bear here. One of us—Berliner—is an Emeritus Regents' professor at Arizona State University. Another—Glass—is currently a research professor at the School of Education, University of Colorado Boulder. The Associates were recruited from among the best and brightest PhD students at both institutions. The opinions expressed here are the result of close collaboration among the 21 individuals who share authorship of this book. Although there are thousands of scholars and scholars-in-training in America's graduate schools, these Associates are distinguished by their experience and their ability to put down in writing convincing reasons for their opinions.

We limited ourselves to 50 myths this time because this book is already thicker than the publisher likes books to be. But the next time, if we can, we will do quite a few more. Education will be helped if we can dispel at least some of the nonsense now being broadcast about public schools and the American education system. We expect to update this book with new arguments and new data in a few years. To help us, please contribute to the next edition. Send us your pet myths, hoaxes, and lies about education and we will investigate them. They could find their way into the next edition of this book.

Myths, Hoaxes, and Outright Lies

Myths are beliefs in things that may or may not be true but that fill the void left by ignorance. We focus here on the pernicious myths, that is, the myths that are untrue and which, if believed, may have unhappy consequences for the believer or others.

They arise in at least two ways: personal experience and observation, which are incapable of unraveling the complex influences that typify causal relationships in an area as broad and encompassing as education. Does a good self-concept cause increased achievement or does increased achievement cause a better self-concept, or do they influence each other, and which is the stronger direction? It is no wonder that weakly justified beliefs based on anecdotes and hearsay—let's call them myths—come to fill the emptiness left by decades of investigation.

One of the hallmarks of myths is that they are greatly influenced by the believer's self-interest. Consider the father of a 5-year-old boy who feels that his own athletic career in high school left something to be desired. This father believes ardently that holding his son back a year so that he begins kindergarten at age 6, or having his son spend 2 years in kindergarten, will be of enormous academic benefit to the child. But in his heart—and even unbeknownst to himself perhaps—he wants his son to be bigger and more mature when he takes to the athletic fields in grade 10.

Hoaxes are of a different stripe. A belief that the believer knows to be dubious still might be pushed because it stands to greatly benefit the believer. Perpetrators of hoaxes evidence a willful blindness to contradictory evidence and choose to remain ignorant of more reliable standards for evaluating empirical claims. A hoax has more than one belief wrapped up in it, and in fact some of the beliefs might even be true. Rather than a myth, which can be summarized in a sentence or two, a hoax tends to be a complete false narrative often supported with theories, stories, and case histories. Examples of hoaxes in education would include things like neurolinguistic programming, the Doman–Delacato Theory of Patterning, or the Orton–Gillingham Approach to reading.

The perpetrators of a hoax typically do not know that in large part the hoax is false, misleading, or even detrimental to others. They are the true believers, and they usually stand to gain in many ways by convincing others to believe.

Believers in myths are merely deluding themselves. But liars are different. And fortunately there are not many of them around who hold credible positions in our education system. But they do exist. The liars don't even believe in what they are saying, but they say it to advance their own self-interest. Individuals who claim vigorously that dressing up all the students in school uniforms will cause them to drop all bad behaviors and soar academically may truly believe it to be true, particularly if they own a uniform company. But that doesn't mean they are liars. Take the example of Michelle Rhee. While she was acting as chancellor of the Washington, DC, schools, the rising test scores of the schools under her management frequently were cited as evidence for the effectiveness of her tough-minded administration. Schools with low test scores could expect changes in principals and teachers. During her no-nonsense, business-oriented tenure, Rhee closed 2 dozen schools and fired 600 teachers and 90 principals for underperformance. When a chorus of whistle-blowers could no longer be ignored, Rhee appointed a commission to look into irregularities in the administration of the achievement tests on which she relied and which determined the fate of numerous teachers and administrators. Years later, after Rhee herself had been replaced, she was asked why she did not heed the findings of the commission that in fact cheating on the tests was widespread. Rhee maintained that she never read the commission's report or if she did she only skimmed it and couldn't recall what was in it. It seems highly unlikely that Rhee ignored or forgot about a report that was so central to her entire management philosophy.

Evidence and claims like this seem to suggest that rather than a myth or a hoax, in this instance we are dealing with a liar.

Tony Bennett served as the very controversial superintendent of schools for the state of Indiana. Bennett was narrowly elected Indiana state superintendent in 2008. The Thomas B. Fordham Institute named Bennett the nation's "reformist reformer" in 2011. The hallmark of Bennett's reform strategies was a school-grading system, based largely on achievement test scores, that aimed to discover and hold accountable "failing schools." "Accountable" in Bennett's system meant potential takeovers by the state. Bennett was defeated for re-election in an upset in his bid for a second term. In 2012, the state of Florida hired Bennett as its state commissioner of education. On August 1, 2013, Bennett resigned his position as commissioner of education for the state of Florida after journalists acquired emails showing that while in his position in Indiana he directed his staff to manipulate Indiana's A–F school-grading system so that the grade of a charter school run by a major Republican donor would be raised from a C to an A. Bennett's behavior has been so universally condemned that even ultra-conservative columnists like Michelle Malkin, writing in the *National Review*, opined:

> [Bennett's] disgraceful grade-fixing scandal is the perfect symbol of all that's wrong with the federal education schemes peddled by Bennett and his mentor, former GOP governor Jeb Bush: phony academic standards, crony contracts, and big-government and big-business collusion masquerading as "reform." . . . As a conservative parent of children educated at public charter schools, I am especially appalled by these pocket-lining GOP elites who are giving grassroots education reformers a bad name and cashing in on their betrayal of limited-government principles.

If people know what they are saying is false and do so to further or protect their self-interest—be it money, a job, reputation, or a beloved ideology—then some are quick to call such persons liars.

Did Mayor Michael Bloomberg of New York City lie when, campaigning for an unprecedented third term as mayor, he ran on his education record? He had been told the data he was using were suspect because the huge gains in achievement that he was citing were highly unusual. He ignored the warnings and soon after the election the New York City data were found to be highly misleading. The tests had been made too easy so that large gains in achievement could appear to be the result of his takeover of the city schools. The *New York Times* believes that both the mayor and his school chancellor, Joel Klein, knew the scores were not believable as the mayoral race heated up. What was a lie and what was delusion? What was a lie and what were really blinders put on to protect self-interest? We will never know. We do know the scores were phony and used to help the mayor keep control of the city and its schools.

Why we wrote this book and how we wrote it.

Why we have written this book should be obvious. The education of America's children is one of its most important priorities. That message has been lost on many Americans. We cannot count the number of even our close acquaintances who recite warped opinions about our nation's public schools: They are inferior to private schools; they are among the worst in the world in math and science; teachers should be fired if their students don't score at the national average, and on and on. Many citizens' conception of K–12 public education in the United States is more myth than reality. It is essential that the truth replace the fiction.

The mythical failure of public education has been created and per-petuated in large part by political and economic interests that stand to gain from the destruction of the traditional system. There is an inten-tional misrepresentation of facts through a rapidly expanding variety of organizations and media that reach deep into the psyche of the nation's citizenry. These myths must be debunked. Our method of debunking these myths and lies is to argue against their logic, or to criticize the data supporting the myth, or to present more credible contradictory data. Where we can, we shall name the promoters of the hoax and point out how their interests are served by encouraging false beliefs.

Myth 29 is an illustration. It's about the lack of benefits of pre-school and why the nation should not support such programs. In the short chapter debunking Myth 29, we first present a logical argument against those who promote the myth, asking why so many middle- and upper-class parents pay so much for expensive preschool if it's not worth the expense. If they think it is so wonderful for their kids, why shouldn't all children get these educational advantages? In addition, we found that the data cited by the opponents of universal, publicly supported preschool were not persuasive and had been criticized by many scholars. We also think that the studies we cite in support of preschool are much more persuasive. Finally, we note that one critic of making universal preschool publicly available is a spokesperson for the Goldwater Institute, and, as noted above, there may be a larger agenda behind their not wanting to support public preschool.

In all 50 myths we try to employ both logic and credible data that make our point. Data from education research are often seemingly in-consistent and no one study is ever perfect or answers all questions. We know that. So we have cited only a few of the studies that back up what we say. We have not filled these essays with reference after reference, although we could have. What we try to provide are enough citations for anyone who wants to check our views to do so. And we hope also to lead anyone interested in the subject matter to more data about the particular issue that interests them.

But as difficult as it is to make sense out of sparse or conflict-ing data, sometimes the data are remarkably consistent. For example, Myths 17 and 18 are about school class size not mattering, and how retaining a child in grade (flunking) will prove to be good for the child. Those who say such things might just as well say baby Jesus rode a dinosaur. They are factually wrong. In both of these cases the data do speak quite clearly. Meta-analyses (statistical integrations of bodies of literature) inform us relatively unambiguously that class size does matter and that flunking children is good neither for them nor for so-ciety. Those who ignore these data to promote corporate interests or personal beliefs are certainly deluded, perhaps lying. In our view they also are hurting children, harming families, and threatening our nation's public schools, and thereby our very democracy.

Whose interests are served by myths about our nation's public schools?

Myths and outright lies have one thing in common. They serve the self-interests of an individual or group. This makes them hard to give up by those who traffic in them. Money, jobs, and reputations are at stake. The myths that surround our nation's public schools arise from a set of circumstances that involve the interests of a large class of people. But first, what is it about America's public schools that excites these interests?

Our public schools are about the last institution where children and families of different wealth, ethnicity, and cultural values come together. While the relatively affluent sector of society has over decades retreated further into gated communities, exclusive country clubs, and homogeneous suburban neighborhoods, at least in public schools children of the majority may still encounter other children on occasion. This is a situation not welcomed by all, and it is disappearing.

America's public education system is expensive. Public schools are usually the biggest item in state and local budgets. As we progress through the first couple of decades of the 21st century, the United States spends approximately a half trillion dollars annually on K–12 public education. Each year in cities and counties across the nation, homeowners open letters from their local government reminding them that the largest portion of their property taxes goes to finance the operation of their public schools.

A thumbnail sketch of the U.S. population looks like this: Aging middle-class Whites experiencing increasing economic pressure due to longer life spans and dwindling income share a country with younger Black and Hispanic families who are responsible for the vast bulk of population growth over the past 30 years. The population of public schools increasingly is made up of Black, Hispanic, and Asian students.

The White middle and governing classes wish both to reduce the cost of public education to themselves and to find protected privilege for their children and grandchildren in segregated schools. Many of the myths that you will encounter in what follows serve both of these ends: Cut the cost of schooling; and further segregate schools to the advantage of the White middle class.

Now, as the U.S. Supreme Court has decreed, corporations are people too. And as a person, a corporation has plenty of self-interest in the form of revenues and stock prices. Both revenues and profits will benefit from lower taxes—much of which will be spent at the state level financing public education—and cheaper labor costs. When a manufacturing plant cannot be relocated to China, the corporation has among its alternatives the lowering of labor costs. Public education has a role to play there. If corporations can influence the public schools to teach precisely those skills the corporations need for their workers, the corporations will not have to spend money training those whom they hire, or at least the training they will have to do will be greatly reduced. Much training in STEM—science, technology, engineering, and mathematics—now so popular in the United States, may serve the labor markets but it is doubtful that it prepares children for a full and satisfying life. And as we make clear in Myth 43 about STEM education, it may not even prepare them for steady work!

Some few corporations view the nation's public education system as a source of potential revenues. In the past, private companies made small change from public school systems: Sell them some chalk, a few reams of paper, supply the cafeteria with some cheap cheese. Modern corporations are beginning to view the public schools as ripe for picking big profits. With expenditures in the area of $10,000 per child, providing all educational services through charter schools or virtual schools is an opportunity not to be overlooked. News Corp CEO Rupert Murdoch has called public education a "$500 billion sector in the U.S. alone that is waiting desperately to be transformed." Transformed into a cash cow for corporations like News Corp, we can assume.

So the interests of both individual adults and corporations are served by various devices that cut the cost of schooling and secure special privileges for the politically powerful class. Dig deeply behind each of the 50 myths that we will be discussing and you are likely to find one or the other of these motives at work.

Where do the myths come from and who perpetuates them?

Some myths about schooling and how to improve it are part of folk wisdom, acquired through personal experience and observation unaided by reliable techniques of producing justified beliefs. The history of education is strewn with these myths, many of which have been discarded. Once in the past it was common knowledge that very intelligent youngsters faced a difficult adulthood: "Early ripe, early rot." "Spare the rod and spoil the child" once held sway in grown-ups' minds. Folk wisdom is as often wrong as right.

Although a few of these folk wisdom myths are still prevalent, modern myths about schools (e.g., private schools offer superior teaching and learning compared with public schools) are likely to be articulated and communicated by organized private interests—by various think tanks and organizations that stand to gain from widespread belief in the myths.

Think tanks are a relatively modern invention. And they overwhelmingly represent politically conservative interests. There was a time not long ago when the federal government in particular was peopled by mainly progressive or liberal civil servants. This was no surprise since the greatest growth in the federal government took place during the four terms of Franklin Roosevelt. But after World War II and the Korean conflict and the turmoil of the 1960s settled down, political conservatives awoke to the fact that they were largely without a voice in public affairs.

The scales fell from the eyes of the conservatives when in 1971 one Lewis F. Powell, Jr., a lawyer and member of 11 corporate boards, sent to the head of the U.S. Chamber of Commerce what has come to be known as the Powell Manifesto. (Powell was appointed to the U.S. Supreme Court within a year of his having transmitted his manifesto.) In brief, Powell urged conservatives to adopt an aggressive stance toward the federal government, to seek to influence legislation in the interest of corporations, and to enlist like-minded scholars in an attack on liberal social critics. These scholars should be brought together in well-funded think tanks to do their work. According to Hedrick Smith, the Powell Manifesto influenced the creation of the Heritage Foundation, the Manhattan Institute, the Cato Institute, Accuracy in Academe, and other powerful organizations. Among the second generation of Right-wing think tanks, one may count the Heartland Institute, the Thomas B. Fordham Institute, the Goldwater Institute, and several others.

These conservative think tanks are sometimes richly endowed and are dedicated to the promulgation of conservative ideology in multiple areas—education, environment, crime, to name only a few. They adopt a tone of scientific inquiry and publish policy briefs and appear in the media. Significant amounts of their budgets are spent on public and media relations. It is fair to say that many of the myths that most threaten our nation's system of public education, that seek to slash its funding and turn a formerly egalitarian institution into a bifurcated system of elite services for the rich and meager services for the poor, have their origin and draw their staying power from the nation's conservative think tanks.

The most recent PDK/Gallup poll of citizens' opinions of K–12 education gives testimony to the power of the conservatives' efforts to shape public perceptions. Even though the only credible studies of charter school effectiveness show them underperforming traditional public schools, and even though charter schools increasingly are run by private, profit-making companies extracting many millions of dollars of public funding from the U.S. education system, almost 70% of adults favor the idea of charter schools. Sixty percent would support a "large increase" in the number of charter schools; and a majority believe that "students receive a better education at a public charter school than at other public schools." Notwithstanding the abysmal record of online schools—virtual schools or cyberschools—the majority of persons polled favor high school students earning credits online (Bushaw & Lopez, 2013).

The Powell Manifesto spawned the powerful American Legislative Exchange Council (ALEC). Formed in 1973, just 2 years after the Powell declaration, ALEC has been without question the most powerful influence on education policy in the United States during the past 3 decades. ALEC's mission in education scarcely hints at the radical agenda of free-market reforms that animates its efforts: "The mission of ALEC's Education Task Force is to promote excellence in the nation's educational system, to advance reforms through parental choice, to support efficiency, accountability, and transparency in all educational institutions, and to ensure America's youth are given the opportunity to succeed." The "Private Chair" of its Education Task Force is an employee of the Goldwater Institute. By the mid-2013 legislative season, 139 ALEC-authored bills affecting education had been introduced in state legislatures around the United States.

Working at the state legislature level, ALEC lobbies politicians to attach free-market reforms to state education laws. Favored legislation includes union busting, voter ID laws, stand-your-ground, and zero-tolerance. ALEC is funded almost entirely by corporations. Its successful pursuit of stricter penalties for law breakers has elevated the private prison systems into one of the most successful businesses in the country. Oregon now spends more money on prisons than on K–12 public education. ALEC hands legislators drafts of the bills it wants passed. Of the 1,000 model bills it causes to be introduced each year, about 20% actually become law. Member legislators who do ALEC's bidding are treated to all-expenses-paid vacations for themselves and their families. Although education represents a minor interest of ALEC —prisons, tobacco, and health insurance rank higher in ALEC priorities—nonetheless the similarity of free-market reform bills introduced by ALEC members from state to state across the United States speaks clearly to their origins.

ALEC's corporate and foundation donors include the Koch brothers, Phillip Morris, the Coors family, Corrections Corporation of America, and dozens of other large entities. Connections Academy, a vendor of online education to K–12 charter schools that recently was acquired by the publishing giant Pearson, once co-chaired the ALEC Education Task Force. To add insult to injury, ALEC is registered with the Internal Revenue Service as a "nonprofit charity"; thus, it pays no taxes and is not required to disclose its contributors or the legislators who are the recipients of its largesse. ALEC is the most effective communicator of many of the 50 myths that are dealt with in what follows.

James Meredith, the heroic young Mississippian who was the first Black student to graduate, on August 18, 1963, from the University of Mississippi, spoke candidly and with passion at the 2013 commencement of Harvard's Graduate School of Education on the occasion of his acceptance of the school's Medal for Educational Impact. "America's public schools are being hijacked and destroyed by greed, fraud and lies," he opined.

> The civil rights issue of our time is to stop unproven so-called education reforms from totally destroying our children's public education and to get parents, teachers, community leaders and elders, the whole "Family of God," to take back control of our children's education from politicians, bureaucrats and for-profits, who have turned our public schools into pawns in a game of money and power.
>
> It is time we as citizens arm ourselves with the best evidence and information and take back control of our schools. (Quoted in Ravitch, 2013)

References

Bushaw, W. J., & Lopez, S. J. (2013). Which way do we go? *Phi Delta Kappan*, *95*(1), 8–25.

Malkin, M. (2013, August 2). Jeb's education racket. *National Review*. Retrieved from tinyurl.com/mbxfu5l

Powell, L. F. (1971). Attack on the American free enterprise system. Memorandum to the U.S. Chamber of Commerce.

Ravitch, D. (2013). James Meredith: Public schools are being "destroyed by greed, fraud, and lies." Retrieved from tinyurl.com/m6j7mn5

Myths and Lies About Who's Best: Charters, Privates, Maybe Finland?

Individuals, corporations, cities, states, and countries like to be the best, numero uno, the big Kahuna. It's a source of personal and civic pride to be the best, or to have the best, or to provide the best for one's family. Thus, debates about the best cars, best physicians, and best football teams are common.

Because education has become so important in contemporary life, parents who can do so search diligently for the best schools or the best neighborhoods for schools. They also spread the word about the best teachers in those schools, and may try to pressure school principals to have their child placed in a particular "best" teacher's class. But the logic and data that drive the search for the best in education are seriously flawed, like the endless arguments over whether private schools are better than public schools. In this part of the book, we address some of these areas of personal and national concern.

We start with a myth of great national concern. Is the United States behind other nations in our educational productivity? This often is accompanied by the question, Are we no longer the best? Certainly those who attack the public schools think we have fallen behind and our nation is in danger—"at risk," as a political report of the Reagan administration once put it. But in truth, because we value so many other things for our youth—sports for boys and girls, school newspaper production, debate teams, chess clubs, community service, and the like—over the past half century we probably have never been number one in academic school achievement. But our economy apparently has never suffered as a result.

Our nation has valued other aspects of development of our young students, not merely academic achievement. Many other nations do not have youth that are at all like ours. The students in Korea and Singapore, who study much more than our students, are quite likely, on average, to beat U.S. students in math and science, although it is not clear they do so in reading. But even then, if we produce more than enough math and science college graduates for our nation's economic system, does it matter?

10

Our purported fall from being the best education system in the world is a myth, as is the purported crisis in production of STEM graduates (science, technology, engineering, and mathematics—see Myth 43). Although we probably are not "the best," that is, the highest achieving nation on average, we really don't do badly given the goals we have for the development of our youth and the contention surrounding the conflicting goals we have for education.

Despite relentless criticism, on some international tests we do quite well. Some of these tests reveal that public school students who attend schools with few students in poverty are among the best in the world. But those same tests reveal what we all know, that students in schools that serve the poor are not achieving well at all. This brings the U.S. average down. Thus, poverty in the United States, rather than overall school achievement, appears to be the more important national problem for us to solve. Finland, for example, often is thought to have one of the best education systems in the world. But does it have a better education system than we do, or are its successes in education due to its remarkably low poverty rate for children? In addition to childhood poverty rates that are dramatically lower than ours, the Finns do better than the United States in international ratings of economic competitiveness, technological advancement, global innovation, national prosperity, reduction of gender gaps, and child health and well-being, and they also have less corruption and greater levels of national happiness. Does any of this matter when it comes to the achievements of a nation's schools? You bet it does!

Judging who has the best school system in the industrialized world, as so many nations have been trying to do, is not easy, and it is very dependent on the context within which a national school system functions. In a big heterogeneous country like the United States, few general statements about quality hold for all our students, all our schools, or all our communities. Thus, our standing in the world is often a misleading average value, and averages hide our nation's enormous variability on just about every dimension, particularly the quality of our schools.

Finding ways to judge private schools, parochial schools, charter schools, and home schooling is as daunting as trying to rate the school systems of countries. Some claim that one or another of these systems is "best." But variability is huge in these different sectors of our education system. The lesson is that you cannot really tell, without a lot more information, which is a "better" system. And even then, questions about the "better" system often lead to further questions: "better for whom?" "better on what criteria?"

There is one sector of schooling, however, that makes claims about its effectiveness that stand out. But it is not because of the truthfulness about enrollments or the achievements of the students. This is the area of cyberschools, that is, full-time online schools, which we discuss in this part. They are new, although in many ways they resemble the old mail-order degree companies that advertised frequently on radio and in "men's" magazines. The modern cyberschool appears to have the same rates as the old mail-order schools for finishing courses and degrees, namely, a negligible number. And the degree, if ever obtained, is of dubious quality, even though it seems so modern, delivered by computer! These schools, warts and all, are making a good deal of money in the unregulated market that education has become in many states.

In the end, when you hold constant all the variables that affect school achievement (variables like family income, family members with college degrees, health care, equity for women, treatment of minorities, and the like), you find that it is much more difficult than it seems to distinguish the best from the worst schools. Big differences in achievement in a parochial school, a charter school, or even a national system of education turn out to be small differences, or nonexistent, when you control for the many variables that affect academic achievement in families, schools, and nations. Questions about which nation's school system, and which form of schooling, is "the best" take up too much time and energy and lead to too much political chicanery, given the difficulty of ever answering these questions sensibly or decisively.

∽ MYTH 1 ∾

International tests show that the United States has a second-rate education system.

The results of international tests, measuring how well students read and what they know about math and science, have been used to benchmark a country's educational performance in relation to international competitors. In the United States, student performance is cast in a negative light. For example, following the release of the 2009 Program for International Student Assessment (PISA) test scores, national media sources declared: "Wake-Up Call: U.S. Students Trail Global Leaders" and "Competitors Still Beat U.S. in Tests." These headlines were accompanied by fresh evidence purportedly demonstrating the U.S. education system to be second-rate, ranking lower than systems in "leading countries" like Finland, Japan, Canada, and South Korea. But the drumbeat of "U.S. students lose in international competition" has been heard for decades, going back as far as the 1960s. An international reading test in the 1970s reported "poor performance" for American

TABLE 1.1. International Tests and Related U.S. Ranking

Test	Test Description	Most Recent U.S. Ranking
PISA—Program for International Student Assessment	Measures reading, science, and math literacy among 15-year-old students. Test content is not linked to curriculum, but focuses on knowledge needed for the emerging global economy, as defined by PISA. First conducted in 2000, and every 3 years thereafter.	In 2009, among 34 countries: 14th in reading. 17th in science. 25th in math.
TIMSS—Trends in Mathematics and Science Study	Evaluates the math and science achievements among 4th- and 8th-grade students. Test content closely matches math and science curriculum. First administered in 1995 and every 4 years thereafter.	In 2011, among 63 countries: Fourth-graders ranked: 11th in math. 7th in science. Eighth-graders ranked: 9th in math. 10th in science.

Source. Author's analysis of results published for PISA 2009 (http://www.oecd.org/pisa/pisa2009keyfindings.htm) and TIMSS 2011 (http://tinyurl.com/qf8m7zo).

pupils—far behind the leading nation, Italy. Italy? Oh, and how did the United States and Italy do in terms of economic growth after we found out in the 1960s we were far from being numero uno?

The frenzied media attention given to international test results, ranking countries from best to worst, has been supported by commentary from apparent experts like U.S. Secretary of Education Arne Duncan, who said the 2009 PISA test results were an "absolute wake-up call for America," showing that "we have to deal with the brutal truth" and "get much more serious about investing in education" (Armario, 2010). Comments like this make it seem as though the United States will slip into oblivion by trailing international peers in standardized tests that measure the knowledge and skills possessed by 4th-graders, 8th-graders, and 15-year-olds. But that may not be so. Two of the most prominent international tests are described in Table 1.1, which also includes the U.S. ranking following the most recent exams.

The "brutal truth" about U.S. performance in these international tests, demonstrating that we are falling behind nations we need to compete with, might appear reasonable at first. But deeper investigation shows that many Americans—news reporters and politicians especially—have been duped into believing the U.S. education system is in crisis. International test scores are poor indicators to use in ranking the quality of national education systems, and even worse, in predicting future national prosperity. This was conceded by Secretary Duncan (2010) himself, who said: "The relationship between education and international competitiveness is a subject rife with myth and misunderstanding" (p. 65), neither of which he has done much to dispel.

One of the ways confusion occurs about the meaning of test scores on international assessments is because of the parallels that have been drawn between the Olympics and tests like PISA or TIMSS. Each of these tests has been likened to the "education Olympics," where the main objective is to take home the gold and beat the competition. Unlike in Olympic sports, however, the United States has never fared well in international comparisons of student achievement in math or science, and in 1964 actually took 11th place among 12 countries participating in the first major international study of student achievement in math (Loveless, 2011). This poor ranking, however, predicted nothing about future economic growth among the 12 nations. Associating national rankings on international standardized tests with rankings in athletic events is simply deeply flawed logic. The point that the United States has never led the world on international achievement tests apparently eluded Michelle Rhee, former chancellor of the Washington, DC, public schools, whose education reform organization released Olympics-themed videos depicting U.S. students as flabby, lazy academic "Olympians" who were unable to measure up to the rest of the world, given that the United States ranked 25th in math and 17th in science in the 2009 PISA results. The garish videos proclaimed, "The once-proud U.S. [education system] has been relying too much upon its reputation" and "can't compete with the rest of the world" (StudentsFirst, 2012). Rhee (2012) suggested that Americans do not understand the "dire situation" of the U.S. ranking in international tests, voicing disappointment in the lack of public outcry: "Can you imagine if, in the [Olympic] medal count, we were below countries like Hungary and Belgium? . . . The American people would be going absolutely nuts, and yet that is where we are right now on the academic front."

Unlike the Olympics, which awards medals based on the performance of an elite few, nations participating in international tests are ranked on the performance of students as a whole. International test results reflect the average, not the top, score for each country, which is problematic for diverse nations like the United States. Although the United States leads the world in the number of high performers on international tests, it has many more students scoring at the lowest levels (Bracey, 2008). David Berliner (2014) explained that the modest U.S. national average is reasonably attributed to a child poverty rate (income below half the national median) that exceeds 20%—considerably higher than comparable countries. Such a high rate of child poverty negatively impacts the average national test score. Comparatively, Finland boasts the best education system in the world, depending on which year's PISA results you look at, but has a child poverty rate of less than 5%. Researchers argue that a more equitable ranking of international test performance could be achieved by comparing average test scores for all students attending public schools with poverty rates that are less than 10%. In the United States, if we looked only at the students who attend schools where child poverty rates are under 10%, we would rank as the number one country in the world, outscoring countries like Finland, Japan, and Korea (Berliner, 2014; Riddile, 2010). In fact, the many millions of public school students who go to schools with fewer than 25% of their students living in poverty have average test scores that are higher than almost all other nations that compete on these tests. Presuming these tests hold meaning for future national accomplishments, another disputed claim, then America's millions of high-scoring students will become the leaders who will boost national productivity.

There is more to consider. The language for international tests varies, based on the country where the test is administered. No one is going to test Turkish students' proficiency in reading by giving them a test written in Dutch. Translation issues abound because tests are carried out in dozens of languages (e.g., Finnish, English, Japanese), introducing complications difficult to overcome. Gerald Bracey (1991) pointed to one test where 98% of Finnish students, but only 50% of American students, scored correctly on a vocabulary question. The students were asked to indicate whether "pessimistic" and "sanguine" were antonyms or synonyms. Because "sanguine" does not exist in the Finnish language, the word "optimistic" was substituted, making the question much easier to answer. Can we rightly say that tests given in different languages are of comparable difficulty? The answer is no (Glass, 2012). The media never ask this question, and test technicians prefer that it not be asked and equivocate in their answers. Common sense tells us that no one can produce two significant passages of text in two different languages and make their cognitive difficulty equal. And yet reporters, politicians, and citizens of various countries bloviate over the fact that Latvia answered 1.5 fewer questions correctly than Spain. If they did, what would it matter?

In the Olympics, participants compete against one another using skills acquired through many years of practice. TIMSS honors this tradition by querying students with science and math questions drawn from elementary and secondary curricula. On the other hand, the more widely reported PISA test is designed to evaluate how well students can apply their knowledge to hypothetical standards that test makers deem necessary for full participation in society. In short, PISA tests are not linked to the school curriculum, presenting challenges in interpreting just what it is that people know when we get their scores. Assessing the application of knowledge, as PISA tries to do with a test that is of no consequence for the American students who take it, may yield results that would be different if we asked our students to apply their knowledge in real-world settings where results would be consequential. But we do not have such assessments, and thus it is fair to ask what the PISA rankings truly mean.

It appears that most beliefs about where U.S. students stand in math and science are derived from reports of TIMSS scores from 20 and 30 years ago. "We're number 19!" some journalists shouted. "Number 18" in math is a figure often repeated. But what lies behind information like that? The early TIMSS results that have become fixed in people's minds were obtained under some bizarre circumstances. First, in the 1970s, four nations decided that their students would not be allowed to use calculators; the United States was one of them. Second, when tests were administered to students in their "next to last year of high school," the meaning of "next to last year" differed from country to country. It turned out that students in Austria, for example, were more than a year older on average than students in the United States, and other nations had different average ages. And third, how was the following problem dealt with? Burma, Liberia, and the United States are the only nations of any size not using the metric system, yet that system was the universal choice for TIMSS testing. Tests in the metric system versus tests in the imperial system are not likely to yield comparable results. The insatiable appetite of the U.S. public for information like that produced by TIMSS (and PISA) surely marks a high point in gullibility.

And for the record, in the 2011 TIMSS results, the average U.S. score in mathematics, in both 4th and 8th grade, for the many millions of children in schools where family poverty rates were less than 50% was higher than the mean scores of Finnish children in those grades. Furthermore, the state of Massachusetts participated in this TIMSS study as a separate entity from the United States as a whole. Massachusetts is ranked relatively high in unionization and in preschool attendance, has a relatively low unemployment rate, and has almost universal health care. In short, it is a progressive state with social policies and practices closer to Finland than, say, Alabama. So how did Massachusetts do? It scored so high that only a few Asian countries beat it, and the mean 8th-grade scores in both mathematics and science, for African American children in Massachusetts public schools, were higher than the mean score of high-scoring Finland. Education systems in the United States obviously differ enormously, and average scores on international tests cannot capture that variation.

According to Michelle Rhee, however, the public is highly attuned to Olympic rankings, while showing indifference to academic rankings. Similarly, Bill Gates (2011) argued that per-student K–12 spending has increased for more than 30 years, even while "student achievement has remained virtually flat" (para. 1). Lost in Gates's analysis is the reality that a majority of the increased spending went toward the creation and support of special education, mandated by Congress in 1975. If special education costs are taken out of the school-funding equation, per-student spending has risen only modestly. Furthermore, student achievement has not been flat; the United States has experienced gains in PISA scores since 2006, most significantly among low-income students. The same is true for all students on TIMSS, since 1995 (Loveless, 2011).

The "brutal truth" is that public angst is unnecessarily intensified by the myth that international tests show the United States to have a second-rate education system. International tests are hardly indicative of the strength of education systems or predictive of future national prosperity. Education reformers like Rhee and Gates capitalize on "dismal" international test results to promote unproven school reforms (e.g., high-stakes testing, charter schools, teacher merit pay, the Common Core State Standards), which are discussed in later chapters. These "reforms" are alleged to boost international test scores to reclaim the United States' rightful place at the top of the test results lists—a position we never held. Relying on national average test scores, using only one or two tests, at a single point in time, is very likely to mislead those who make state- and national-level policy decisions. The secrets to economic progress and general well-being are not likely to be found in the scores from a few paper-and-pencil tests.

References

Armario, C. (2010, December 7). *'Wake-up call': U.S. students trail global leaders.* Associated Press Wire. Retrieved from tinyurl.com/prelqy6

Berliner, D. C. (2014). Effects of inequality and poverty vs. teachers and schooling on America's youth. *Teachers College Record, 116*(1). Retrieved from tcrecord.org/PrintContent.asp?ContentID=16889

Bracey, G. W. (1991). Why can't they be like we were? *Phi Delta Kappan, 73*(2), 104–117.

Bracey, G. W. (2008, December 8). International comparisons: More fizzle than fizz. *The Huffington Post.* Retrieved from tinyurl.com/6roo3r

Duncan, A. (2010). Back to school: Enhancing U.S. education and competitiveness. *Foreign Affairs, 89*(6), 65–74.

Gates, B. (2011, February 28). How teacher development could revolutionize our schools. *The Washington Post.* Retrieved from tinyurl.com/47mxu7e

Glass, G. V (2012, February 17). Among the many things wrong with international achievement comparisons. Retrieved from tinyurl.com/nl9su27

Loveless, T. (2011). *The 2010 Brown Center report on American education: How well are American students learning?* (Vol. II, No. 5). Washington, DC: Brown Center on Education Policy at Brookings. Retrieved from tinyurl.com/q5coey6

Rhee, M. (2012, August 30). *The politics of education with Michelle Rhee* [Radio transcript]. Retrieved from tinyurl.com/nhdepq2

Riddile, M. (2010, December 15). PISA: It's poverty not stupid. *The Principal Difference.* Retrieved from tinyurl.com/2emf66q

StudentsFirst. (2012). The U.S. education system vs. the world. Retrieved from www.studentsfirst.org/pages/Olympics

⤚ MYTH 2 ⤚

Private schools are better than public schools.

Policymakers, parents, and the general public have long been told that students who attend private schools receive a better education than their peers in public schools. For many parents who seek to provide their children with a high-quality education, whether for religious or other reasons, private schools may seem worth the associated tuition costs. This is especially likely if the schools attract other high-performing students and presumably better teachers than nearby public schools. Often parents also assume that private schools possess greater autonomy in terms of curricular design and access to resources (OECD, 2011).

These largely unchallenged assumptions have prompted policies intended to increase private school enrollment through vouchers, particularly for low-income, minority students in urban areas (Lubienski, Crane, & Lubienski, 2008). Yet little evidence exists suggesting that private school students are better prepared academically than their public school counterparts, particularly once other factors attributed to student achievement, such as demographics, family characteristics, and other nonschool factors, are considered (C. & S. T. Lubienski, 2013; S. T. & C. Lubienski, 2005). Despite the lack of evidence, many parents continue to choose private education for their children. About 5.5 million students are enrolled in private schools in grades prekindergarten through 12th grade. Private schools enroll approximately 10% of all elementary and secondary pupils in the United States, a rate that has been reasonably constant for years (Aud et al., 2013).

In reality, private and public schools are serving different populations of students. When compared on characteristics such as race/ethnicity, parents' level of education, need for special education services, and English language proficiency, private schools enroll fewer disadvantaged students than do public schools (Perie, Vanneman, & Goldstein, 2005). Researchers also compared the respective private and public school populations participating in the National Assessment of Educational Progress (NAEP) from 2000 to 2005. Private schools enrolled a higher percentage of White students and a lower percentage of Black and Hispanic students than did public schools in all grades (4th, 8th, and 12th) and subject areas (reading, writing, mathematics, and science). In addition, these researchers found that a greater percentage of 8th-grade students who attended private schools reported that at least one parent had postsecondary education, and there were fewer students with disabilities and limited English proficiency enrolled in the private schools. Not surprisingly, over the 5 years studied by these researchers, students in all three types of private schools examined scored, on average, higher on the NAEP than did public school students.

The use of standardized assessment data such as the NAEP actually perpetuates the myth of the "private school effect" without considering other factors attributable to higher student achievement (Lubienski & Lubienski, 2005). Because students' eligibility for free and reduced lunch typically is used as a proxy for socioeconomic status (SES), Lubienski and Lubienski (2005) combined multiple variables (e.g., available reading material and computer access in students' homes, Title I eligibility, parents' education level, etc.) to more precisely measure the extent to which SES differences account for the private school achievement advantage among elementary students. Consistently higher overall achievement among students, in this case among 4th- and 8th-grade students on the 2000 NAEP mathematics assessment, seemed to validate claims of superior academic achievement among students enrolled in private schools. However, once having accounted for the enrollment of higher-SES students in private schools, and considering other variables such as race/ethnicity and disability status, C. Lubienski and S. T. Lubienski (2013) and S. T. Lubienski and C. Lubienski (2005) found that public school students on average outperformed their peers in private schools.

The inability to measure student achievement over time poses another challenge when relying on NAEP data to compare public and private school student achievement. Using a nationally representative, longitudinal database of students and schools (the National Educational Longitudinal Study of 1988–2000, or NELS), Wenglinsky (2007) determined that students enrolled in independent (or secular) private high schools, most types of parochial schools, and public magnet or "choice" schools did not perform any better than students in traditional public high schools, when considering family background characteristics. Interestingly, it also was found that students who had attended private schools were no more likely to go to college, and did not report higher job satisfaction at age 26, than their public school peers. And in addition, private and public school graduates at the same age differed little in their engagement in civic activities.

International assessment data also indicated little difference in achievement between private and public school students, again after SES factors were considered. Based on the 2009 Program for International Student Assessment (PISA) reading scores in 26 OECD countries and other partner economies, the typical private school student outperformed the typical public school student at a rate equivalent to three-quarters of a year of schooling (OECD, 2011). Approximately one-tenth of this "private school advantage" can be attributed to competition between schools, curricular autonomy, and additional resources; however, the ability of private schools to attract and recruit more socioeconomically advantaged and often high-performing students accounts for more than three-quarters of the difference in achievement (OECD, 2011).

Given that autonomy over curricula and resource allocation accounts for only a small portion of the difference in achievement that is not attributable to SES, it is not surprising that the "private school advantage" seen in PISA assessment results disappears in 13 out of 16 OECD countries when public schools are afforded comparable autonomy and resources (OECD, 2011). Given this evidence, critics suggest that some parents who chose private education for their children are perhaps unwittingly "selecting the greater probability that their child will attend classes with peers of similar or higher socio-economic status, [and] that the resources devoted to those classes, in the form of teachers and materials, will be of higher quality" (OECD, 2011, p. 4).

Despite evidence that suggests private schools, on average, do not offer students a competitive edge in academic performance over their peers in public schools, some parents choose private education based on other perceptions. Charles (2011) found that parental perceptions of private school quality were statistically higher among parents of children in private schools than among parents whose children attended public schools in terms of quality of instruction, support for student learning, school climate, and parent–school relationships. While private school students do not academically outperform students of similar backgrounds in public schools, parents' perceptions about these other areas of school life prompt advantaged families to choose private education, ultimately increasing racial/ethnic and socioeconomic segregation in public schools. This continuing trend does little to improve educational opportunities for the middle- and low-income students "left behind" in public schools. And it also separates the wealthier students from a more diverse peer group, defeating the goals of a democratic society, which prospers when there is integration across class, race, and ethnic lines.

References

Aud, S., Wilkinson-Flicker, S., Kristapovich, P., Rathbun, A., Wang, X., & Zhang, J. (2013). *The condition of education 2013* (NCES 2013-037). Washington, DC: U.S. Department of Education, National Center for Education Statistics. Retrieved from tinyurl.com/po7hajq

Charles, G. W. (2011). *Parental perceptions of school quality in public and private schools.* A doctoral dissertation retrieved from ProQuest dissertations and theses, Accession Order No. AAT 3447723.

Lubienski, C., Crane, C., & Lubienski, S. T. (2008). What do we know about school effectiveness? Academic gains in public and private schools. *Phi Delta Kappan, 89*(9), 689–695.

Lubienski, C., & Lubienski, S. T. (2013). *The public school advantage: Why public schools outperform private schools.* Chicago, IL: University of Chicago Press.

Lubienski, S. T., & Lubienski, C. (2005). A new look at public and private schools: Student background and mathematics achievement. *Phi Delta Kappan, 86*(9), 696–699.

OECD. (2011). *Private schools: Who benefits?* PISA in Focus, No. 7. Retrieved from www.oecd.org/pisa/pisainfocus/48482894.pdf

Perie, M., Vanneman, A., & Goldstein, A. (2005). *Student achievement in private schools: Results from NAEP 2000–2005* (NCES 2006-459). Washington, DC: U.S. Government Printing Office. Retrieved from tinyurl.com/nnontcz

Wenglinsky, H. (2007). *Are private high schools better academically than public high schools?* Washington, DC: Center on Education Policy. Retrieved from tinyurl.com/njg4zgo

৵ MYTH 3 ৵

Charter schools are better than traditional public schools.

Charter schools are by far the most prevalent form of school choice for parents and their children. They enroll far more students than do school voucher and district open enrollment programs, two other forms of school choice. In 2010–11, the U.S. Department of Education reported that there were almost 1.8 million students enrolled in more than 5,000 charter schools operating in 40 states and the District of Columbia—particularly in such states as Arizona, California, Florida, Michigan, Ohio, Pennsylvania, and Texas (Aud et al., 2013). Proponents of charter schools can be found on both sides of the political aisle and among parents with high- and low-economic means, living in both inner-city and suburban communities. A broad coalition of support exists for these publicly funded, quasi-privately operated schools, purportedly providing parents with more control over their children's education while also reforming traditional public schools. Apparently charter schools are seen as a gift to our citizens from free-market advocates such as Nobel-winning economist Milton Friedman, the father of this movement (Friedman Foundation for Educational Choice, 2013).

The growth and expansion of charter schools over the past 2 decades have given them a mythical status in the education arena, without much data to support the hype. The rhetoric of success fuels the myth, but reality is much more sobering. Myth spreaders conflate parental agency and school choice, concealing research that traditional public schools typically outperform charter schools; play down the impact of charter school failures; and promote the diversion of resources from traditional public schools that educate most of the kids in this country.

Some would have it that the only parents who really choose their child's education are the parents who choose to leave traditional public schools. In this view, parents are only true agents of rational economic choice when they choose to exit traditional schools. However, more than 85% of K–8 students in Arizona, a state heavily invested in charter schools, remain in traditional public schools even when charter options are widely available (Garcia, 2010). This trend is also true in other states. Keeping one's children in traditional public schools is, of course, also a choice and should not be overlooked when talking about parents' options when choosing the schools that they believe best fit their and their children's needs.

While the research is clear that most parents consider academic performance the top priority in school selection, the literature also suggests that other things, like school safety, extracurricular offerings, convenience, and resource limitations (transportation, parental volunteer requirements, and program fees), also play a role in choosing a school, particularly among minority parents (Haynes, Phillips, & Goldring, 2010).

The promise of charters fervently heralded by many policymakers and education reformers was confronted by reality when the results of the first national assessment of charter school impact were released by the Center for Research on Education Outcomes (CREDO) at Stanford University in 2009. That report found that more than 80% of charter schools are either no better or worse than traditional public schools at securing math and reading gains for their students. It is interesting to note that the states most associated with extensive charter school laws, parental choice, and accountability systems (Arizona, Florida, Ohio, and Texas) rank highest among the states where traditional public school students outperform charter school students. The same report found that Black and Latino charter students at all levels and charter students in high school perform worse in both math and reading than do their peers in traditional public schools. This is significant considering that charter schools on average enroll almost twice as many Black students (29%) as do traditional public schools (15%) in the 27 states that enroll 95% of the nation's charter school students. The CREDO report released in 2013 updates 2009 data and reveals that, overall, traditional public schools outperform charters in math and reading. This is especially true when comparing traditional public schools with new charter schools (those that opened after 2008 and were not included in the 2009 assessment). In some cases, new charter school performance is tantamount to 22 fewer days of learning than traditional public schools. But the 2013 CREDO report does reflect some positive results for charters: Charter schools do better at serving students in poverty and English language learners.

Separating hype from reality in the world of charter schools is nearly a full-time job. The *Chicago Tribune*, in March 2013, hoaxed the public by passing on an apparent invention by charter school advocates who claimed that 19,000 children were on waiting lists to be admitted to charter schools in the city; hence, let's have more charter schools. The reality was that this 19,000 number was not children but applications, with many children applying to 2, 3, 4, or even more charters. And many of these children had already entered a traditional public school or been turned down by a charter. Moreover, the phony waiting list number was at odds with the fact that the existing charter schools in Chicago were reporting numbers of vacant seats in the thousands.

The subtle exclusion from charter schools of students with special needs is common. A Minnesota mother reported her experience with the same charter school in which one of her children was enrolled: "My daughter is a mainstream student and has been attending Minnesota School of Science since they opened. For 2 years in a row I have been trying to enroll my son, who is a special-needs student, but have been told by the school both years not to enroll him because the special education program is lacking and that my son's needs will not get met and was told he is better off in a Minneapolis public school, not a charter school."

For the most part, charter schools that are touted in the media as making conspicuous academic progress achieve their reputation by discouraging enrollment of students who might not score well on tests. In the case of one charter school, the Tucson BASIS school, prospective students were asked to submit a long research paper, an original short story, or an essay on some historical figure they admire. There were interviews of applicants and entrance tests. Parents were asked to fill out a long survey and answer questions such as: "Will you volunteer time each week to help at the school?" Significantly, many of those parents were never asked to make good on their commitment. Strauss (2013) reports more abuses, including an Arizona charter that has applications available for parents only for a few hours per year, and only some people are informed when that will be.

One chain of charter schools has captured national attention—even touted by *U.S. News & World Report* as one of the top 10 high schools in the nation—by the ruthless selection of incoming students and the subsequent "flunking" out of all but the most able. In a grade 6–12 school with enrollment of more than 500 students, one year's graduating class was fewer than 2 dozen students. The name of this chain of schools? BASIS Schools, founded by an economics professor from the University of Arizona.

Although charter school expansion seems inevitable, there are glimmers of resistance. In April 2013, the District of Columbia Public Charter School Board rejected the application of BASIS to open a school in the District. Collecting big fees and constantly testing little children didn't appeal to the Board, apparently. And some years previously, BASIS attempted to open a private school in Scottsdale, Arizona, an affluent city near Phoenix. Attracted, perhaps, by the hefty private school fees of the area, BASIS had pinpointed Scottsdale as a prime target for increased revenues. When only seven students had signed up by the fall opening of this BASIS private school, the executives of BASIS Schools quickly converted the enterprise into a charter school—free to students, but not to the general public, who must foot the bill. This failure of the free market had to be a bitter pill for the BASIS leadership to swallow. The bad taste was surely relieved by the handsome revenues resulting from requiring the state's taxpayers to purchase the services they offered.

It is fair to ask, given the mission of many charter schools, how a student who is at once minority, poor, and needing special services fares in a charter high school. These students have been less studied, and that may be because they are less likely to be admitted to a charter school. Due to the autonomy that charter schools are granted, they influence enrollment through a series of practices, such as placement testing, marketing, specialized curricular emphasis, and geographical site selection, that attract and retain students from higher socioeconomic backgrounds. This practice, known as "creaming," seeks to skim off the highest performing students from traditional public schools. These practices restrict ethnic, social class, and intellectual diversity, and contribute to the resegregation of public schools.

There is a tendency to point to academic outliers as evidence that charter schools are working, much the same way someone might tell rags-to-riches stories to convince us that the American dream is alive and well. But for the millions of Americans who have seen their incomes stall or decline in recent decades, the "pull yourself up by the bootstraps" rhetoric does not hold the same promise it once did. Likewise, millions of American parents are not so easily convinced that charter schools are the answer to their concerns about their children's education. Scholarly research, news reports, and blogs have captured the voices of parents whose experiences with charter schools have left them disappointed, and in some cases angry. When charter schools close, proponents say this is a healthy sign that the free market is working and that the surviving charters must be excellent. "Disruption," the coming and going of corporations, is believed to help a free market attain efficiency. But disruption in education, meaning the closure of charter or ordinary public schools, is a disaster for children, families, and communities. The 2013 CREDO report notes that 193 charter schools included in the 2009 report had closed by the time data collection began for the new study. For young children, seeking stability is a far better goal than is the pursuit of disruption. Furthermore, genuinely free markets exist only in the fantasies of hide-bound conservative economists, and every consumer knows that just because a company is in business does not mean that it is either a good or an efficient company. In sum, Americans may not really want a free market in education, a market that is as unregulated as a local restaurant. Public utilities (like power and water supplies) and public schools are not restaurants or Silicon Valley start-ups. They should not be "disrupted."

Student success is the result of many influences, but the governing structure of the school is not likely to top the list. There is nothing that inherently makes charter schools better than traditional public schools. Alas, the strongest predictor of students' success is related to their social circumstances. The social, intellectual, and fiscal resources, or "capital," students bring with them into schools, whether charter or traditional, are much more important than the structure of the school or even the quality of the teachers (see Myth 9). But even with that noted, the data we have support the statement that traditional public schools do a better job in most instances of educating all students, regardless of their demographic and socioeconomic backgrounds. The myth that charter schools are better than traditional public schools is part of a bigger agenda, best articulated by Ronald Reagan decades ago: " . . . government is not the solution to our problem; government is the problem." Charter schools may not be the solution to our public school problems either, and in many ways the increased funding for new and new types of (i.e., virtual) charter schools, especially those with unproven records of success, may exacerbate problems with our public schools.

References

Aud, S., Wilkinson-Flicker, S., Kristapovich, P., Rathbun, A., Wang, X., & Zhang, J. (2013). *The condition of education 2013* (NCES 2013-037). Washington, DC: U.S. Department of Education, National Center for Education Statistics. Retrieved from nces.ed.gov/pubsearch/pubsinfo. asp?pubid=2013037

Center for Research on Education Outcomes. (2009). *Multiple choice: Charter school performance in 16 states.* Palo Alto, CA: Stanford University.

Center for Research on Education Outcomes. (2013). *National charter schools study.* Palo Alto, CA: Stanford University.

Friedman Foundation for Educational Choice. (2013). Retrieved from www. edchoice.org

Garcia, D. (2010). School reenrollment: Choosing to stay. *Policy Points* 2(4). Retrieved from arizonaindicators.org/sites/default/files/content/publications/PolicyPoints-vol2-issue4.pdf

Haynes, K. T., Phillips, K. J. R., & Goldring, E. (2010). Latino parents' choice of magnet school: How school choice differs across racial and ethnic boundaries. *Education and Urban Society, 42*(6), 758–789.

Strauss, V. (2013, February 16). How charter schools choose desirable students. *The Washington Post.* Retrieved from tinyurl.com/mghkl9f

∽ MYTH 4 ≈

Charter schools are private schools.

You know that charter school down the street? The one you drive by, with its uniform-clad students neatly lined up outside before school? Or the one advertised on the radio or television, marketed as a "rigorous" educational alternative? Although these charter schools may "walk and talk" like private schools, they are actually public schools that receive taxpayer dollars to operate. That means that as a taxpayer, you may have your child or your grandchild attend free of charge—and the same goes for your neighbor. And, because they are public schools, charter schools cannot by law exclude students from enrolling by setting entrance requirements or charging tuition or fees. Even though some charters have found ways to work around the laws under which they operate, as public schools they should all be operating in accordance with the public's expectations.

Unlike your neighborhood public school, charter schools can operate practically anywhere—on church property, in strip malls, out of a house, or online. Many use names that give the perception that they offer an exclusive or private education, such as "academy," "collegiate," or "preparatory school." Odds are that the general public will think that a school called "Star Academy" is private. One of my colleagues doing research in charter schools even discovered a charter school teacher who believed that the school was private.

So what, then, distinguishes a charter school from your local, traditional public school? Charter schools operate under a state legislative contract, or charter, that outlines their mission, curriculum, management structure, and how they will be held accountable. Unlike traditional public schools that must answer to a local school board and state authorities, charter schools have nearly complete control over what they teach, how they teach it, whom they hire and fire, and how they spend their money. And, although charter schools typically receive a large portion of their funding from the state, most charter schools are not held accountable to all of the state or federal education standards, rules, and legislation to which your local public school must attend.

Public charter schools are considered part of a growing national education reform movement based in part on myths and lies about poor school performance and the advantages of competition (see Myth 1). The charter movement took off in 1991, when Minnesota became the first state to pass legislation allowing charter schools to operate. Over the past 20 years, similar laws have been passed across the country;

charter schools now operate in 40 states and the District of Columbia, representing approximately 5% of all public schools and enrolling over 1.6 million students nationally (U.S. Department of Education, 2012). More than half of America's charter schools are elementary schools and more than half are located in cities. In 110 districts, over 10% of the school-age population is enrolled in charter schools, and in seven districts (New Orleans, Detroit, Washington, DC, Kansas City [Missouri], Flint, Gary, and St. Louis), more than 30% of all public school students are enrolled in charter schools (National Alliance for Public Charter Schools, 2012).

Applying market principles to education, these "schools of choice" claim to give parents more educational options for their children. The competition to enroll students is believed to spur all schools to improve academic outcomes—or so the story goes. Education reformers often tout charter schools as a solution to broken, failing, or incompetent public schools—myths we address elsewhere (see Myths 2 and 3). Free-market advocacy is seen, for example, when the San Antonio–based George W. Brackenridge Foundation advocates for increased charter school funding based on the argument that "billions of philanthropic dollars have disappeared into public school districts with no aggregate impact," pointing out the "highly bureaucratic and politicized nature of districts run by elected boards" (Michels, 2012). Free markets, apparently, never waste money, or end up bureaucratized.

The public-yet-private nature of charter schools contributes to the perpetuation of the private school myth. Like private schools, charter schools have some decisionmaking authority, such as control over facilities, teachers, and curricula. Charter schools also are able to make their own rules about dress codes, requiring school uniforms, or promoting heavy-handed suspension and expulsion procedures. They may be run by a management company outside of the authority of a district school board, or they can be part of chain run by either a nonprofit or a for-profit educational management organization (EMO). In fact, EMOs oversee approximately 30% of all charter schools nationally. So, while charter schools officially must answer to accreditation organizations and state departments of education, they are usually outside of the public school bureaucratic administration. And, while charter schools are funded based on the number of students enrolled, this funding is often insufficient to operate the school as planned, much less to purchase facilities, which necessitates asking families and the community for additional financial support. For many charter schools, these contributions from families, businesses, and foundations are what keep their doors open.

The myth that charter schools are private is further reinforced by several recent court decisions that found that charter schools are, in some instances, really not public. The Ninth Circuit Court ruled in 2010 that charter schools in Arizona were not state actors like traditional public schools (Walsh, 2010). This ruling could threaten the federally guaranteed rights of charter school students, which protect all public school students from unreasonable search and seizure, and unfair disciplinary policies, and ensure freedom of speech. In addition, the Internal Revenue Service recently has questioned whether charter school teachers can participate in state pension systems. Many charter school teachers are not allowed to form or participate in a union (McNeil & Cavanagh, 2012); when their right to unionize has been brought to court and upheld, charter school companies have argued that they should not be subject to the laws of the state that apply to public institutions because they—the charter schools—are private. Families are often unaware that by exercising their choice to have their children attend a charter school, they in fact may be promoting a system with fewer rights and protections for their children and for the educators who serve them.

Overall, charter school students attend more racially and ethnically segregated schools than do students who attend traditional public schools (Frankenberg, Siegel-Hawley, & Wang, 2010). Particularly in more affluent communities, charter schools are enrolling primarily White, non-Hispanic children. This has led some charter school critics to regard the charters in such areas as promoters of "White flight" from the traditional public school system. An important reason for this is that in order for a child to attend, a family must learn about the existence of the school, gather information, make a conscious decision to send the child there, and navigate the registration process. Many charter schools also require some type of parental involvement, such as 20 volunteer hours per school year. Researchers have determined that such requirements work to exclude lower income and single-parent families, and then, ironically, the requirement often is not enforced after the child is enrolled. In addition, busing is not provided for most charter schools. Consequently, a natural, but legal, "filtering" function is created that makes charter schools self-selecting and homogeneous in a number of ways (Simon, 2012; Welner, 2013). More-affluent families have the social, cultural, and financial "capital" to send their children to a charter school compared with lower income families, who may not know about the registration deadlines and requirements, the additional financial obligations (e.g., uniforms or textbook purchases), or time commitments (e.g., transportation, volunteering).

Researching whether charter schools are as effective or more effective than traditional public schools at educating students is difficult to do. This is in part because charter schools are extremely diverse in terms of management and pedagogy. Some charter schools have a "college-prep" focus, while others cater to "at-risk" students or students who have been expelled from traditional public schools. Charter schools also vary greatly by instructional methods (traditional classroom or online education), teacher training and certification, student-to-teacher ratios, and mission. For these reasons, obtaining a definitive answer on the effectiveness and quality of charter schools as a whole is challenging, although what has emerged is not very supportive of their claims (see Myth 3). What the charter school research reliably does show is that charter school teachers are less experienced, are less likely to be certified, are paid less well, and have higher turnover rates than traditional public school teachers (National Conference of State Legislatures, 2012). These differences add to the perception that charter schools have more in common with private schools and are not public schools.

The myth that charter schools are private institutions has serious implications for public education in general. All public institutions, and that is what charter schools are, should be held to the same high standards that traditional public schools are held to. They should be required to meet the same local, state, and federal rules and requirements, and to serve all types of students by engaging in transparent enrollment and discipline practices, just like traditional public schools. Furthermore, families should demand that charter school teachers have the same rights and protections as other public employees. Families should be encouraged to look beyond the often-inflated claims of exclusivity, academic excellence, individualized attention, and "rigorous" coursework. These are the kinds of claims that private schools make in their marketing efforts, even if less than true. But, when these kinds of claims are made by a charter school, they violate the public trust, the intent of the charter. Charter schools should be judged like any other public school—based on the experience of their teachers, the quality of their school leadership, curriculum, learning environment, and the breadth and excellence of the ancillary services they provide.

References

Chubb, J. E., & Moe, T. M. (1990). *Politics, markets, and America's schools.* Washington, DC: Brookings Institution.

Frankenberg, E., Siegel-Hawley, G., & Wang, J. (2010, January). *Choice without equity: Charter school segregation and the need for civil rights standards.*

Los Angeles: Civil Rights Project/Proyecto Derechos Civiles at University of California at Los Angeles. Retrieved from civilrightsproject.ucla.edu/research/k-12-education/integration-and-diversity/choice-without-equity-2009-report/?searchterm=Choice%20without%20equity)

Glass, G. V., & Rud, A. G. (2012). The struggle between individualism and communitarianism: The pressure of population, prejudice, and the purse. *Review of Research in Education, 36*(1), 95–112.

Gleason, P., Clark, M., Tuttle, C. C., & Dwoyer, E. (2010). *The evaluation of charter school impacts: Final report* (NCEE 2010-4029). Washington, DC: National Center for Educational Evaluation and Regional Assistance, Institute of Education Sciences, U.S. Department of Education.

McNeil, M., & Cavanagh, S. (2012, February 2). Charter advocates claim rules in works would affect pensions [Web page]. *Education Week* blog. Retrieved from tinyurl.com/pbpxq4t

Michels, P. (2012, December 13). San Antonio donors court a charter school with a record of serving wealthy White students. *The Texas Observer.* Retrieved from tinyurl.com/aa4zq5k

National Alliance for Public Charter Schools. (2012). *New report identifies 110 districts with 10 percent of students enrolled in public charter schools.* Retrieved from tinyurl.com/od6fflq

National Conference of State Legislatures. (2012). *Teaching in charter schools.* Washington, DC: Author. Retrieved from tinyurl.com/ntx5xvw

Simon, S. (2012, February 15). Special report: Class struggle—how charter schools get students they want. *Reuters.* Retrieved from tinyurl.com/c2lh57r

U.S. Department of Education. (2012). *Condition of education.* Washington, DC: National Center for Education Statistics.

Walsh, M. (2010). Charter school not a 'state actor,' court rules [Web page]. *Education Week.* Retrieved from tinyurl.com/q2ez78d

Welner, K. G. (2013, April). *The dirty dozen: How charter schools influence student enrollment.* Retrieved from nepc.colorado.edu/publication/TCR-Dirty-Dozen

⋘ MYTH 5 ⋙

Cyberschools are an efficient, cost-saving, and highly effective means of delivering education.

There is a long history of students being taught by distant teachers. Correspondence courses using postal mail for shut-ins or those in military service have been around for almost a century. But the invention of the World Wide Web in the 1990s was the game-changer. The web browser brought courses to students in a form that resembled conventional textbooks, and email let students ask questions of teachers maybe hundreds of miles away. At first, companies arose to provide advanced placement courses to schools in rural areas that couldn't afford to offer AP programs. And then the same companies began to offer "credit recovery" courses to students who failed a face-to-face course, in algebra, for example, and could recover the credit by passing an online version of an algebra course. But these first small steps were soon dwarfed by the rise of full-time online charter schools delivered completely over the Internet. Cyberschools are now the fastest growing, percentagewise, alternative to traditional brick-and-mortar public education.

In the past decade, a small number of private companies have taken advantage of a market in cyberschooling that has presented itself from the convergence of home schooling, charter schools, and the Internet. By obtaining a charter in those states with permissive charter school legislation, often written by the American Legislative Exchange Council, and vigorously recruiting home schooled students, companies like K12 Inc. in Herndon, Virginia, and Connections Education of Baltimore have able to enroll significant numbers of students in full-time schooling delivered entirely over the Internet. These cyberschools, with names like Colorado Virtual Academy or Pennsylvania Cyber Charter School, quickly began to earn significant profits. The precise authority under which they operate varies depending on state laws. In some states, profit-making companies are not awarded charters to operate schools. In such states, the outside corporations might open a nonprofit foundation in the state, receive a charter, and then purchase all services (courses, administrative record-keeping, human resources) from the distant parent corporation. In other states, they have entered into contracts with tiny rural school districts to enroll students from elsewhere in the state under lax open enrollment laws. The ingenuity of companies seeking to increase revenues knows few bounds.

Spurred on by the search for profits and the need to keep stockholders happy, these companies have launched sophisticated advertising campaigns to attract new students, even buying ad time during the Super Bowl. Ads promise a first-class education individualized for every child at no cost (since state funds pay the cost of educating children in charter schools). One of the largest cyberschooling companies spent half a million dollars on advertising and lobbying in 2010. Researchers at the National Education Policy Center estimated that in 2013 more than 300 full-time virtual public schools enrolled more than 200,000 students in the United States. Most of these students are enrolled in cyberschools operated by profit-making companies, foremost among the latter being K12 Inc. and Connections Education, recently acquired by the U.K. publishing conglomerate Pearson. Pearson earned approximately $1.5 billion in 2011, on sales of nearly $6 billion, two-thirds of which were in education (Molnar, 2013). Not a bad year's work!

The reality of the cyberschool is quite different from the impression created by slick television ads that praise the individual attention and joys of being a student in a charter cyberschool. A handsome young boy peers through goggles while holding a test tube of blue liquid and smiles at the camera as an off-screen voice extols the virtues of individualized, self-paced learning. The thought of a child as young as 6 or 7 years attending "school" full-time on a laptop on the family's kitchen table sends chills up the spines of many professional educators. Physical education—so badly needed in these days of sedentary life for young people—music, art, lab sciences, and the like, all take a back seat to drill-and-kill basic skills instruction. In one cynical attempt to sidestep state laws that disallowed 100% online instruction, a cyberschool company mailed jump ropes to its enrolled students. One assumes that the physical education course in this "school" consisted of being told to skip rope.

When the performance of the children who receive their education at cyberschools is assessed, the results are dismal. Dropout rates during the school year are staggering, often exceeding 50%. Graduation rates are abysmal, and achievement lags far behind that of their peers in brick-and-mortar schools. For the 2012–13 school year, Tennessee Virtual Academy—operated by K12 Inc.—scored lower than any of the other 1,300 elementary schools on the state standardized test. Efforts by authorities to close the school have run into strong political opposition, and the school looks to collect $5 million during the 2013–14 school year.

Questions about the quality of instructional staff in these cyberschools also have been raised. One applicant was asked 10 questions in her job interview, eight of which concerned how she could recruit more students. Student–teacher ratios can be as high as 200 to 1, making the individualized instruction of the television ads an empty promise. Persons working as teachers in the industry have reported being overwhelmed by the numbers of emails they are required to answer. Instead, their supervisors have instructed them to send regular emails to students' parents praising the students' progress so that they will not drop out. In California, any teacher in a charter school must be certified by the state just like any other public school teacher. Some cyberschools operating in California have dodged this law by hiring one or two certified teachers and calling all their other employees "teacher aides." A large cyberschool enrolling more than 5,000 students was discovered "outsourcing" essay grading to India. Not unexpectedly, teacher turnover in cyberschools is extraordinarily high.

Cyberschooling at the K–12 level is big business. K12 Inc., one of the largest companies in cyberschooling and publicly traded on the New York Stock Exchange, reported revenues of approximately three-quarters of a billion dollars in fiscal year 2012. The industry is projected to have revenues of approximately $25 billion by 2015. All of these funds come from state coffers for the education of children in charter schools. Most states pay less for a student in a charter school than for a student in a traditional brick-and-mortar school. Charter schools generally are staffed at much lower levels of service (lacking nurses, psychologists, special education services, and the like). And cyber charter schools lack physical facilities. Legislators are often big proponents of cyberschooling, for which they can pay a fraction of the cost of educating a child in a traditional brick-and-mortar school. In spite of this, the cyberschool industry continues to argue that it deserves 100% of the per-pupil expenditure in the states in which its schools operate.

How, one might wonder, could an industry about which so many questions could be raised, be allowed to function in the United States without political, if not legal, intervention? The cyberschool industry operates in the grand tradition of crony capitalism, essentially buying the support of politicians through such things as campaign contributions and personal perks like junkets to foreign countries (e.g., Brazil) to study other education systems. The growth of the cyberschooling industry depends on favorable legislation at the level of individual states. State laws often must be created or amended to remove a cap on the number of charter schools, for example, or to permit charter schools to be entirely online, or to change open enrollment laws to allow recruiting students statewide into a cyberschool based in some small rural district administered by a compliant school superintendent.

To accomplish the industry's legislative agenda, the American Legislative Exchange Council is supported financially in part by a few large cyberschooling companies. ALEC writes the bills that favor the growth of the industry and lobbies state legislatures for their passage. These bills generally are devoid of any effective accountability regulations. Regulations, it is argued, will stifle creativity. But lack of regulations, history shows, breeds corruption. Given great freedom from oversight, some public school districts also have become entrepreneurial, in the worst sense of the word. On the prairie in southeastern Colorado, a third of a mile north of the New Mexico border, sits the tiny town of Branson. Branson has no grocery store and no gas station; in 2000, it had a population of 77 persons in 43 domiciles. Branson is a most unlikely place to have received over $15 million in state support for its 1,000 virtual students from around the state who attended Branson School Online in its first 4 years (2001–2005).

In the early years of the cyberschool movement, state education authorities showed little interest in regulating the industry. As abuses have risen to the attention of journalists and law enforcement, the malfeasances of an industry gone crazy with its own success have been impossible to ignore. Some states have enacted moratoria on the creation of charter online schools. In February 2013, the Secretary of Education for the Commonwealth of Pennsylvania rejected applications for eight new charter cyberschools. In June 2013, Governor Pat Quinn of Illinois signed a law that enacted a 1-year moratorium on virtual charters, based on studies that showed that these charters get poor results—high dropout rates, low achievement scores, and low graduation rates.

Following an FBI raid in 2012 of the school's offices, Nicholas Trombetta, founder of the 10,000-student Pennsylvania Cyber Charter School, was indicted in August 2013 by federal authorities on 11 tax and fraud charges. The Pennsylvania Cyber Charter School has annual revenues above $100 million. Trombetta, a former school superintendent and wrestling coach, is alleged to have stolen almost $1 million. The modus operandi is common to the bottom dwellers in the charter school industry: Form private businesses and purchase services from them, essentially doing business with oneself, and hire family members or purchase services from them at exorbitant rates. To some audiences, these unsavory details might seem irrelevant or merely signs of the minor imperfections of the free market. But to federal authorities, they can land one in prison.

But who really cares if what is being delivered over the Internet to a quarter million children is superb education that gives them the knowledge and skills needed to succeed in postsecondary education and in life beyond? In fact, there is scant evidence that this is the case. The turnover in enrollment in these cyberschools within the school year is distressingly high. As many as a third of the students who begin a school year are not around at its end. Enrollments in grades 9–12 are much lower than enrollments in kindergarten through grade 8, presumably as parents realize that the offerings of the cyberschool fail to match the offerings of their local traditional brick-and-mortar schools.

Only about a quarter of online cyberschools meet "adequate yearly progress" as defined by the No Child Left Behind act, as compared with about 50% of traditional brick-and-mortar schools. In 2011–12, state department of education ratings of virtual schools' academic performance showed that more than 70% were rated academically unacceptable. Students in cyberschools consistently have scored substantially lower than their counterparts in traditional brick-and-mortar schools in math and reading. The on-time graduation rate for students in cyberschools is about two-thirds the rate for traditional schools (Molnar, 2013).

Cyberschooling for young people must look like a success to stock-holders of the cyberschooling corporations, and surely the key actors in these few corporations consider themselves successful indeed. Have these successes been shared by the hundreds of thousands of families and young people touched by the industry to date? Do the taxpayers, whose billions of dollars of funds for public education now line the pockets of far away corporate big wigs, consider the cyberschool movement a success?

References

Glass, G. V, & Welner, K. G. (2011) *Online K–12 schooling in the U.S.: Uncertain private ventures in need of public regulation.* Boulder, CO: National Education Policy Center. Retrieved from tinyurl.com/6t3wddx

Glass, G. V (2009). *The realities of K–12 virtual education.* Boulder, CO, & Tempe, AZ: Education and the Public Interest Center & Education Policy Research Unit. Retrieved from tinyurl.com/oh83ndw

Miron, G., & Urschel, J. L. (2012). *Understanding and improving full-time virtual schools: A study of student characteristics, school finance, and school performance in schools operated by K–12 Inc.* Boulder, CO: National Education Policy Center. Retrieved from tinyurl.com/75pqkom

Molnar, A. (Ed.). (2013). *Virtual schools in the U.S. 2013: Politics, performance, policy, and research evidence.* Boulder, CO: National Education Policy Center. Retrieved from tinyurl.com/pg5kgjj

✎ MYTH 6 ✎

Home schooled children are better educated than those who attend regular public schools.

Home schooling has grown in popularity and in practice over the past 2 decades. Michael Apple once named it the fastest growing alternative to public education. In 2007, football star Tim Tebow, one of home schooling's high-profile supporters, won the Heisman Trophy playing for the University of Florida. Home schooling supporters cheered a dual victory for their cause. After all, Tebow's public persona challenges stereotypes that home schooled children are socially inept, and his biography illustrates that home schooled children can make it to, in, and beyond college, and accomplish more than first place in an occasional spelling or geography bee.

Tebow's access to high school sports in spite of his being home schooled inspired some "what if" discussions about equal access to extracurricular activities for home schooled students, especially those

in high school who seek more sophisticated sports, equipment, materials, and opportunities than parents are able to provide on their own.
For instance, what if Nease High School had not allowed the home
schooled Tebow to play on its football team? Would this NFL star have
even made it to the NFL? But is Tebow, the poster boy, an exception
rather than the rule for home schooling? Seldom are the backgrounds
of children featured in other home school success stories considered.
This oversight distorts our understanding of the phenomenon of home
schooling. The question we should ask is whether the average, not the
occasional, home schooled child is educated as well as or better than
children who attend regular public schools.

So, what if Tim Tebow was born into a family:

- that had one parent instead of two (like 35% of U.S families)?
  (Kids Count, 2013)
- that spoke a language other than English in the home (like 24%
  of U.S families)? (Skinner, Wight, Aratani, Cooper, & Thampi,
  2010)
- that had a household income for a family of four under about
  $23,550? (like the 22% of children in the United States who
  live below the federal poverty line)? (National Center for Children in Poverty, 2013)

And what if the Tebow family had been geographically isolated
from libraries, community centers, museums, and parks? What if his
parents lacked social connections, networks, consistent access to
transportation, or the "cultural capital" to get him "in the game," or
what if they had little or no experience with postsecondary education,
much less advanced degrees of their own? Would his home schooling
experience have been successful? Would it have even been attempted?

We will never know. But this exercise in imagining other possibilities should remind us of the fact that some children, from some
families, have access to fully supported home school environments.
Others do not. Issues of family educational background and fiscal resources, access (e.g., transportation), and opportunity (e.g., museums)
to supplement the home environment are important to consider in the
education of all children, traditional and home schooled. These factors
strongly influence student outcomes.

How are claims for the superiority of home schooling supported?
Outstanding performances in contests like national spelling and geography bees and in scholarship competitions often are cited to make the
home schooled population as a whole look exceptional (Lyman, 2002).
At first glance, the superiority of home schooling appeared to be veri-

fied by Rudner (1999). His survey provided a comprehensive report on the standardized test scores of home schooled students and compared them with the scores of more traditionally schooled peers. The home schoolers' scores were often in the 70th and 80th percentiles, and 25% of the home schoolers tested one or more grades above grade level. This was great news for parents who want to—and are able to—create schools at home for their children, and for anyone else in search of another way to attack and undermine the public schools. But one must read the whole study to understand that these figures do not speak for themselves. The study does not support the argument that the schooling of children in the home, as opposed to the public school, is a superior form of education.

Right in the abstract of the much ballyhooed Rudner article, the author warns: "This study does *not* demonstrate that home schooling is superior to public or private schools and the results must be interpreted with caution" (pp. 1–2, emphasis added). So, let's be cautious. Let's examine the surveys and test scores of 20,760 children across the United States and see whether the lesser told story about home schooling merits consideration.

First of all, the parents who participated in the survey that Rudner analyzed were only about half of the potential population, probably those most confident of their children's scores. And those parents participating in the survey had more formal education than parents in the general population. Brian Ray (2000, 2002, 2004), who has published research in support of home schooling since the 1980s, relies on the Rudner study in several publications, but even he acknowledges that "home school parents apparently average two or three years more of formal education" than parents who do not home school their children (1988, p. 19). The Associated Press and the U.S. Department of Education repeat this important finding (Lyman, 2002). Does parental education matter in the grand scheme of a child's academic success? You bet it does! Research demonstrating that children whose parents have postsecondary degrees are more successful on standardized assessments than those whose parents do not is not news, nor is the positive relationship between parents' educational attainment and their level of income.

This brings us to a second fact that is often ignored in the analyses of the statistical reports on home schooling. Rudner (1999) explained that participating parents had a significantly higher median income than those of all U.S. families with children. Like traditional schools, home schools need resources. Both schooling environments require a great deal of time, energy, and funding, as well as appropriate facilities, a sound intellectual infrastructure, and competent teachers. All of this is a lot for a pair of parents to shoulder on their own, so much so that home schooling might not even be possible for a single parent to consider. Many two-parent households cannot support home schooling either, because their incomes are low and the time they are required to work outside the home is excessive. Which brings us to another important point that Rudner makes, namely, that participating parents in his survey were most often home schooling in two-parent households, another finding confirmed by Ray (1988, 2002), as well as the Associated Press and the U.S. Department of Education (Lyman, 2002).

Without appropriately acknowledging the background characteristics of families who can develop outstanding schools at home, home schooling itself might seem to be the key to higher test scores. But family background matters a great deal, both in whether children are afforded a high-quality home school and in whether they will excel on standardized tests. Home schooled children have a distinct testing advantage when they come from families who have the academic, cultural, and financial capital that is associated with higher scores on standardized assessments, just like their traditionally schooled peers. It is not likely that children of poorly educated parents who are home schooling because of religious objections to the curriculum, using texts and materials that are scientifically dubious, and relying heavily on materials from content providers delivered by television, will produce the same positive results that home schooling advocates like to publicize.

Of course, home schooling might provide a great option for some families. After all, schooling in the home offers flexibility, customizable curriculum, and one-on-one pupil attention that might be less apparent or available in public schools. Home schooling may safeguard children from perspectives, viewpoints, and practices that parents would rather filter through their own belief system or religious views. Parents who have children with special needs may feel that the programming available in public schools is underfunded or inadequate. And for many children, especially those who are born into affluent families with parents who can provide resources that many children in home schools and in public schools cannot even dream of, the home school simply has more to offer than the public school—more guest speakers, more fieldtrips, more advanced technologies, more music lessons, more second-language tutors . . . more than any child living in poverty is likely to benefit from in either of these educational environments. Just like some children in public schools, some home schooled children simply have more opportunities than others. The vast majority of parents, however, are ill-equipped to teach their children analytic geometry or to turn the kitchen into a chemistry lab. Consequently, the home schooling population shrinks dramatically after the elementary and middle school grades, when parents send their children back into the public school system to be educated by professionals.

The consequences of the myth that home schooled children are better educated than children who attend regular public schools, are detrimental to all students, teachers, and families. The myth:

- Wrongfully targets all public schools as institutions that provide a second-rate education, in comparison to the alternatives.
- Supports the kind of thinking that "defunds" public education.
- Promotes the naïve belief that all parents have the same academic, cultural, and financial capacity to sustain an excellent schooling environment in their home.
- Contributes to the "deprofessionalization" of teachers, especially those in early childhood and elementary education. Think that just anybody can be a teacher? Try it sometime.

Tim Tebow needed public school football because his family did not have access to their own high school football team. Millions of children need access to excellent public schools for other reasons. Damning and defunding our nation's public education system because some home schooled children do well and some publicly schooled children do not is logically untenable. There will never be one answer to the question of how to best educate the citizenry. Our time and energy would be spent more fruitfully not in arguing over which school type is inherently better, but in advocating instead for adequate funding, resources, and support for the education of all children.

References

Kids Count. (2013). *Kids count data book.* Baltimore, MD: Annie E. Casey Foundation. Retrieved from tinyurl.com/owuhjxm

Lyman, I. (2002). Answers to homeschool questions. *The New American, 18*(9), 31.

National Center for Children in Poverty. (2013). *Child poverty.* Retrieved from www.nccp.org/topics/childpoverty.html

Ray, B. D. (1988). Home schools: A synthesis of research on characteristics and learner outcomes. *Education and Urban Society, 21*(1), 16–31.

Ray, B. D. (2000). Home schooling: The ameliorator of negative influences on learning? *Peabody Journal of Education, 75*(1–2), 71–106.

Ray, B. D. (2002). Customization through homeschooling. *Educational Leadership, 59*(1), 50–54.

Ray, B. D. (2004). Homeschoolers on to college: What research shows us. *The Journal of College Admissions, 185*, 5–11.

Rudner, L. M. (1999). Scholastic achievement and demographic characteristics of home school students in 1998. *Educational Policy Analysis Archives,* 7(8), 1–33.

Skinner, C., Wight, V. R., Aratani, Y., Cooper, J. L., & Thampi, K. (2010). *English language proficiency, family economic security, and child development.* New York, NY: National Center for Children in Poverty. Retrieved from tinyurl.com/pbscfaj

∽ MYTH 7 ∾

School choice and competition work to improve all schools. Vouchers, tuition tax credits, and charter schools inject competition into the education system and "raise all boats."

If there is one thing that the majority of U.S. politicians seem to agree on, it is that public schools are failing and that the remedy is school choice. And politicians aren't the only ones. Films like *Waiting for Superman* made the case that school choice is only fair. Why should the right to choose a school for one's child be available only to families that can afford to live in affluent suburban school districts or to pay private school tuitions? Media reports on highly acclaimed charter school networks like KIPP suggest that school choice is simply logical. Shouldn't we be doing everything we can to support innovative, hardworking educators who are helping kids in places like south Los Angeles actually graduate from high school and go to college? Business leaders contend that the evidence for competition, and hence school choice, is obvious in every other aspect of American life. When, they ask, does a government monopoly ever benefit consumers? Aren't you glad that the U.S. Postal Service has to compete with FedEx and UPS to provide you with quality service at the best prices? Research reports from Stanford and Harvard and various think tanks argue that the data are clear: Charter schools and private school voucher programs "lift all ships" by forcing traditional public schools to become more effective and efficient (Hoxby, 2001). In an era of intense political polarization, Americans of many stripes seem united in their belief that our nation's children and taxpayers will be better served by introducing choice and competition into the public school system.

Before we accept school choice as a panacea to the troubles of our public schools, however, it would be wise to consider two key questions about what is actually happening in regions where school choice programs are being implemented:

1. Has school choice increased academic achievement across the board by forcing traditional public schools to compete with charter and private schools?
2. Has school choice increased equality of educational opportunities for low-income and minority students by giving all families the chance to choose a school for their children, regardless of location or cost?

The answers to these questions, in turn, raise two additional questions: What are the motivations of the politicians and businesspeople who are promoting free-market ideology and funding the research to prove its effectiveness in education? And, does competition in the educational sector exacerbate rather than solve our most difficult challenges in public education?

Consider academic achievement. It is widely assumed that private and charter schools outperform public schools, and that the goal is to get public schools to perform more like these autonomous schools. But a growing and very convincing body of research is calling that assumption into question. Private schools do produce higher test scores—but they also serve a significantly more privileged student population (see Myth 2). It turns out that when you compare apples to apples—that is, similar student populations—public schools actually are outperforming private schools (Lubienski & Lubienski, 2013). This might be because private school teachers tend to have fewer credentials and to cling to traditional teaching styles, such as lecturing while students sit in rows and take notes. Public school teachers, by contrast, are much more likely to be certified, to hold higher degrees, and to embrace research-based innovations in curriculum and pedagogy (Lubienski & Lubienski, 2013). Perhaps for reasons like these, results from Ohio and Wisconsin show that students who used vouchers to attend private schools did no better academically than comparable students who remained in public schools (Richards, 2010; Witte, Sterr, & Thorn, 1995). A long list of studies also has demonstrated that public schools perform on par with or better than charter schools, despite the fact that public schools serve a larger percentage of students who are harder to teach because of disabilities, English language learning needs, or behavioral and other challenges (see Myths 3 and 4). Once again, this may be linked to the comparatively weak credentials of charter school teachers and administrators. All of this research calls into question the very idea that public schools even *need* to be competing with private and charter schools in the first place.

That's the big picture. What about local contexts where the neighborhood public school is floundering and some students have been able to transfer to local charter schools or to private schools through voucher programs? Do the public school administrators and teachers, seeing families "vote with their feet," and feeling the threat of "going out of business," finally get their act together and provide students with better instruction?

Not quite. The students who leave are often the ones with the most resources: better academic skills and higher motivation; more involved and better educated parents with valuable social networks and connections; and access to personal transportation every day so they can get to and from schools that are not in their neighborhood. Along with the funds local and state governments pay for their tuition, these students take with them the positive contributions that they have been making to their public school community, including positive peer influence on their lower achieving classmates, and the effects of parent involvement and volunteerism. In their absence, the public school finds itself struggling even more for resources that are so badly needed to serve their now increasingly poor and underperforming students: special education services, English language learning resources, counselors, school psychologists, and a wide array of instructional supports. In this challenging environment, it becomes harder to attract and retain experienced teachers and to foster achievement that attracts and retains parents equipped to exercise their right to school choice. How can a public school possibly compete with private and charter schools that, unlike the public school, have no obligation to accept every student, regardless of learning needs and challenges?

Some public schools have found two ways to compete. They may subtly practice the same exclusionary practices as their autonomous school counterparts, or they may divert funds from instruction into marketing targeted at parents of high-performing, well-resourced students (Heilig, 2012).

Has school choice increased educational opportunities for low-income and minority students? The promise of school choice as a civil right—as an acceptable way to tackle the seemingly intractable segregation that has persisted in our schools even after *Brown v. Board of Education*—has been one of the more appealing arguments in favor of choice. Choice proponents have long argued that allowing children to attend schools outside of their neighborhoods would allow low-income and minority students to go to school with their affluent and White peers. Unfortunately, what actually has happened as a result of school choice policies is exactly the opposite; school segregation has increased, often leaving the most disadvantaged students in even more under-resourced public schools. The integration picture is no better at charter schools, where students are even more isolated by race and class than are their traditional public school peers (Frankenberg, Siegel-Hawley, & Wang, 2011).

This increased segregation seems to have three causes: (1) Parents choose to enroll their children in schools that mirror their own demographic; (2) schools of choice choose which students they want to enroll and retain; and (3) private schools set their own tuition costs. The first cause is most evident in the case of White and upper-income parents who choose private or charter schools that enroll few low-income or minority students. Since the school's test performance is invariably higher when the percentage of low-income and minority students is lower, privileged parents prioritize academic performance and choose a school that reflects their own race and class. While parental choice plays a role, segregation seems to be intensifying mainly because school choice gives schools more power to choose.

School choice is supposed to allow parents to choose a school that best suits their child. In practice, schools of choice—private and charter schools—regularly flip that equation and choose students that will best suit the goals of the school. In a competitive environment, schools face increased pressure to outperform their neighbors, and one of the best ways to do that is to choose students who perform well. More important, it is critical to not enroll or retain students who will bring down test scores, threaten the school culture, or use up too many school resources. While private schools can advertise their admissions requirements more freely, charter schools practice exclusion more subtly. Interested parents of students with special needs may be subtly discouraged from applying, counseled to consider that the charter school has many fewer special education resources than the neighboring public school. Many charter schools also require that students demonstrate motivation to succeed in school, and that parents sign contracts agreeing to check students' homework, volunteer a certain number of hours to the school each year, and attend parent–teacher conferences. While these requirements certainly foster student achievement, they also weed out students who most need school to find motivation and provide the academic support that their parents cannot.

Although particular charter schools may enroll large percentages of African American and Latino students, a close look at the socioeconomic breakdown of those students, compared with their counterparts in the neighborhood public school, often reveals that the students with the most challenging life circumstances are the ones left after their comparatively more well-off peers have been admitted to nearby charter schools. When charter and private schools enroll students whose behavior or work ethic becomes problematic, those students usually are asked to leave. Retention policies, like admissions policies, reflect the great power of choice afforded to schools instead of parents. For example, based on its test scores, one charter school in Arizona was lauded as the best high school in the state. It had class enrollments in grades 5–11 that showed this pattern: 152, 138, 110, 94, 42, 30, 23. Finally, in the senior year of high school, eight students were enrolled, and 100% of them graduated. Apparently, somewhere along the way, many students were told to leave (Strauss, 2012).

The enthusiasm for "school choice" has its roots in the philosophies and arguments of free-market economists, most notably Milton Friedman, seen by some as the father of the school voucher movement. One of Friedman's last public statements before his death in 2006 was on the occasion of Hurricane Katrina. In a *Wall Street Journal* op-ed, Friedman (2005) wrote, "Most New Orleans schools are in ruins as are the homes of the children who have attended them. The children are now scattered all over the country. This is a tragedy. It is also an opportunity." The opportunity was afforded to companies that rushed into the devastation and set up private schools, taking advantage of the voucher system created by state and local politicians. The effects of this takeover will not be known for years, but it is already mired in controversy and court cases concerning support for religious schools and violation of segregation orders. And the achievement test score data coming out of these schools are not at all what the free-market advocates expected. In one recent evaluation there were 15 state-run schools and 42 charters in the Recovery School District of New Orleans, schools formed by the "opportunity" offered by Katrina. When these schools, which are wholeheartedly supported by the state, were graded using an evaluation system designed by the state, heavily weighted by achievement test scores, 100% of the former and 79% of the latter group of schools received grades of F or D (Strauss, 2012).

Free-market philosophy imagines actors rationally choosing to maximize their self-interest from among a variety of options. The application of such a philosophy to the case of parents choosing schools for their children has long been known to be problematic. The famous economist Kenneth Boulding argued some 40 years ago that parents might make the choice but students are the recipients of the services in education. The feedback from child to parents is anything but perfect. And simple free-market philosophies ignore the reality that one person's successful pursuit of self-interest can lead to a second person's loss.

Do all children deserve the right to attend excellent schools that will prepare them for college? Should educators be striving to provide their students and families with the best possible education? Should taxpayers expect that schools use funds efficiently and effectively? Yes, of course. School choice and competition, however, simply have not helped to achieve these goals, neither in the United States nor in countries like Chile that have wholeheartedly embraced these principles. Rather than offering all students better opportunities, vouchers and charter schools have used tax dollars to help some students while leaving many others even more segregated and disadvantaged. Our nation and our children need a well-funded public school system that provides equal support to all its schools. That is the tide that will really lift all ships.

References

Frankenberg, E., Siegel-Hawley, G., & Wang, J. (2011). Choice without equity: Charter school segregation. *Educational Policy Analysis Archives, 19*(1). Retrieved from epaa.asu.edu/ojs/article/view/779

Friedman, M. (2005, December 5). The promise of vouchers. *The Wall Street Journal.* Retrieved from tinyurl.com/njftmwc

Heilig, J. V. (2012, November 8). *Supporting public schools: Are vouchers a panacea or problematic? Pt. IV.* Retrieved from tinyurl.com/qftg5k9

Hoxby, C. M. (2001). Rising tide: New evidence on competition and the public schools. *Education Next, 4*(1). Retrieved from educationnext.org/rising-tide/

Lubienski, C., & Lubienski, S. T. (2013). *The public school advantage: Why public schools outperform private schools.* Chicago, IL: University of Chicago Press.

Richards, J. S. (2010, September 23). Voucher results mixed. *The Columbus Dispatch.* Retrieved from tinyurl.com/ppwd63g

Strauss, V. (2012, August 28). To: Sec. Duncan re: what you said about New Orleans schools. *The Washington Post.* Retrieved from tinyurl.com/ncysmv3

Witte, J. F., Sterr, T. D., & Thorn, C. A. (1995). *Fifth-year report Milwaukee Parental Choice Program.* Madison: Robert M. La Follette Institute of Public Affairs, University of Wisconsin. Retrieved from tinyurl.com/qj9es8g

✀ MYTH 8 ✀

Want to find the best high schools in America?
Ask *Newsweek* or *U.S. News.*

The print media discovered a gold mine a few years back. Rank the nation's colleges or graduate schools from best to worst and copies of their magazines would fly off the shelves. Nearly everyone loves a good ranking. Major league baseball updates the rankings every day; so does the Association of Tennis Professionals. Who doesn't love to see who's number one? It was only a matter of time until *Newsweek* and *U.S. News* ranked high schools, so that for the price of a magazine we could all know who was on top. Of course, separating the wheat from the chaff proves not to be as simple when what is being evaluated is as complex as schools.

Newsweek was particularly inept at this task. It sent its survey to 5,000 schools; about half returned filled-out forms. The nation has about 20,000 high schools. So maybe the ones who didn't respond had something to hide and wouldn't be in the highest echelon anyway, so no harm done . . . maybe. *Newsweek* asked for self-reports of six statistical indices: graduation rate (weighted 25% of the total score); college acceptance rate (25%); SAT/ACT average (10%); advanced placement/ International Baccalaureate/Advanced International Certificate of Education (AP/IB/AICE) tests per student (25%); AP/IB/AICE (10%); and percent students enrolled in an AP/IB/AICE course (5%).

It's obvious to anyone, except a journalist perhaps, that if you rank schools on these numbers you will be ranking schools by wealth, ethnicity, and exclusivity, not by how well schools work with whomever society asks them to educate. Try this thought experiment on for size: School A admits Johnny, whose parents are professors at the local college making $150,000 a year and who had 3 years of preschool under his belt before he ever entered that intimate Montessori elementary school on campus. School B admits Juan, whose parents are divorced, whose parents and grandparents speak primarily Spanish at home, and who was held out of 2 years of elementary school due to illness and family relocation. Any fool knows that Johnny could be told to go sit in the library for 3 years and he would still greatly exceed Juan's performance on *Newsweek*'s golden half dozen criteria. Is School A composed of better educators than School B? *Newsweek* thinks so. But in reality, School A merely finds itself to be located in more favorable circumstances than School B.

If magazine readers really aren't interested in where the best educators work but simply want to find that place where the tiger moms send their children, or where lucky kids go to school, then *Newsweek* has served them well. And there are many readers so motivated; that's why school rankings—often emanating from *Newsweek*-like operations of state education departments—are used by Realtors more than any other audience. Realtors are enjoined by law from discussing racial composition of neighborhoods with their clients, but school test scores do the job of directing home buyers to privileged neighborhoods just as well as red-lining used to do.

U.S. News & World Report is another magazine that loves rankings, and the sales they produce. It continues to make a fortune from annual publications of college, grad school, and public school rankings. Try to find a copy of the annual rankings editions a week after publication and you'll end up paying a fee to view them online. Admittedly, *U.S. News* does a better job of finding the "best" high schools than *Newsweek*, that is, if being more statistically sophisticated in an invalid endeavor can be said to be done "better." *U.S. News* uses publicly reported data and attempts to measure performance in light of expected performance based on some socioeconomic characteristics of the schools. Of course, it succeeds in this no better than similar attempts to grade teachers on their students' test score gains.

Consider an example that should give any objective individual pause in interpreting the hoax associated with *U.S. News* high school rankings. BASIS Schools is an Arizona-based charter school company started by a university economics professor of libertarian free-market temperament, we can assume. It has campuses in several locations in Arizona and elsewhere. It announces proudly on its website that its "campuses are ranked in the top ten in the nation by *Newsweek*, *The Washington Post*, and *U.S. News & World Report*"; and indeed that is true. Top 10! But to all who know BASIS Schools firsthand, the reality is anything but "top 10." Although a typical BASIS school starts off with hundreds of students in elementary grades, the number who survive the gauntlet of tests and requirements for promotion, and make it to middle school and high school, is hugely reduced. Slow students are counseled to go off and lower the statistics of regular high schools —but not in those words, surely. Special-needs students need not even attempt the required admissions essay.

And at the end of this Darwinian ordeal, a few dozen make it to graduation from one of the nation's "top 10" high schools. Here are the enrollments by grade at the BASIS Tucson charter school for 2011–12:

Grade 5—121
Grade 6—125
Grade 7—125
Grade 8—102
Grade 9—58
Grade 10—57
Grade 11—34
Grade 12—21

After the relentless shifting and winnowing of wheat from chaff, fewer than two dozen students were around at graduation day. Just about any large suburban high school in America could collect a few dozen graduates who aced their AP courses and topped their SATs. But measures like "percent graduates accepted to college" make schools like BASIS appear to be in the top 10. There is much less to these ratings than meets the eye.

Myths and Lies About Teachers and the Teaching Profession: Teachers Are "Everything," That's Why We Blame Them and Their Unions

Somewhere, almost every day, police are heroes, yet often, on the same day, they are vilified in the press of some community. Military personnel are respected and honored, yet there is near constant protest of our military in communities across the United States. So it is with teachers. Often revered individually and honored locally, they are castigated regularly by both politicians and the press. Teachers too frequently are assigned blame for all manner of perceived faults in our society.

Lost a factory to Bangladesh? Blame our teachers! Surely we don't want to blame the political and economic system that gives tax breaks for moving jobs overseas, which in turn helps manufacturers to reduce the costs of their labor at home. Those moves also allow many manufacturers to increase their profits and hide their gains overseas so that they do not have to pay a fair share of the taxes needed to support our nation's schools, police, and military. But surely the captains of industry are not to blame; our economic problems must be the fault of our teachers!

Have to train a worker for a complex job? Let's blame the teachers for their failure to have workers ready to jump into any of the jobs that become available. Don't blame the company that wants its new workers trained in public schools at public expense.

Can't get people to behave appropriately, or to operate the cash registers and computers at a job that pays $7.50 an hour? Blame the teachers! Let's not blame the companies that create temporary, part-time, and low-paying jobs, and still expect to attract talented and "job ready" graduates of our schools as their employees. In spite of their pay policies, these corporations expect all their employees to care deeply about their work. The complaints of these companies have nothing to do with the quality of our nation's teachers. Mind-numbing, low-paid work without benefits will produce nothing but dispirited workers, regardless of how the nation's education system prepares them.

Teachers have become the punching bag for all sorts of problems faced by our nation, but these are problems teachers cannot influence. It is illogical to lay so much blame for so many of the ills of society on a profession with so little power to affect much more than the lives of 30 or so students in a class. Our 3.3 million public school teachers show remarkably high rates of educating our youth humanely and competently, even though hampered in doing that by government policies such as No Child Left Behind, Race to the Top, and other actions that have curtailed both their humanity and their competency. For their efforts, teachers frequently confront critics who argue they are overpaid. This too is a complicated issue to sort out, but the bottom line is that this is a myth that we take head-on here.

In this part, we deal with a number of the myths and lies about teachers and teaching commonly reported in newspapers and discussed on talk radio. We start with a myth that underlies much misbegotten educational policy: Teachers are the most important factor in a student's achievement. Although teachers often influence individual students' lives quite dramatically, they actually are much less powerful than are family and neighborhood influences. So lauding them or blaming them for students' success or lack of success on achievement measures is really blaming the weaker contributor to those outcomes. Even the belief that teachers are the most important in-school influence on student achievement may be false. It may well be the classroom peer group and school-level factors that have the greater influence on overall classroom achievement.

No one wants to diminish teachers' responsibility for classroom achievement, but they are not alone in producing those effects, and to hold them solely responsible for those effects is unfair.

In this part we also report on myths, lies, and misunderstandings associated with the role of teachers' unions, so often reviled by education critics. In addition, we address what may be the worst idea of the decade—merit pay for teachers. And we present a balanced but critical view of the controversial program called Teach For America. As will be clear throughout this part, there is less evidence and logic than meets the eye to support many of the beliefs we cherish!

⤝ MYTH 9 ⤞

Teachers are the most important influence in a child's education.

Teachers are important. They provide instruction to students, give them valuable emotional and social support, and are often generous with their time and energy to support a variety of extracurricular activities for the benefit of students. They also labor in the shadow of this myth—a myth that appears to celebrate teachers, but that in reality hangs an unrealistic responsibility around their necks. The importance of teachers has been mythologized to the point that it burdens teachers, restricts their ability to serve students in ways they deem appropriate, and may be driving some of the best teachers out of the classroom.

The myth that teachers are the most important influence in a child's education grows out of research that points to the impact teaching has on student learning. Good teachers make a difference in the academic growth of students. Bad teachers can slow down a student's academic progress. This is not news. If teachers were not important, parents would just leave students in a room full of books and other materials and let them learn. No reasonable person believes that this is the best way to organize education of children. What teachers do is important for student learning.

As obvious as it is to note the importance of good teaching, research makes it equally clear that teachers are not the most important influence in a child's education. In fact, most research indicates that less than 30% of a student's academic success in school is attributable to schools, and teachers are only a part of that overall school effect, perhaps not even the most important part. Student achievement is most strongly associated with other variables, the major one being socioeconomic status. Other important factors that relate to student learning include the neighborhood the student lives in, language use and language complexity in the home, whether the student lives in a psychologically and physically healthy environment with access to competent medical care, and access to books, games, and activities that prepare the student for school. These outside-of-school factors, having nothing to do with teacher competency, appear to have at least twice the weight in predicting student achievement as do the inside-of-school factors, of which teachers are only a part (Berliner, 2012).

Nevertheless, we hear politicians and education reformers argue that those factors are outside of the control of policymakers, or that it is unrealistic to think that we can change the social dynamics related to class and race. Policymakers argue that holding teachers accountable for student success is the best option for improving education. The mythological importance of teachers in determining student achievement is then promoted, as policymakers strive to show that what they are doing is best for children, namely, holding teachers accountable for student success. This illusion of "doing something," even if it is not likely to cause the desired changes, allows many politicians and citizens to close their eyes to the larger social and economic problems that affect classrooms and schools more than do teachers.

Because of the myth, teacher accountability has become a central part of education reform. The federal government, through promotion of "Race to the Top," has enticed many states to adopt programs that tie teachers' evaluations to student achievement on standardized tests, called value-added measurement, or VAMs (see Myth 11). Increasingly, and often using VAMs, school districts are implementing merit pay, basing at least part of a teacher's compensation on student test scores. These "reforms" flow from two myths. The first is that pay-for-performance is an effective way to motivate workers. But it is not. The second myth, examined more closely in this chapter, is that teachers are the most important factor in a child's education and that what, and how much, the child learns, is predominantly under the control of that child's teacher.

It would be reasonable, if we were sure that teachers were the most important factor in determining student achievement, to promote policies holding them accountable for what students learn. But accountability policies built on this premise are a hoax because it is assumed that teachers have more control over student achievement than they actually do. Teachers do not have any power over the conditions of students' lives outside of school, and it is those conditions that account for much of the difference in student achievement. In addition, teachers are often among the most powerless in the school when it comes to making decisions that affect student achievement. For example, under the new Common Core State Standards, currently adopted by 45 states, teachers have little control over the curriculum they teach and the time they can allocate for instruction. In addition, they have no control over the classroom and school resources (including textbooks and counselors) that support instruction, and they have little say in how many, or which, students are in their classrooms. All these factors impact the quality of instruction a teacher can provide.

As a result, policies flowing from this myth of the all-important teacher put teachers in an untenable position. They are asked to overcome many problems outside of their control, and this can lead to devastating consequences for both students and teachers. As the pressure increases on teachers (and their administrators) to improve student performance, so does their temptation to game and to cheat the system to show improvement in student achievement. Cheating scandals in Atlanta, Washington, DC, Denver, and elsewhere point not just to the possibility of this regrettable situation, but to its reality (Nichols & Berliner, 2007; Ravitch, 2010). Gaming and cheating to show the gains desired in achievement are also harmful to students. Imagine believing that you were a high-achieving student at one grade level or in one district, only to find out that your test scores plummet the following year, with a different teacher, or in a different district. Or as is also common, you are a high school graduate in one state with high school graduation tests that are easy to pass, so the graduation rates of the schools will look good, and then find that you are unprepared for college in another state.

The policies growing out of the myth of extremely powerful teachers also can result in lower teacher morale and push talented people away from considering a career in teaching. Working in an environment where you are evaluated on outcomes that are largely outside of your control is a recipe first for anxiety, and eventually for abandonment of the profession. And, to the extent that these accountability policies measure teachers against one another, they can foster an environment that discourages cooperation among professionals. Talented people considering a career in teaching may think twice about entering the profession if the working conditions of teachers continue to worsen, and their salaries remain lower than for others with similar levels of education (see Myth 10).

None of this means that accountability, and in particular accountability for teachers, must be abandoned. Teachers vary in quality, and it is not helpful to ignore that fact. A small number of teachers do seem to consistently have a greater impact on student achievement than others, although we know that their efficacy will vary year by year as the composition of their classrooms changes (Baker, 2012; Berliner, 2014). There are benefits in recognizing these teachers, rewarding them, and encouraging those with the potential to succeed in these ways to enter teaching. But we also have to abandon the myth about how much control a teacher has over student learning. Instead, accountability measures should grow out of a realistic perspective on the important work that teachers do, and recognize that accountability for student achievement is broadly shared. Families, communities, school boards, state and federal governments—society in general—all bear responsibility for student achievement. Asking teachers to bear more than their share is harmful.

References

Baker, B. (2012). On the stability (or not) of being irreplaceable. *School Finance 101*. Retrieved from tinyurl.com/o3qnpb8

Berliner, D. C. (2012). Effects of inequality and poverty vs. teachers and schooling on America's youth. *Teachers College Record, 116*(1). Retrieved from tinyurl.com/q3qfkyt

Berliner, D. C. (2014). Exogenous variables and value-added assessments: A fatal flaw. *Teachers College Record*. Retrieved from www.tcrecord.org/Content.asp?ContentId=17293

Nichols, S. N., & Berliner, D. C. (2007). *Collateral damage: How high-stakes testing corrupts America's schools.* Cambridge, MA: Harvard Education Press.

Ravitch, D. (2010). *The death and life of the great American school system: How testing and choice are undermining education.* New York, NY: Basic Books.

⤚ MYTH 10 ⤚

Teachers in the United States are well-paid.

An educated, stable teaching force serves as the linchpin in an effective public school system, usually representing the greater portion of expenditures in many communities in the United States and abroad. To recruit high-quality teachers into the profession, and retain them, most American public school districts are challenged to offer competitive salaries and improve working conditions. This is a particularly daunting task for schools serving the highest needs students, often in low-income communities. It is also daunting in a nation that strives for very low tax rates, thus working hard to hold teacher salaries to a minimum. This low-tax philosophy has effects: Teacher salary, as a percent of average gross domestic product per capita, has fallen 2% a year every year from 1970 on. In fact, in 1970, in New York City, a starting lawyer at a prestigious firm and a starting teacher in a public school had a differential in their salaries of about $2,000. But 2 years ago, including salary and bonus, that starting lawyer made $160,000, while teachers beginning their careers in New York City made roughly $45,000 (Auguste, Kihn, & Miller, 2010).

Nevertheless, some critics of teachers' salaries cite higher than average pay for teachers in the United States compared with their counterparts in some other industrialized nations who have similar years of experience and who teach at similar grade levels. But that is not true. In reality, American teachers are paid less than teachers in many other countries (1) relative to the wages of other workers with similar levels of education; (2) based on the amount of time spent teaching each day; (3) in terms of the salary differentials between starting and experienced teachers; and (4) in relation to salary trends over the past decade.

Common sense also enters into this argument. Have you ever encountered an American college student who professed his or her desire to become a teacher to earn lots of money? More than likely, aspiring teachers cite their love of learning, desire to help children succeed, or other nonmonetary motivators for entering the profession despite the relatively low pay over one's career. Noble sentiments about wanting to be a physician are not used as a justification to limit the salaries of physicians. But those same noble sentiments sometimes are used to justify the low pay of teachers: "Since they love to teach, we don't have to pay them as much!"

In recent decades, teachers in many other industrialized countries have in fact chosen to teach because of the good pay and working conditions. Our neighbor, Alberta, Canada, for example, pays those with a bachelor's degree in education and 10 years of experience approximately $92,500, plus another $7,000+ in benefits, in a province that underwrites all medical care as well. At the time of this writing, the Canadian dollar is close to parity with the U.S. dollar. In South Korea, teachers earn somewhere between the salaries paid to doctors and to engineers. And in Singapore, every few years, on top of decent salaries, teachers get large bonuses ($10,000+) for staying in the profession (Auguste et al., 2010). Although relative wages and the quality of working conditions in schools vary considerably around the world, it is nevertheless true that the United States is trailing some of our international competitors in wages paid to teachers and, maybe more important, the quality of the academic talent that is recruited to teaching. In her book *The Smartest Kids in the World: And How They Got That Way*, Amanda Ripley (2013) makes the point that the academic talent that enters the teaching profession is a major driver of national success in education. And, of course, the way to attract academic talent is through salaries, benefits, and working conditions.

Teacher salary data and other measures of compensation in the United States and more than 35 member countries in the Organisation for Economic Co-operation and Development (OECD) indicate that the average American teacher with more than 15 years of experience earns an annual salary of between $45,050 and $48,450 U.S. depending on whether he or she teaches at the primary, lower secondary, or upper secondary level (OECD, 2012). These teachers typically earn a higher annual salary than the average for OECD teachers. But given their years of experience and grade-level assignments, these teacher salaries are disproportionately lower than those of other full-time, full-year workers (ages 25–64) in the United States with comparable levels of postsecondary education. For example, teachers employed in U.S. public schools who meet the minimum training requirements and have more than 10 years of experience receive an average annual salary ranging from 28% less at the upper secondary level to 33% less at the primary level than that of other similarly educated workers (OECD,

2012). Teachers in many other OECD countries earn annual salaries that are more comparable to those of college-educated workers in those nations' other professions, ranging from 10% less at the secondary level to 18% less at the primary level (OECD, 2012).

Some critics justify teachers' relatively lower wages as appropriate, given the flexibility and additional vacation time often built into the schedules of the American public schools. But teachers in several other OECD countries, with similar flexibility and vacation time, enjoy higher salaries per hour than U.S. teachers typically earn. For example, the average salary per hour (based on net contract or teaching time) for U.S. teachers with at least 15 years of experience is lower than the OECD average (OECD, 2012). Specifically, American teachers with that level of experience earn on average about $43 U.S. per hour of teaching, at the primary and upper secondary levels. But on average, OECD teachers earn $49 and $65 U.S. per hour at the same grade levels (OECD, 2012). Because upper secondary teachers abroad often are required to teach fewer hours than primary teachers, their salaries per hour are actually even higher, including those in countries that have seemingly similar hourly pay rates across grade-level assignments. Thus, upper secondary teachers in Belgium, Denmark, Germany, and Japan reach an hourly salary up to $90 U.S. or more (OECD, 2012).

Teachers in most OECD countries, including the United States, earn higher wages based on their years of experience and the grade level that they teach; however, the top salaries and length of time required to reach those levels of pay vary considerably by country (Ladd, 2007; OECD, 2012). Intended as an incentive for starting teachers to continue in the profession, the slow increase in pay in the United States yields top salaries approximately 40% to 50% higher than starting salaries within grade-level assignments (OECD, 2012). While this may seem like a considerable increase in pay, the average OECD teacher earns 60% to 63% more at the top of the salary scale compared with starting salaries within grade-level assignments (OECD, 2012). In some countries, including Korea and Japan, teachers earn double their starting salary at the top of the scale, although they work on average 34 years to reach this salary (OECD, 2012). Teachers in other countries, such as Estonia, New Zealand, and Scotland, also reach top salaries of 45% to 60% more than starting salaries in less than 8 years (OECD, 2012). Some teachers will earn top wages in less than a decade, while the average OECD teacher will work nearly 2.5 times as long to achieve such a salary (OECD, 2012).

Teacher salary trends also influence college students who might consider entering the profession (Ladd, 2007). When compared with the average salary of OECD teachers with at least 15 years of experience in 2000, salaries for U.S. teachers had increased on average only 3% by 2010 across all grade levels (i.e., primary, lower secondary, and upper secondary) (OECD, 2012). In fact, upper secondary teachers' wages were actually 1–2% lower between 2005 and 2007 than wages in 2000 (OECD, 2012). The relatively stagnant and even declining wages in the United States further discourage highly qualified college students from pursuing a career in education. Milanowski (2003) found that pay levels for starting teachers would need to be increased by nearly 50% to attract significant numbers of undergraduate science and technology majors into teaching. Auguste et al. (2010) also concluded that the top-performing school systems in the world, namely, Singapore, Finland, and South Korea, actively recruit and work earnestly to retain new teachers who are in the top third of their academic cohort. Similar strategies in the United States to attract, develop, reward, and retain effective teachers from the "top third" would prove highly cost-effective (although not inexpensive), especially in high-needs schools, when compared with the return on less effective K–12 reforms (Auguste et al., 2010).

Despite the reality of relatively low pay and little professional prestige, each year enthusiastic American college students with respectable academic qualifications choose to enter teacher-preparation programs in hopes of making a difference in the lives of children. Most of them are probably aware that they will work extra hours per week at home, both weeknights and weekends. Most probably are also aware that their "summer off" usually will require additional courses, seminars, and curriculum preparation for the new school year. And they probably are also aware that they will earn relatively lower wages than many of their college-educated peers and lower salaries than starting teachers in a few other industrialized countries. They may even be aware that teachers spend some of their own money on their students, because districts and schools do not supply all that is needed for their classrooms to function well. For example, the average teacher spends around $500 per year, but about 10% of our teachers spend over a $1,000 of their own money to do their job. So 1 or 2% of teachers' salaries is used to subsidize the education system in which they work.

Nevertheless, the desire to help children learn may always draw a pool of young, new teachers into the profession. But without adequate increases in their compensation as they gain experience and become better teachers, the real challenge may be to retain them in the classroom year after year as they gain experience and become better instructors.

References

Auguste, B., Kihn, P., & Miller, M. (2010). *Closing the talent gap: Attracting and retaining top-third graduates to careers in teaching.* New York, NY: McKinsey.

Ladd, H. F. (2007). Teacher labor markets in developed countries. *Excellence in the Classroom 17*(1), 201–218.

Milanowski, A. (2003). An exploration of the pay levels needed to attract students with mathematics, science and technology skills to a career in K–12 teaching, *Education Policy Analysis Archives, 11*(50), 1–25. Retrieved from epaa.asu.edu/ojs/article/view/278

Organisation for Economic Co-operation and Development (OECD). (2012). *Education at a glance 2012: OECD indicators.* Paris, France: OECD Publishing. Retrieved from tinyurl.com/ohawndp

Ripley, A. (2013). *The smartest kids in the world: And how they got that way.* New York, NY: Simon & Schuster.

⤚ MYTH 11 ⤙

Merit pay is a good way to increase the performance of teachers. Teachers should be evaluated on the basis of the performance of their students. Rewarding and punishing schools for the performance of their students will improve our nation's schools.

Since the enactment of the No Child Left Behind (NCLB) act in 2001, student, teacher, and school accountability measures have dominated school reform debates. Advocates assert that the way to improve the education system is to test more often and increase the stakes attached to the scores. The theory seems to be that a no-nonsense, rough-and-tough treatment is what is needed to whip those careless students and lazy teachers into shape! Students are being held back ("flunked," in other words), teachers are being fired, and schools are being shut down. But more than a decade of NCLB implementation has resulted in no changes in the achievement gap between poor and wealthy students, and gains on achievement tests are small, even after extensive time has been allocated in schools across the nation for direct preparation for the tests. President Obama's recent school reform initiative, Race to the Top, adds yet another seemingly sensible, but actually reprehensible, policy to the list of pressures on teachers: pay-for-performance, or merit pay. One of the stipulations of the RttT grant was that states had to implement a merit pay system based, in significant part, on student achievement scores. States also are encouraged to base other personnel decisions (e.g., retention, tenure, termination, etc.) on student growth data. For example, in four states—Delaware, Louisiana, Rhode Island, and Tennessee—some teachers seeking to update their licenses must meet certain criteria for their students' test scores. At the time of this writing, 44 states and the District of Columbia have submitted Race to the Top applications.

Most states have adopted a value-added measurement (VAM) method to statistically measure teacher performance based on student test scores. VAMs are designed to measure student growth from year to year by controlling for nonteacher influences, such as student social class standing or English language competency. But a host of other variables that are known to affect the growth of classroom achievement in any one year are totally unaccounted for (Berliner, 2014). Researchers and classroom teachers alike have warned against the use of merit pay systems in public schools. On top of major validity problems with the instruments used to determine merit, such systems can promote corruption and also impede teacher collaboration, one of the well-documented characteristics that make many schools good places in which to teach and learn (Leana, 2011). High-stakes tests, upon which VAMs rely, are known to narrow the curriculum in many schools and to foster what has come to be known as drill-and-kill test preparation. Regardless of the warnings about pay-for-performance that come from theoreticians and workers in schools and in business, educational policymakers have been promoting the myth that merit pay is an effective way to increase teacher performance. This is a hoax: Most contemporary businesses are too smart for such simple-minded solutions to the ever-present concern everyone has for productivity.

Advocates for merit pay have praised the use of competition among teachers and schools. They assume that a bit of rivalry will encourage teachers to be better teachers, which, in turn, will boost student achievement. The basic premise is that better teachers, as defined by standardized achievement tests, will be paid more money than their colleagues, thereby creating the incentive for other teachers to do better themselves. But it is hard to think of teachers as motivated primarily by money (see Myth 10). Moreover, teachers do not simply make things or sell things; they teach children everything from two-column addition to morality and citizenship. They teach how to play nicely and write persuasive essays. Much of what teachers do is hard to measure accurately, and thus bonuses dependent on objective measures, such as automobiles sold per week, phone calls made per day, or tomatoes picked per hour, seem totally inappropriate. This is where the business-minded folks miss the boat.

Nobody but the most selfish of parents and politicians really wants winners and losers among teachers and students. The American goal is for good teachers and successful students in every classroom. Even if it were possible to use student test scores to validly identify a few of the best and worst teachers in a school or district, that would do little to assure us that we had competent teachers in every class (Berliner, 2014; Darling-Hammond, Amrein-Beardsley, Haertel, & Rothstein, 2012).

Think about a situation where competition is appropriate, perhaps a baseball league. Coaches vie for the championship trophy each year, hoping for the sweet victory over their opponents. It's simple: There are winners and there are losers. Coaches of opposing teams don't share pitching strategies or practice regimens. They don't meet on their off days to reflect on their decisions and discuss opportunities for improvement. They don't pore over data together to develop strategic plans for fostering group and individual progress. Why? Because they want to win, and in order to win, others must lose. They recognize that winning coaches need two things: good coaching techniques, and, more important, good players. So they recruit. They search for the fastest, strongest, smartest players they can find. They look for players who have winning records, and players who spend time at home practicing, possibly with a private trainer. It helps if the players have a supportive family who take the time to chauffeur them to each practice and the money to feed them a decent meal before the game. The coach needs players who are willing to put in 110% effort at all times and who will battle through nerves during the bottom of the ninth. Coaches need this because to be the best, they need to start with the "better." This appears to be the strategy of many charter school operators, who pursue high test scores and high rates of graduation by dumping the weakest of their students and keeping the "better" ones (see Myth 3).

With VAMs, teachers, like coaches, are pushed to score the highest, which means, as in baseball, others must lose. It means that many teachers are likely to abandon their collaborative efforts of helping students of all classrooms succeed, in order to increase the chances of their own classrooms' success. It means that teachers who seek a bonus, or fear getting fired, must plot to get the most affluent students because, as history shows, these are the students with winning records. In Houston, with a history of merit pay, teachers talk about the "money kids," the kids who get them the big bonuses (Amrein-Beardsley & Collins, 2012). These are middle-class or wealthy children with low average scores from the year before. They are expected to grow the most. Definitely to be avoided are kids who won't score well, such as English language learners, special education students, and students who are gifted and talented. The latter are to be avoided because most tests do not have enough "ceiling" in them to track the gains made by students who are well ahead of their grade level. They actually may gain a lot, of course, but it won't show on the tests because gifted children often perform well above what is measured at their particular grade. So teachers seeking bonuses have learned to avoid them!

In addition, when the stakes are high, cheating is inevitable (Nichols & Berliner, 2007). In sports we can point to Sammy Sosa and Lance Armstrong; in education it's the superintendents of schools in Atlanta, Washington, DC, and a dozen other cities. Competition is appropriate in some arenas, but in education it is a repugnant motivator that will alienate teachers from one another and decrease the chances of all students succeeding. Competition is about winners and losers among teachers and their students. A Darwinian survival of the fittest, applied to education, cannot be healthy for an education system inside a democracy.

Despite movies such as *Waiting for Superman* and *Won't Back Down*, or school reform advocates like Michelle Rhee, the problem with public education is not that schools are populated with lazy, careless, I-love-my-summers-off kinds of teachers. Of course they exist, just as do some bad doctors, police officers, lawyers, and, dare we imagine, politicians. But in truth, schools are filled with dedicated, highly educated, competent teachers. The real challenge to public education is that teachers and schools have only a relatively small impact on student achievement. The major predictors of student achievement scores are outside-of-school factors, chief among them being family social class standing. Yet, legislators and the business community enact policies requiring teachers to triumph over the well-established facts about the sources of student test score achievement, demanding that all students, regardless of their circumstances, succeed in their classrooms.

Simple-minded merit pay systems based on test scores are what the politically powerful impose on the politically weak. Attempt to pay doctors or hospitals based on the recovery and survival of their patients, without taking into account the nature of the medical problems they present with, and you will soon discover that the "best" doctors and the "best" hospitals never treat the toughest cases. Or propose a merit pay system for legislators based on how many of their bills pass, and you quickly will be informed that the work of politicians is far too complex and multifaceted to be evaluated in such a crude manner. Those who have never walked in a teacher's shoes have no idea how complex and multifaceted classroom life actually is. Policymakers need to come to terms with the realities faced by teachers on a daily basis and consider that reality in discussions about evaluating teacher performance. Teachers do have an impact on their students, and good teachers matter; but to assume that teachers perform a simple service, and are the number one influence in student achievement, is simply not true (see Myth 9).

Suspend rational belief for a moment and assume that competition is good for teachers (and students) and that teachers should be measured by the test scores of their students. We still encounter the problem of accurate measures of teacher effectiveness. The value-added measurement methods that states have adopted promise to control for the outside influences, such as socioeconomic status and race. However, educators around the country, including education scholars and classroom teachers, have vehemently condemned the use of VAMs, as was made vividly public during the 2012 Chicago teacher strike. These educators did not fight against being evaluated per se, but they argued against the fairness of VAMs as the means of doing so. They understand the intricacies of teaching on a level that policymakers and the general public do not. They understand that a classroom test score says little about a student's overall achievements for the year, and that such scores are incapable of capturing the realities of classroom life faced by the teacher (and the student). Test scores are influenced by the realities of family affection, income and hardships, neighborhood crime rates and after-school facilities, hunger and hormones (Berliner, 2012). Teachers have witnessed high-achieving students fall victim to test anxiety, and they have witnessed low-achieving students excel against all odds. They know that one testing day is different from the last and that the two scores should be compared with caution. And researchers back them up in that understanding. VAM scores vary erratically from year to year for the same teacher who teaches in the same way (Newton, Darling-Hammond, Haertel, & Thomas, 2010).

Beyond what these educators recognize about the over-reliance on student test scores to measure student achievement, they also are keenly aware of the validity issues involved in using these test scores in teacher and school evaluations. They have watched as teachers and schools serving our nation's most vulnerable students, including minority and poor students, English language learners, and students in special education, perpetually are labeled as low achieving. As Houston teachers have discovered, teaching a homogeneous group of motivated and affluent students is the best chance of earning big bonuses. It now seems clear that when merit pay is linked to student test scores, with their reliability and validity both questionable, such schemes cannot be justified. Other ways to evaluate teachers exist; for example, observations by peers or supervisors, portfolios, earning National Board

Certification, parent surveys, and so forth. But even then, linking these alternative methods of evaluation to merit pay will harm the profession and not serve students well.

Furthermore, we live in a 21st-century world and expect our students to have 21st-century skills, but we keep assessing our students and their teachers with methods best suited for a 19th-century model of education, one based on the simple transmission of knowledge. Texts, and what teachers say, are what students memorize, and memory of the knowledge and skills transmitted in these ways is tested. Modern companies, including modern factories, have begun to realize the potential of collaboration and have incorporated this method of work into their daily routines. Take Google, for example. Everything from the building architecture to the staff meetings encourages collaboration among the "Googlers." They recognize that they can do bigger and better things when people work together instead of against one another, and that the best results are produced when many brains are working on a problem instead of one. They have capitalized on what it means to do business in the 21st century. If policymakers want to use a business model to improve education rather than merely beat up on teachers' unions, then they should focus on the companies that are defining the future of work. Those companies seek skills not measured by today's tests of either our students or our teachers.

References

Amrein-Beardsley, A., & Collins, C. (2012). The SAS education value-added assessment system (SAS® EVAAS®) in the Houston Independent School District (HISD): Intended and unintended consequences. *Education Policy Analysis Archives, 20*(12). Retrieved from epaa.asu.edu/ojs/article/view/1096

Berliner, D. C. (2012). Effects of inequality and poverty vs. teachers and schooling on America's youth. *Teachers College Record,116*(1) Retrieved from www.tcrecord.org/PrintContent.asp?ContentID=16889

Berliner, D. C. (2014). Exogenous variables and value-added assessments: A fatal flaw. *Teachers College Record.* Retrieved from www.tcrecord.org/Content.asp?ContentId=17293

Darling-Hammond, L., Amrein-Beardsley, A., Haertel, E., & Rothstein, J. (2012, March). Evaluating teacher evaluation. *Phi Delta Kappan, 93*(6), 8–15.

Leana, C. R. (2011, Fall). The missing link in school reform. *Stanford Social Innovation Review.* Retrieved from tinyurl.com/4yanqed

Newton, X., Darling-Hammond, L., Haertel, E., & Thomas, E. (2010). Value added modeling of teacher effectiveness: An exploration of stability across models and contexts. *Educational Policy Analysis Archives, 18*(23). Retrieved from epaa.asu.edu/ojs/article/view/810

Nichols, S. L., & Berliner, D. C. (2007). *Collateral damage: How high-stakes testing corrupts America's schools.* Cambridge, MA: Harvard Education Press.

Rothstein, J., & Mathis, W. J. (2013). *Review of two culminating reports from the MET project.* Boulder, CO: National Education Policy Center. Retrieved from tinyurl.com/acuahee

⋘ MYTH 12 ⋙

Teachers in schools that serve the poor are not very talented.

The debate over teacher quality in schools that serve mostly poor and working-class children is a complex one. So complex, in fact, that the two parts of this myth actually seem to contradict each other. On the one hand, there are many incredibly talented, effective, and committed teachers working in poor schools. On the other hand, they are certainly not as qualified or prepared as their peers in schools that serve the rich. However, any gap in the quality or effectiveness between these two groups of teachers, as measured by their students' standardized test scores, is probably not due to a difference in talent, drive, or effort, but rather is due to structural inequities: intentional, constructed unfairness that produces predictable and unequal results in terms of student achievement. These inequities are hiding in plain sight in teacher-preparation programs and school systems. The training of teachers who end up in poor and working-class schools hardly prepared them for the challenges of working with students who live in poverty. Once they earn their posts, they receive less support and lower salaries, and have many incentives to leave these schools for jobs in wealthier communities (Berliner, 2006).

It is no secret that students with the most pressing needs often sit in classrooms staffed by the least prepared teachers, while students who come to school with access to the most resources outside of school often have access to highly qualified teachers inside their schools (Darling-Hammond, Holtzman, Gatlin, & Heilig, 2005). The distribution of teachers is certainly an example of the rich getting richer. But make no mistake; this is not a random distribution. Structural inequities at all levels of teacher preparation, development, support, and professional activity allow for, if not promote, a system where teaching in poor and working-class communities is seen as a stepping stone to positions in more affluent communities. The excellent work of teachers who persist in poor and working-class schools is not made visible by most indicators of so-called "teacher effectiveness" (Duncan-Andrade, 2005).

The rigged system of teacher preparation, development, and support begins in traditional and alternative certification programs. Most traditional programs do an adequate job of preparing teachers for positions in middle-class and suburban schools, where students do not bring to school the challenges that come with living in poverty. It is hard to find traditional teacher education programs with a specific emphasis on working with poor and working-class children that stretch beyond one elective course, or modifications to core curriculum made by individual instructors (Darling-Hammond & Bransford, 2005).

Take, for instance, the experiences of students in one of the largest teacher-preparation institutions in the country, who have two traditional paths to becoming a teacher. Students can earn either a bachelor's degree in education or a bachelor's degree in a content area, then pass necessary licensure exams to become a classroom teacher. In the bachelor's of education program at this particular university, there are no required courses that focus specifically on supporting the learning of children living in poverty. There are no classes that build the skills, knowledge, or even the dispositions needed to offer poor and working-class students a quality education. For the content-based degree, since these programs are housed in colleges and departments that are not education focused, students may not take any courses that focus specifically on teaching, let alone teaching in a low-income community. This lack of preparation does not prohibit either of these groups of teachers from taking a position in a low-income community, as most of the jobs available to them after graduation are indeed in schools and school districts that serve the poor. In fact, many states offer incentives to new teachers to teach in these schools by forgiving loans or offering grants for further education as long as they teach in these schools for a few years. So, even though the university did not prepare these candidates for teaching in a low-income community, most of the university's graduates will indeed find themselves in one of these schools in their first job.

Alternative certification programs are also available to people who wish to become teachers. These programs, including Teach For America, The New Teacher Project, the New York Teaching Fellows, and other similar programs, usually emphasize working with children in low-income communities, yet these programs are often stripped down preparation programs that focus on efficiency, rather than deep learning. Teach For America, for instance, offers only a 5-week crash course to its candidates, which might include being a lead teacher for less than an hour a day only 4 days a week. Although these programs may emphasize working in poor schools, they have not been found to be any better than traditional programs at developing effective teachers as measured by student achievement or other measures of teacher quality (Darling-Hammond et al., 2005).

Structural inequities ensure that schools in low-income communities are staffed with teachers who were not prepared for working in these communities. Once they arrive in these schools, these teachers face even more challenges. Due to funding disparities, they are likely to have less access to support, development, and resources than teachers in middle-class and affluent communities. They are more likely to teach in an overcrowded classroom in an aging building, and to teach students who have experienced the stress of living in poverty their entire life.

It doesn't take long for these teachers to begin to look for positions in more affluent communities—positions that previously were denied to them due to their lack of experience. These are also the positions they actually were prepared to take when they studied to become a teacher in the years before their first placements. In these "better" positions, they are more likely to experience success and feelings of self-efficacy, and also will receive a larger salary due to an increase in base pay as well as increases that come with the years of experience they bring. These teachers probably completed the requirement of teaching in a Title I school that came with loan forgiveness, if they needed that. They also experienced a great deal of turnover in school and district leadership in their first placements. Outside of their professional life, they are probably more likely to want to buy a home in more affluent communities and, given the massive under-representation of undergraduates from low-income communities, they are more likely to "return home" when they take one of these positions. Why wouldn't these teachers "graduate" to more affluent schools? Schools in poor and working-class communities are continually staffed with a stream of new, beginning, and underprepared teachers, while schools in affluent areas draw from a pool of experienced and well-prepared teachers.

But what of the teachers who stay in their original placements in schools in low-income communities or, rarer still, leave positions in affluent communities to teach poor and working-class students? These folks teach with a cause, often feeling what a leading scholar on urban teachers, Jeff Duncan-Andrade (2005), calls a "duty" to working with these children. It is easy to argue that these teachers are actually more talented, committed, and dedicated, and of higher quality than their suburban peers, especially when we take into consideration the challenges they face in raising levels of student achievement and educational attainment. Urban teachers are given beat-up cars full of potential, and told to make them run better if they can. Suburban teachers are given the keys to a BMW and told not to wreck it. Which sounds like the more difficult task?

References

Berliner, D. C. (2006). Our impoverished view of education reform. *Teachers College Record, 108*(6). Retrieved from www.tcrecord.org/Content. asp?contentid=12106

Darling-Hammond, L., & Bransford, J. (Eds.). (2005). *Preparing teachers for a changing world: What teachers should learn and be able to do.* San Francisco, CA: Jossey-Bass.

Darling-Hammond, L., Holtzman, D. J., Gatlin, S. J., & Heilig, J. V. (2005). Does teacher preparation matter? Evidence about teacher certification, Teach For America, and teacher effectiveness. *Education Policy Analysis Archives, 13*(42). Retrieved from epaa.asu.edu/epaa/v13n42/

Duncan-Andrade, J. M. R. (2005). Developing social justice educators. *Education Leadership, 62*(6), 70–73.

∽ MYTH 13 ∾

Teach For America teachers are well trained, highly qualified, and get amazing results.

I, Victor Diaz, am a proud Teach For America alum and a current full-time staff member. I have high expectations for TFA and I can point out many examples of how this organization has failed to meet these expectations and not kept its promise to poor and working-class communities across this nation. I also can point out many examples of the times it has, and you've probably heard that story already in the media. So, I write this chapter as a critical friend of TFA, offering a loving critique of a complicated program.

Like any social program of substance and importance, understanding and evaluating TFA are complicated. They're complicated because of its history, its supporters and critics, its methods, and the nature of its mission. So, when we think about the effectiveness of TFA teachers, we also must attempt to understand the complexity of the whole system.

TFA ascended from a college senior thesis to a multimillion-dollar national nonprofit over the course of about 12 months in 1990, led by founder and former CEO Wendy Kopp. In the decade before Kopp's thesis, President Reagan sought to fulfill his campaign promise to dismantle the U.S. Department of Education by commissioning a blue-ribbon panel called the National Commission on Excellence in Education to report on the sorry state of the nation's education systems. In 1983, this panel produced *A Nation at Risk: The Imperative for Educational*

Reform. The commissioners argued our nation was a small step away from losing its place in the world due to an ineffective and inefficient education system. The culprits? Teachers who didn't know the subjects they were supposed to teach or how to teach them, and the universities that prepared them. The report was sensational and filled with inaccuracies (Berliner & Biddle, 1996), yet still highly influential on approaches to education reform that followed for the next 2 decades.

In this climate of fear, panic, and despair, TFA argued that the education system described in *A Nation at Risk* and similar reports could be fixed by recruiting the nation's best and brightest to lead us out of the darkness. If they taught for 2 years, then used that frontline experience to fight for systematic change in the education system, the so-called achievement gap between rich and poor, minority and majority could be closed.

To legitimize its entry onto the scene, TFA needed a villain. A community doesn't need TFA to set up shop unless it believes those who teach their children and run their schools can't do the job themselves. So, intentionally and unintentionally, the organization cast several groups as the Banditos of the Education System: teachers, teachers' unions, teacher educators, teacher-preparation programs, and school and district leadership. TFA spinoffs like The New Teacher Project, the Knowledge Is Power Project (KIPP), the Relay Graduate School of Education, and even the chancellorship of Michelle Rhee in Washington, DC, all reflect TFA's beliefs about the limitations of working within the system and the need to overhaul public education from top to bottom. Even today, when reading through cover letters in application essays, we see that those who hope to join TFA often compose melodramas. Data we analyzed (Fischman & Diaz, 2012) led to the conclusion that recruits seek acceptance to TFA because they feel that teachers aren't doing their jobs well, or systems are failing communities, or unions are holding the system hostage, or they remember the bad teachers they had when they were in school.

As crucial as the villains are in TFA's heroic story, recognizing those who are not cast in the role of villain is more important: business leaders, elected officials, philanthropic foundations, and wealthy institutions and individuals. Bad teaching is the enemy, not the dismantling of public assistance programs meant to combat poverty and redistribute wealth. Low-quality teacher education programs are the villains, not local chambers of commerce that fight for lower tax burdens for corporations that shrink public coffers. Teachers' unions are "terrorist organizations," as Secretary of Education Rod Paige publicly called them, but at the same time philanthropic foundations that use their wealth to push an ideology of privatization and limited government are to be respected. The administration of George W. Bush was among the most vocal supporters of TFA, even commending the organization in a State of the Union address. Providing more publicity and support, First Lady Laura Bush, and her daughter Jenna, donated all the profits of a children's book they authored to TFA.

It is important, though, to understand not only the bad guys in TFA's heroic tale, but the good guys as well. At the same time that the Reagan administration rolled back support of public programs and engaged in class warfare with the poor and working class, the so-called "me" generation was coming of age in our nation's most prestigious universities. Although most of this generation seemed to seek private, individual, material wealth at any cost, others were described by Kopp as feeling that corporate America wasn't the place for them. But these ambitious young people didn't know what else to do with their talents. Some of these misfits also felt both gratitude and guilt for their elevated social position. What better way to assuage that guilt and give back to their country than to fix a prominent social issue by committing 2 years to be a teacher in a low-income rural or urban community?

In one of the first books about TFA, curriculum theorist and professor Thomas Popkewitz (1998) described the majority of corps members as privileged people "struggling for the soul": simultaneously trying to save themselves from the damnation of corporate greed and the legacy of institutionalized racism while saving the souls of unfortunate youth born into poverty through no fault of their own. Others, less generously, have described teacher corps members as nothing more than "résumé builders." In the words of Kopp (2001) herself, "If top recent college graduates devoted two years to teaching in public schools, they could have a real impact on the lives of disadvantaged kids. Because they themselves excelled academically, they would be relentless in their efforts to ensure their students achieved. They would throw themselves into their jobs, working investment-banking hours in classrooms instead of skyscrapers on Wall Street. They would question the way things are and fight to do what's right for children" (p. 6).

Rhetoric aside, Teach For America is founded on one very problematic assumption, namely, that TFA first- and second-year teachers are better than other teachers. TFA teachers are expected to teach more effectively and efficiently, and to lead their students to higher academic achievement than the people who otherwise might hold their positions in a school. The experience, training, and commitment of those other people do not matter. In the early days of TFA, this was thought to be a no-brainer. Many of the positions held by corps members otherwise would be held by other beginners with more training and preparation, re-tread teachers who were scraped from the bottom of the barrel, or, in many cases, long-term substitutes. The organization and its supporters operated under a "there is no alternative" approach to hiring TFA teachers in under-resourced schools. Twenty years later, this approach has not changed much, as TFA continues to grow in both size and reach, expanding from 20 to 46 regions of the country in the past 10 years.

The best answer to the question, "How good are TFA teachers?" is "It depends." The data on TFA teacher effectiveness are incongruent and contradictory. Some studies indicate that TFA teachers are as effective as or slightly less effective than beginning teachers who have graduated from traditional university teacher training programs, while other studies show they are slightly more effective. TFA's website features a review of studies conducted by research institutes and state departments of education that support the effectiveness of TFA teachers, entirely contradicted by a review published by the National Education Policy Center (Heilig & Jez, 2010). Perhaps all these reports are right. In some places, TFA teachers do better than their peers, and in other places, TFA does worse. And when we explore what we mean by "peers," we add even more to the complexity of finding an answer to the question, "How good are TFA teachers?"

Consider two TFA teachers at a middle school in Phoenix, Arizona. "Martha" is the 7th-grade language arts teacher, while another first-year corps member named "Byron" is the 8th-grade language arts teacher. Each teaches his or her entire grade level, including students with special needs who spend time in mainstream classrooms. This means that these two corps members are the entire middle school language arts team at their school and are responsible for all reading and writing instruction for the middle school.

Early in their first year, both teachers struggled. Martha's students constantly disrupted her lessons by speaking out inappropriately, and since most students did not do their homework, Martha stopped assigning it. In fact, 4 weeks into school, she had not entered a single grade in the grade book and she couldn't fully explain what the students would be learning the next week. In Byron's classroom, students stole his cellphone, which he didn't notice until the end of the day. The next day, he yelled at the students before each class, calling them "thieves." By the end of the day, his phone mysteriously reappeared on his desk. For the first few weeks of school, after surveying students for their interests, he read newspaper and magazine articles with his students about fashion and sports, as well as a story or two from a teenage literary magazine. While his students certainly have found the articles interesting, it is not entirely clear what they have been learning. Like Martha, he also doesn't assign homework nor does he have grades in his grade book halfway through the first quarter.

Both Martha and Byron were very aware of their struggles, which they attributed to a lack of support from their school and district. The school used a discipline system that accomplished little. The instructional coaches who were supposed to work with them had been mostly unavailable, due to both taking maternity leave, then being assigned administrative tasks because the school was short of office staff. Martha and Byron, though, found support from the staff of TFA. Each week, they attended 3-hour sessions after school about unit planning, lesson planning, and setting a clear vision for their classroom. On a Saturday, Martha went to her TFA support provider's home to spend the entire day planning for her classes and developing systems to help her maintain control of the class. Most of the short stories, learning activities, and graphic organizers Martha and Byron used in their class come from other TFA teachers or an online bank of resources on TFA's website.

For their entire first year, Martha and Byron continued to struggle on all fronts. This phenomenon is not unique to these two teachers, as research has shown similar levels of frustration over a lack of support in other TFA teachers in Phoenix, some of whom simply felt abandoned by TFA after the school year began (Veltri, 2010). Given these kinds of struggles, these first-year teachers were certainly not highly qualified by any measure. In fact, the majority of TFA teachers do not reach "highly qualified" status, as defined by state certifying bodies, until the end of their 2-year commitment, after completing the necessary coursework during the 2 years. Sadly, this is around the time that many TFA teachers finish their commitments. It seemed obvious that these teachers were not well trained and would not achieve excellent academic results with their students.

Adding to the complexity of assessing the competence of TFA teachers is this: Despite their struggles, based on data reported on the Arizona Department of Education website, in the year that Martha and Byron taught them, 7th- and 8th-graders at their school passed the state's test of standards at levels comparable to 7th- and 8th-graders the year before! In addition, the cohort of students they taught scored about the same as they had the year before.

It is hard to say whether TFA teachers are better or worse than other teachers. But we certainly can say the assumption that the entire organization rests on—that its first- and second-year teachers will be the force in schools that will bridge the achievement gap—is surely faulty, as the case of Martha and Byron makes clear. In addition, as many critics of TFA have pointed out, TFA problematically and significantly has contributed to the mission of conservative, neo-liberal movements to destroy unions and public education (Hartman, 2011). TFA adds weight to the notion that any smart, young person can outperform old, tired, union dues-paying school teachers. Smart, young people also cost less money and are not likely to complain as much when the pensions and health care programs of older teachers are gutted. And, if teaching school is nothing but a trade that anyone can be trained to do in a 5-week summer program, it hardly deserves the autonomy, respect, and pay accorded to real professionals. Nearly every TFA success can be cited as a justification for nontraditional teacher certification programs that condense teacher training to a few months or a few online courses. Thus, in Texas, filled with neo-conservative policymakers, 40% of all new teachers now come out of TFA and other nontraditional teacher education programs (Smith & Pandolfo, 2011). These novice teachers have experienced enormously variable training, and almost all of them teach poor and minority students. The set of beliefs that are the cornerstone of TFA, along with data suggesting that relatively untrained teachers of the poor may be as good as traditionally trained teachers, provide neo-conservative reformers support for their negative views about teachers and public institutions, and help mask their indifference to economic injustice.

But TFA success stories are not just a counterpoint to the stories of failure; they also stand as proof that poor and working-class children have the same potential as their more privileged peers. Given the right resources, poor children can achieve well in school. This demonstration is significant, as it humanizes groups of people who often are seen as culturally deficient at best and incapable or defective at worst.

Stories of TFA corps members who win teacher-of-the-year awards and stories like Martha's and Byron's make it clear that TFA is neither hero nor villain. The cheerleaders for TFA will latch onto the heroic tales of successful corps members and alumni of the program—and there are many—while the harshest critics will attack TFA for its role in the conservative attack on public education and the ineffectiveness of many corps members like Martha and Byron.

In fact, Summer 2013 brought with it a new round of attacks on TFA from some familiar places, as well as a new source: some of its alumni. The TFA critics were especially angry over their organization's role in support of the privatization of education. They saw privatization, ultimately, as the goal of Chicago Mayor Rahm Emanuel's decision in 2013 to close 48 schools and lay off 850 teachers and staff. But at the same time, he planned to welcome 350 new corps members. This is of concern to the Chicago TFA teachers, the Chicago Teachers Association, and the public, who have serious questions about TFA's role in Emanuel's and other "reformers'" plans in this city as well as others. Perhaps in the next edition of this volume, concerns over TFA's role in the privatization of public education will be a more prominent topic than the preparation and effectiveness of its teachers.

As noted at the start of this chapter, because articulate and convincing defenders and critics of the program exist, the evaluation of TFA is complicated, and its politics hotly contested. The vast majority of the 20,000 young people who have been TFA teachers have entered classrooms with a little bit of knowledge, but most have acted with the best of intentions. TFA is driven by people's sense of hope and altruism. Although there may be controversies whirling around TFA, we can't pretend for a moment that the situation in public education was just fine for poor and working-class kids before Wendy Kopp's senior thesis. The state of public education in the communities that employ TFA probably would not be any better today if TFA were simply to vanish.

References

Berliner, D. C., & Biddle, B. J. (1996). *The manufactured crisis: Myths, fraud and the attack on America's public schools.* New York, NY: Basic Books.

Fischman, G. E., & Diaz, V. H. (2012). Teach for what America? Beginning teachers' reflections about their professional choices and the economic crisis. In D. R. Cole (Ed.), *Surviving economic crises through education* (pp. 79–94) . New York, NY: Peter Lang.

Hartman, A. (2011). Teach For America: Liberal mission helps conservative agenda. *The Washington Post.* Retrieved from tinyurl.com/qju79fe

Heilig, J. V., & Jez, S. J. (2010). *Teach For America: A review of the evidence.* Boulder, CO, & Tempe, AZ: Education and the Public Interest Center & Education Policy Research Unit. Retrieved from tinyurl.com/pwsyzrl

Kopp, W. (2001). *One day, all children . . . : The unlikely triumph of Teach for America and what I learned along the way.* New York, NY: Public Affairs.

National Commission on Excellence in Education. (1983). *A nation at risk: The imperatives for educational reform.* Washington, DC: U.S. Department of Education.

Popkewitz, T. S. (1998). *Struggling for the soul: the politics of schooling and the construction of the teacher.* New York, NY: Teachers College Press.

Smith, M., & Pandolfo, N. (2011, November 26). For-profit certification for teachers is booming. *The New York Times.* Retrieved from www.nytimes.com/2011/11/27/us/for-profit-certification-for-teachers-in-texas-is-booming.html?pagewanted=all&_r=0

Veltri, B. T. (2010). *Learning on other people's kids: Becoming a Teach For America teacher.* Charlotte, NC: Information Age.

❧ MYTH 14 ❧

Subject matter knowledge is the most important asset
a teacher can possess.

Subject matter knowledge is an important characteristic of successful teachers. But content knowledge alone is not enough to make a good teacher. We can all imagine, or know, a "nutty professor." This person may be thought of as brilliant, perhaps a leading expert in his or her field. But when such people attempt to describe concepts and teach applications to their students, the class is confused. Teaching is not just about the transfer of knowledge; it's also about being able to guide students to develop their own knowledge, skills, attitudes, and beliefs. And even if it were solely about the transfer of knowledge, not everyone knows how to transfer knowledge well.

Despite the problems in defining excellent teaching, common sense suggests that it is an amalgam of many skills and dispositions. Of course, subject area knowledge is one of them. Another necessary characteristic of those we consider to be good teachers is teaching or instructional skill. This includes classroom management and the quality of the presentations made. Perhaps we would add dispositions like passion for education, or a love of children, or a love of a subject matter area, like biology, or love of a particular topic, like a Shakespeare play. None of these skills and dispositions matters much, however, if students do not want to learn. So in certain communities, and with certain students, the ability to motivate may be a necessary teaching skill. In the end, good teaching requires that educators possess a set of characteristics, and those that argue subject matter knowledge is all a teacher needs to know, will do harm to children and the education profession. That was the proposal of Governor Fife Symington of Arizona, before being convicted of financial crimes and sent to jail. He tried to get laws passed so that teachers would not be required to be certified or attend colleges of education. All they need, he said, is "a college degree, a good mind, a clean background check and a desire to teach" (Symington, 1995). Symington, and those like him, are wrong. But to be fair, beginning teachers from most teacher training institutions, and those with no teacher education, all struggle their first few years. The issue is what teachers learn as they develop, if they choose to stay in the profession.

Despite the U.S. having so many who advocate abandoning teacher education, educational agencies throughout the world continue to make commitments to train new teachers. Almost all these nations require preservice teachers to take courses on pedagogy, emphasizing teaching or instructional skills appropriate for different age groups, alongside courses for learning content knowledge in depth. Teaching skills are necessary for teachers to choose and then impart the important concepts in a particular subject area, create a learning environment where students feel comfortable and competent, and to develop the dispositions and mindsets of students that are required in order to learn x or y at a high level.

Content knowledge without coursework or training in these other matters is insufficient if we seek excellence in teaching. Let us take a simple example: classrooms where management looks easy and discipline is never a problem. A simple inference is that something about a teacher's charisma and personality produces that state of affairs. It looks like some teachers have it, and some don't! But good management is almost always the function of routines taught to students over the first few weeks of school, so that when observed later in the school year, it all looks seamless. These routines are learned in preservice education coursework and during student teaching. Possessing content knowledge is necessary, but it is not at all sufficient for becoming a teacher whose classes learn well what they are supposed to.

Those who continue to believe that content knowledge is both necessary and sufficient to achieve excellence as a teacher always face quite legitimate arguments about the need for instructional skills to help students acquire their knowledge. Telling, talking, lecturing, showing PowerPoints, putting students online, or showing films is not what makes a teacher good. Those ways of communicating subject matter knowledge need to be augmented by a large number of instructional skills. Teachers need to learn how to start a lesson; motivate students; design and act on information from formative assessments, some of which is collected in real time as instruction occurs; design tests and give feedback on the students' performance that leads to improved performance; handle students not attending; cope with students that are noncompliant or disrespectful; and dozens of other tasks related to instruction. Textbooks in education list hundreds of skills that research suggests are helpful to teachers, and these are quite separate from content knowledge (Gage & Berliner, 1998; Hattie, 2009).

The clinical wisdom gained by other teachers is also a source of instructional knowledge. We have heard, for example, that on rainy days teachers should keep the pace of classroom instruction quite fast, because the students cannot go outside for recess and burn off energy. So if you slow instruction down, the students get "wild." We also have heard that lunch on Mondays in elementary schools should be moved up an hour or more, since many children have not been well fed over the weekend and they do not learn much when they are hungry. None of the teaching skills mentioned, nor these insights by experienced teachers, has anything to do with content knowledge. But without this kind of craft knowledge, the transfer of content knowledge from teachers who know their content would be seriously hampered.

The scholars that study teaching also suggest that, besides dispositions, there is something more than instructional knowledge and content knowledge, and it goes by the peculiar name of "pedagogical content knowledge," or PCK (Shulman, 1986). This form of knowledge is hard to define, but may be thought of as teachers' interpretations and transformations of subject matter knowledge to fit the context they are in. Teaching children in a suburban honors physics class requires a different presentation, different examples, maybe even a different method than does teaching physics to ordinary students in an inner city. This special ability to vary content knowledge by setting, by makeup of the class, and even for different children in a class, is separate both from content knowledge and from a teacher's general instructional skill. The teachers with a developed sense of PCK will use a baseball example for one student, a cooking example for another, and an example related to automobiles for a third. This is a special knack that is neither taught easily nor acquired by every teacher. But it is often what makes one teacher seem exceptional and another one ordinary. PCK is also about having knowledge of different ways to represent subject matter (a drawing as well as an equation, a metaphor that makes things clear). It is also about understanding students' conceptions of the subject and thus understanding where they are going to make errors in acquiring that subject matter. Teachers' PCK has been assessed in the subject of mathematics. It was found to be a very strong predictor of student success, over and above the teachers' content knowledge (Baumert et al., 2010).

PCK depends on, but is different from, content knowledge. This kind of knowledge is deeply rooted in classroom life, acquired by conscientious, thoughtful teachers over a considerable period of time. Some call it craft knowledge. A White middle-class teacher teaching in an inner-city minority neighborhood who has acquired PCK finds ways of teaching that are culturally relevant for students who are not of the same culture and social class as the teacher.

Pedagogical content knowledge is part content knowledge and part pedagogical or instructional knowledge, but it is also neither and both; a bit of a chimera. But most researchers concerned with teaching believe that it is real, a special form of an educator's professional knowing, akin to the professional wisdom you hope your physician and your automobile mechanic have each acquired. This is also known as case knowledge, the knowledge derived from succeeding or failing at solving professional problems. You cannot be a great physician or a great auto mechanic without picking up a good deal of case knowledge earned through reflection about why you succeeded or failed in solving problems arising out of your practice. Some research suggests that it is case knowledge that most distinguishes expert from novice teachers (Berliner, 1994).

We may hope that those who come in to education for a short period of time have content knowledge. They also may pick up some pedagogical knowledge from coursework and their initial experience, but they are likely never to acquire PCK or the case knowledge needed to become an expert. That is one of the reasons so many experienced educators dislike Teach For America and other alternative certification programs, where undertrained novice teachers expect to be in education for a short period of time (see Myth 13). These teachers are likely never to have had instruction that could help build PCK, and they rarely stay long enough to acquire the case knowledge they need to develop expertise as a teacher.

One more issue about this myth is relevant. Old notions of teachers as the "sage on the stage" thankfully are being replaced by a vision of our best teachers acting more like a "guide on the side." That is, we are witnessing an end to the dominance of a simple transmission model of teaching. In this traditional model the teachers have the content knowledge and transfer it from their heads to their students' heads, and then the quality of the transfer is measured by the students' ability to give back on tests a close approximation of the content obtained from teachers and textbooks. But educators are asked by many in the business community to develop in our students the skills deemed important for the 21st century: independent thinking, debate, working in groups, participating in projects of depth and duration, developing creative solutions to common problems, and so forth. So the best teachers of the coming age will need to know their content, of course, as they always needed to. But if that is their only asset, they will fail as teachers and fail the country.

References

Baumert, J., Kunter, M., Blum, W., Brunner, M., Voss, T., Jordan, A., Klusmann, U., Krauss, S., Neubrand, M.,&. Tsai, Y-M. (2010). Teachers' mathematical knowledge, cognitive activation in the classroom, and student progress. *American Educational Research Journal, 47*(1), 133–180.

Berliner, D. C. (1994). Expertise: The wonders of exemplary performance. In J. N. Mangieri & C. Collins Block (Eds.), *Creating powerful thinking in teachers and students* (pp. 141–186). Ft. Worth, TX: Holt, Rinehart and Winston.

Gage, N. L., & Berliner, D. C. (1998). *Educational psychology* (6th ed.). Boston, MA: Houghton Mifflin.
Hattie, J. (2009). *Visible learning: A synthesis of over 800 meta-analyses relating to achievement*. Abingdon, United Kingdom: Routledge.
Shulman, L. S. (1986). Those who understand: Knowledge growth in teaching. *Educational Researcher, 15*(2), 4–14.
Symington, F. (1995, October 26). Retrieved from tinyurl.com/mdlnroa

⤝ MYTH 15 ⤞

Teachers' unions are responsible for much poor school performance. Incompetent teachers cannot be fired if they have tenure.

If you have stumbled across any form of education debate over the past decade, then there is a good chance that you have heard someone throw around the union boogeyman myth, as if there were substantial evidence to support the ground on which it stood. School reform advocates, whose mantra habitually takes some form of pro-accountability stand, blame teachers' unions for public education's supposed failures. Speaking to a crowd of sympathetic "reformers" in Minneapolis in 2013, a magnet school principal from Connecticut, Steve Perry, called teachers' unions "roaches," while former secretary of education Rod Paige described the NEA as a "terrorist organization."

Anti-union sentiments have taken root in the public narrative about teachers, often showing up in newspaper articles, political debates, and popular documentaries. The lazy teacher sits with feet propped up on the desk, newspaper in hand, students running amok, and the poor principal has her or his hands tied because of the teachers' union–protected tenure. This story, stylized a bit differently for various contexts but always with the same motif, has tugged at America's heartstrings. It stereotypically pairs the incompetent teacher with the neediest of students and places the frustrated principal in a state of perpetual despair. The message is always clear: Unions protect bad teachers and hurt students. In Arizona, for example, this rhetoric is common in the legislature and newspapers, even though the conservative Fordham Institute ranks the Arizona union as the weakest/least influential union in America (Winkler, Scull, & Zeehandelaar, 2012). The unfortunate part of this anti-union campaign is that the public has heard the message so often and from so many sources, it has begun to believe it, when in fact the message isn't just deceptive, it is entirely not true.

Teachers' unions, like other workers' unions, have figured prominently in the history of the United States and have helped shape the working conditions that we know today (e.g., minimum wages, 40-hour work week, child labor laws, and the like). The two largest teachers' unions are the National Education Association (NEA) and the American Federation of Teachers (AFT), both of which have been supported by many educators for their efforts to improve pay, benefits, and working conditions for teachers. They also have worked toward the professionalization of teaching and teacher-preparation standards. According to the Bureau of Labor Statistics, 35% of teachers (including those involved in training activities and library work) belonged to a union in 2012 (Bureau of Labor, 2013). Unions have various degrees of influence across the country in terms of collective bargaining, contract agreements, and political clout. They are essentially banned in some states, including Texas, Georgia, Virginia, North Carolina, and South Carolina, where collective bargaining is prohibited; and several more "right-to-work" states do not have binding contracts for teachers. So unions are quite powerless in many U.S. states (Winkler et al., 2012).

Teachers' unions have faced controversy since the beginning of their time; but in the wake of the accountability wars of the past decade or so, unions have been placed at the center of attention, in part because they stood in opposition to education reform zealots who most educators believe are supporting destructive models of teacher accountability. The union opposition to the Bush era high-stakes accountability that was the core of the No Child Left Behind act turns out to have been totally justified. Districts and states, as well as the U.S. Department of Education, its former champion, now abandon it as its failures have become obvious. And unions rightly have noted that many "reformers" view education as a multibillion-dollar industry, ripe for privatization, but with one big obstacle in their way—unions.

Two of the powerful myths about unions have dominated public discourse: that teachers' unions impede student academic growth, and that unions protect bad teachers from being terminated. To begin, let's examine the first of these beliefs, which is not grounded in empirical evidence. Quite to the contrary, states that do not have binding contracts for teachers typically fare among the lowest in terms of student achievement, while states that are more heavily unionized tend to have higher achievement scores (Strauss, 2010). This also rings true internationally, such as in the high-performing countries of Finland and Canada, where nearly all teachers are part of a professional union.

The no-union ideology has almost completely dominated the charter school movement. Charter schools often pride themselves on hiring only nonunion teachers. Yet mounting research has shown that students of charter schools perform about the same as, and in many cases worse than, their public school peers (see Myth 3). Following the logic of the anti-union enthusiasts and the charter school leaders, one would assume that the charter schools would be blowing public schools out of the water in terms of student achievement. At this point, no such claim can be substantiated. The insidious and continual assertion that unions hinder student achievement is lacking any evidential backing. The anti-union forces have no acceptable explanation for why unionized states and countries outperform their nonunionized neighbors, a consistent finding over many years, conveniently ignored by those who are working to dismantle the unions.

Now let's look at the second belief, that unions protect bad teachers. It is false, as stated, but needs to be more carefully examined. The claim is that principals are unable to fire teachers who are protected by unions. The truth is that principals absolutely can fire poor teachers; they just have to go through due process to do it. Yes, it is expensive and it is also time-consuming. But few object when the issue is to ensure justice and the court battles to do that take extended time and require the expenditures of money as well. Tenure is not to protect the job of poor teachers; it is to ensure that a principal or district is not capricious and unjust in its handling of employees. Union protections are not evil, but they ought not to be an obstacle to removing teachers who are unworthy of holding their positions.

Organizations like schools, which serve diverse populations with diverse needs, can be breeding grounds for controversy; consequently, there is a need for responsible advocacy by teachers. This isn't a bad thing; perhaps it is even a cornerstone of our democracy. Controversy can lead to the challenging of stagnant views, thinking outside of the box, and improving practice. The assurance of due process in termination procedures allows teachers to voice their opinions, advocate for their students, and challenge inequities without fear of capricious retaliation by principals, superintendents, and school boards. Because teachers know their students better than anyone else in the school, they can be put in a vulnerable position at certain times. For example, think about the 3rd-grade teacher who has to beg for math manipulatives because she knows they will provide her students with a greater depth of understanding, but her request comes at a time when the school's budget is tight. Or the special education teacher who challenges conventional ways of schooling and opts for inclusive teaching methods over his superior's tried and failed methods, supported only by the supervisor's belief that he knows what is best for his students. And what about the teacher that refuses a principal's request to change a C to an A for a particular child? Or the one that demands to teach evolution despite community pressure not to do so? These teachers should not have to put their jobs at risk to advocate for what they believe is right. Without the protection of due process negotiated by their union, they might feel that the risk involved in speaking up is too high and choose to teach as required, ignoring what they see as the best interests of their students or their community. Due process was not intended to protect bad teachers. It is designed to protect good teachers, affording them opportunities to make decisions based on what they perceive to be the best interests of their students, schools, and communities. Due process means that districts and principals cannot fire teachers simply for disagreeing with them about what is best for students.

It is worth noting, however, that tenure has been abolished in some states, and due process has been done away with in places like the Denver Public Schools, Chicago, the state of North Carolina, and elsewhere. This will harm the profession. Neither unions nor administrators should protect teachers who are poor instructors or morally compromised. And unions and districts should agree on a process for bringing help to improve a poorly performing teacher, before a decision to fire that teacher is made. But after help is offered and improvements are not forthcoming, then the process to fire teachers must be made easier and less expensive. Of course, this is hard to do. But the abandonment of due process, as is occurring now in many U.S. school systems, would be a terrible loss to our society. The current anti-union movement is likely to throw out the baby, due process, with the bathwater, tenure.

The ideological opponents of unions, among whom are large corporations, conservative politicians, and Right-wing think tanks, decry the political action of the "wealthy" NEA and AFT. But in fact, the $60 million contributed to political campaigns by these two unions over a decade is a tiny fraction of the money spent by anti-union forces to advance their agenda. Anti-union forces close ranks to defeat pro-union politicians and thwart legislation that would advance the professional status of teachers. As Brill (2011) makes clear, the slingshot of "David"—NEA and AFT—is useless against "Goliath"—Rupert Murdoch (NewsCorp), the Walton Family (Wal-Mart), Fisher (The Gap), Langone (Home Depot), Arnold (Enron), former New York City Mayor Bloomberg (Bloomberg Inc.), and Eli Broad (SunAmerica–AIG).

The pervasive myth that unions are hurting our schools and hindering a good education for students is pitting teachers against society today unlike at any other time in history. The anti-union rhetoric is sullying the reputation of teachers and misleading the public to believe that teachers who fight for due process also must be against the best interests of students. Those leading the anti-union movement are often the same group of people who see money to be made from public education and will do whatever it takes to make profits from public education—especially a nonunionized profession of educators.

America's public education system is one of its most valuable civic institutions—and the ones who understand its operations better than any outsider possibly could, the teachers, deserve to be treated as professionals. And if they are accorded that courtesy, they are expected to behave like professionals. As such, after a 3- to 5-year probationary period (depending on the state), they should be afforded the protection of due process in order to feel safe about making the hard decisions they face each day. It is not only in the best interest of the teaching profession and our students, but also for the betterment of our society as a whole.

References

Brill, S. (2011). *Class warfare: Inside the fight to fix America's schools.* New York, NY: Simon & Schuster.

Bureau of Labor. (2013, January 1). *Economic news release: Union members summary.* Retrieved from www.bls.gov/news.release/union2.nr0.htm.

Strauss, V. (2010, October 25). The real effect of teachers union contracts. *The Washington Post.* Retrieved from tinyurl.com/pfatmsn

Winkler A. M., Scull, J., & Zeehandelaar, D. (2012). *How strong are U.S. teacher unions? A state-by-state comparison.* Washington, DC: Thomas B. Fordham Foundation. Retrieved from www.edexcellence-media.net/publications/2012/20121029-How-Strong-Are-US-Teacher-Unions/20121029-Union-Strength-Full-Report.pdf

❧ MYTH 16 ❧

Judging teacher education programs by means of the scores that their teachers' students get on state tests is a good way to judge the quality of the teacher education program.

Can foolishness be squared? In Myth 11, we debunk the trend toward using value-added measurement (VAMs) to judge teacher effectiveness. The VAMs have logical problems, their reliability is low, and their validity is worse. But data rarely stop critics of education. The proponents of VAMs recently have pushed their foolishness further. Now they want to use student test scores of teachers to judge the institution that trained the teachers. That is foolishness squared!

Consider the Teach For America (TFA) program (Myth 13). Those teachers are placed with low-income and minority children. As a group, those students always score poorly on standardized tests. Their absolute scores are low and the growth they make per year of schooling is lower than that made by middle-class children. Thus, almost all the hot-shot TFAers from Yale, Princeton, Harvard, Berkeley, and the like, will be labeled as poorly trained teachers. That actually appears to be the case (see Myth 13), so perhaps no harm is done. But almost every other teacher in the same environment will be labeled as a poor teacher, and therefore their university programs will be considered deficient when their students' test scores are examined.

There is no getting around it. The kind of student that new teachers end up teaching will determine a good deal of the score that the institution they attended will get. There surely are poor teacher training institutions. We certainly need ways to identify them and either fix them or close them. But student test scores will be more harmful than helpful in identifying them.

The recent "school-grading systems" hoax is promoted by former governor Jeb Bush and his acolytes, including Tony Bennett, the man who "fixes" school grades, apparently for contributions to his political campaigns. Bennett is an ex-superintendent of schools in Florida and Indiana, and put into place Indiana's school-grading system. But according to policy analyst Matt Di Carlo (2012), here is how that school-grading system works: Almost 85% of the schools with the lowest poverty rates among its students receive an A or a B rating, and virtually none gets a D or an F rating. On the other hand, among the schools with the poorest students, a little over half are assigned an F or a D, compared with about 22% across all schools. When the 125 elementary and middle schools that got an F grade in 2012 were looked at, 100 of them were in the highest poverty quartile. Only eight F grades were assigned to schools that were above the median in terms of the wealth of the student body. Only 25% of the poorest schools got an A or a B, compared with almost 60% overall. Di Carlo notes that this is not at all surprising. It is "baked into this system." Roughly the same thing happens in other states that use school-rating systems. The school's scores in the rating systems usually are determined by absolute student performance (test passing rates), and these are heavily influenced by student demographics, particularly poverty. The result is almost always a rating system that orders the schools by the wealth of the parents served by them.

All the insanity of the school-grading systems now embraced by the education-denigration lobby, in turn, will be visited on the heads of the college and university programs that train teachers to teach our neediest students.

So whether we deal with grading teachers, grading schools, or grading schools of education, it is hard to escape the effects of the social class and circumstances of the child and the child's class on the test that generated the data used for grading. Researchers continually inform policymakers that student test scores are much less the result of teachers and schools, and much more the result of influences in the student's family and neighborhood, employment and health opportunities in the community, language status and special education status of students, and so forth. This is not in dispute. So placing too much credence in grading teachers, schools, and teacher training institutions on the basis of student test scores is foolish, if not shameful.

There is also the problem of size of the cohort being measured. What sample size of teachers with student test data is needed to judge the efficacy of a teacher education program? Are 25 teachers enough to provide a stable mean difference in the efficacy scores of Institution X versus Institution Y? That's not an easy question to answer.

Louisiana rates teacher education institutions based on student test scores. It does use 25 teachers as the minimum sample size. Because of that, not a single New Orleans–based teacher training program was consistently included in its ratings since the programs at the University of New Orleans, Xavier University, Southern University at New Orleans, and Our Lady of Holy Cross were missing data. Only the University of New Orleans had a cohort of 25 or more teachers, and then only in its undergraduate social studies and math certification programs.

This problem exists in part because many teacher education programs serve very few students. If 50 teachers at College X are new teachers each year, only about 20 of them actually might have student test data to report, as other graduates of the institution will teach in fields such as art, history, music, or physical education. These fields are not usually tested and so there are no data available to judge the adequacy of these practicing teachers. Still other recent graduates of the institution will be teaching in grades that are untested, at least in states that do not test in every grade every year. The question then arises whether one can make a valid inference about a school's entire teacher education program based on a sample of its graduates that is nonrandom as well as small in size and teaching in different grades.

There are more problems if student data from teachers in their first few years of teaching are used to judge an institution. Over time, teachers get better at what they do in many ways, including helping their students attain higher test scores. So if a teacher education program graduates teachers for the toughest placements in under-resourced schools serving poor and minority students, we know that those teachers are (1) likely to generate test scores that are low, and (2) likely to leave the profession sooner than teachers in affluent areas. So a teacher training program that chooses to place its students in difficult circumstances will be at a disadvantage for score growth and will lose, on average, its more successful and more experienced teachers over a few years, usually replacing them with newer, less successful teachers. Therefore, if student test scores are used to judge a teacher training program, it would be better for that program to place teachers in the easy-to-teach-at schools and not the hard-to-teach-at schools. This unfortunate side effect is a distinct possibility when assessments are high-stakes, such as when a state threatens to close down or cut the funds of a school of education.

Finally, there are two logical reasons known to every practicing teacher that make new teacher evaluations using student test scores an invalid method for judging either the teachers or the institutions that trained them. First, a teacher's performance in his or her first year is not typical performance. It is common for almost all experienced teachers to confess how many mistakes they made the first year or two, how stressed they were, how they handled student discipline poorly, how they were constantly behind on everything, how little sleep they got, how much weight they gained or lost, how their social relations suffered, and so forth. If the job of first-year teachers is so difficult and stressful, for virtually all teachers regardless of where they were trained, then student test scores from first- and even second-year teachers are not likely to be indicative of how those teachers ultimately will perform. The contributions of their training institution to their career achievements will not be known. Student test scores from first-year teachers are likely to give a distorted view of their capabilities.

No one seems to blame the medical schools when the adjusted mortality rates rise 4% in July and August at major research hospitals as students become interns, interns become residents, and residents become practicing physicians. The first years of medical training result in 8 to 14 more deaths each summer at all the great research hospitals because novices take on greater responsibility. Beginners in complex fields are just that, *beginners*, and neither medical schools nor schools of education can ever do a perfect job of preparing novices for the complexities of the real world. So it's not really sensible to measure the impact of the training programs in either field at that time in the novice's career. What we really seek in medicine or in education is the teaching institution's contribution to a novice's ability to learn by experience. A first-year teacher's student test scores will not give us that.

The second logical problem is that some districts do and some districts don't provide support for first-year teachers. The best of the districts have released time for National Board Certified teachers, or other expert teachers, to visit and help novice teachers survive the first year. Many times in wealthier teacher training institutions, a cadre of first-year teaching coaches work with recent graduates. Some new teachers have neither of these kinds of support. If they do poorly their first year, the inference is that the teacher training program is at fault. But instead, it may be that no one in the district, state, or university will pay for first-year coaches. And in the poorest school districts, where many of the new teaching vacancies occur, support systems for new teachers are harder to provide. The inference from student test data that one teacher education institution was good, and another bad, is easily confounded by the intensity of the coaching first-year teachers receive at one site or another.

In short, the VAM-like systems for inferring the quality of the teacher training received by a new teacher are not sensible. But the issue is even bigger. Some of our nation's finest scholars gathered a few years back to look at the decisions that are made using any of the contemporary versions of VAM scores (Rothstein et al., 2010). They said cautiously what we now say boldly. At present, the use of VAMs for evaluating teachers and teacher training institutions is simply junk science used to serve political ends.

References

Di Carlo, M. (2012, November 1). *The structural curve in Indiana's new school grading system.* Retrieved from shankerblog.org/?p=7090

Rothstein, R., Ladd, H. F., Ravitch, D., Baker, E. L., Barton, P. E., Darling-Hammond, L., Haertle, E., Linn, R. L., Shavelson, R. J., & Shepard, L. A. (2010). *Problems with the use of student test scores to evaluate teachers.* Washington, DC: Economic Policy Institute. Retrieved from www.epi.org/publication/bp278

IV

Myths and Lies About How to Make Our Nation's Schools Better

Everyone seems to have a solution to the purported crises in our schools, crises that put our nation at risk, and have been doing so for at least 150 years! But most of the solutions put forward are inadequate, sometimes totally contradicted by research, and occasionally just plain stupid or motivated by greed! An example of a program to make our schools better embodying all three of these characteristics are the policies to leave children back, to flunk them if they are not keeping up with their age mates. About a dozen states now have passed legislation allowing for "retaining pupils in grade," the popular euphemism for flunking. We note that this policy is shortsighted, costly, meanspirited, and contradicted by the preponderance of research. Aside from that, holding kids back is a fine idea!

Other seemingly "smart" solutions to school problems turn out to be less beneficial than parents or politicians believe them to be. For example, everybody we know thinks that time spent in educational pursuits is likely to be time well spent. But adding minutes to the school day turns out not to have the kinds of effects desired. We try in this part and throughout this book to distinguish between facts and myths—and the many failures of the policies derived from those myths.

Much as we might like it, there simply is no automatic correspondence between some of our beliefs and some of the education policies that follow from those beliefs. Consider zero-tolerance policies for school infractions. This makes parents happy. Such policies are signals to parents that their child will be safe in school. But the application of a zero-tolerance policy is fraught with difficulties, often is applied in a discriminatory way to non-White and poorer students, and has not always had the effects desired. Despite our hopes, the implementation of a policy is rarely without problems. Life is complicated.

In this part, we also deal with some parental beliefs that we think are absolutely correct. However, some politicians and corporations refute these justified beliefs by promoting myths, if not outright lies.

These justified arguments made by parents are refuted primarily because some politicians and businesspeople won't pay the "up-front" costs for what, admittedly, are more expensive programs. For example, it is argued quite vigorously by some that school class size should not be a concern because research does not support the idea that smaller class sizes yield increases in school achievement. That is simple hooey! Similarly, it also is argued that preschool is not worth the money because its effects on later academic achievement are small, transitory, or nonexistent. This too is hooey! Nevertheless, politicians and some taxpayers make these arguments, failing to cite the preponderance of the literature that refutes their claims, and always failing to note two other very important considerations.

Most wealthy parents in the United States seek schools with small class sizes and make extensive use of preschools. These wealthy parents are often willing to pay exorbitant amounts of money to back up their belief that these are important influences on the development of their own children. Sadly, some of these people do not think these are good programs for other people's children!

A second and often overlooked consideration in the arguments about class size reductions and attendance at preschool is that economists and other researchers have discovered that small class sizes (especially in the early grades and especially for poorer children) and high-quality preschools (especially for poorer children) have long-term benefits. So the up-front costs can be fully paid back as the benefits of these programs kick in through later school completion rates and greater economic success for students participating in these programs. Parents are right to fight for these programs.

Many other ideas that are supposed to make our schools better (school uniforms, academic tracking, immersion programs for English language learners, switching governance to mayoral control, and the like) are addressed in this part. We also address a common belief that we find untrue, namely, that the schools have been dumbing down the curriculum for decades. We try to confront the myths, hoaxes, half-truths, and occasional lies associated with criticisms of our schools and the many suggestions to improve them. In the end, we are forced to conclude that it is extremely difficult to change the outcomes of schooling in the United States, because the biggest causes of school problems lie outside the education system. Some might call this conclusion a cop-out; we call it reality.

◦§ MYTH 17 ◦

Class size does not matter;
reducing class sizes will not result in more learning.

The task of educating our nation's youth is an expensive endeavor, and in a time of ever-increasing financial constraints on school budgets, it is no wonder schools frequently opt to increase class sizes. It appears to be both a simple and an easy way to cut budgets; fewer teachers providing instruction to more students means lower expenditures on salaries, which constitute the bulk of a school district's expenses. Larger class sizes, even if only by two students, can enable districts to cut their budgets dramatically. To support these decisions, education critics and legislators concerned with school budgets argue that class size does not really matter. A well-trained and highly qualified teacher can engage students regardless of the number, so they argue. But what are the true costs of these decisions and who really pays for them?

Both sides of the class size debate use student achievement in their arguments. Those arguing for smaller class sizes assert that they contribute to increased student achievement as well as some additional desirable long-term outcomes, while those arguing against a reduction in class size maintain that smaller classes are too costly and that the research in support of smaller class sizes is equivocal.

The debate surrounding the benefits of class size reduction on pupil achievement can be traced back to the early 20th century and continually resurfaces as educational jurisdictions negotiate the costs of providing a free public education. Yet for decades, the entire corpus of studies on the impacts of class size on student achievement had been largely ignored. For every assertion that smaller classes equate to improved student achievement, another study would be cited arguing the opposite. A meta-analysis, a quantitative synthesis of nearly 100 studies reported over 7 decades, was published in 1982 (Glass, Cahen, Smith, & Filby, 1982). It established the considerable benefits of smaller classes; but one person's facts are another person's fancy, and facts rarely end ideological debates.

In 1985, however, the Tennessee legislature authorized funding for Project STAR (student/teacher achievement ratio), one of the best-designed and most respected studies examining the effects of class size reduction. This 4-year longitudinal program clearly demonstrated that smaller class sizes, those with fewer than 18 students, had significant impact for students in grades K–3 (Mosteller, 1995). These students scored better on standardized tests, earned better grades in their classes, and exhibited continued improvement beyond the early grades. Furthermore, minority students in small classes in the lower grades benefited by nearly double the amount of the average student (Mosteller, 1995; Nye, Hedges, & Konstantopolous, 2000). Similarly positive long-term results were obtained from a study in Wisconsin (Molnar et al., 2000) and another in England (Blatchford, Bassett, & Brown, 2011). The latter found that for every additional five students there was a 25% increase in off-task behavior by class members—almost exactly what, for decades, teachers have been telling all who would listen.

Why do critics continue to argue the irrelevance of class size despite pervasive evidence to the contrary (Hanushek, 1999; Slavin, 1989)? Their position on this issue may be politically motivated, as choosing smaller class sizes has significant economic impacts. Smaller classes require more teachers, more materials, and, additionally, more space; hence, they are more expensive, thus requiring more tax money.

The debate about class size in many ways can be better understood from the perspective of teacher workload. As is true for many public service professionals, the day-to-day duties of teachers are continually increasing while salary and benefits rise more slowly, if at all. But one simple equation tells the story: "More students in the classroom" equals "more work for any conscientious teacher." To effectively educate our children, teachers must continually assess their learning. Contemporary teachers are taught to do a great deal of formative assessment. These are on-the-fly assessments, integrated into what they teach, so they can have real-time estimations about where a student or a whole class is in understanding what is being taught. Formative assessment lets a teacher modify instruction, and research overwhelmingly supports its use (Black & Wiliam, 1998). But the larger the class, the more likely the inferences drawn about student understanding of a lesson will be wrong, limiting the usually positive effects of formative assessment.

Other student assessments come in the form of tests, essays, research papers, or presentations, and require the teacher's time to develop and grade. This is all done in addition to creating lesson plans, monitoring students' academic progress, attending parent–teacher conferences and faculty meetings, probably serving as a faculty advisor on student-run organizations, or coaching sports teams or the school yearbook. The more students a teacher is responsible for, the greater the demand on the teacher's time in school, and this inevitably impacts his or her life outside of work. Designing an educational policy resulting in more work for the same pay has consequences. Teachers are less likely to remain in the profession, leading to higher rates of turnover by experienced teachers and, in the end, fewer highly trained, qualified, and experienced teachers in schools educating our nation's children. Teacher experience is one of the factors that make a difference in students' achievement, so any policy that reduces the number of experienced teachers is quite likely to reduce student achievement.

With smaller classes, teachers believe they are able to contribute more significantly to their students' learning, and research backs up that claim. As teachers attempt to engage their students individually, as we hope they will, teachers need time to understand the needs of their students. This is less likely to occur if class sizes rise too much. In those situations, teachers will have less time and less energy to invest in the individual needs, desires, and aspirations of their students. Individualized and creative curricula are likely to be replaced by more canned curriculum, computer-assisted curriculum, and workbook exercises, commonly referred to as drill-and-kill. Curricula that feature critical thinking, discussion, debate, and group projects, the kind of curricula called for to develop 21st-century skills, necessarily will be curtailed. So, large class sizes may hinder our production of citizens suited for the modern world.

Interestingly, average class sizes in the United States are reportedly in the low to mid-20s. Yet these figures may not represent the experiences of many of the nation's children. This average includes special education classrooms, which often consist of only a handful of students. The low class size figure also comes about by combining rural, suburban, and urban schools. But the ratio of teachers to students in all communities is not the same. Nebraska has 17.5 students per teacher; Arizona has 24.5; in 2013, 26,545 of Chicago's littlest learners—in kindergarten, 1st grade, or 2nd grade—were in classrooms with 29 or more students; and the principal of a Beaverton, Oregon, high school posted a large protest sign *himself*, since his daughter was in an Algebra II class in his school with over 50 students, and dozens of other classrooms at his school were also over 50 in size.

Regardless, let us consider teacher workload in a reportedly moderate average size class. For teachers in the higher grades, 25 students per classroom is not uncommon. This figure is multiplied by 4–6, the number of separate classes taught per day. This makes one teacher responsible for anywhere from 100 to 150 students in a given day, and some of those classes may be quite different, such as honors algebra and business arithmetic. Given the impossibility of keeping track of this many students, in multiple curriculum areas, it is no surprise that some students get lost in the shuffle. Those who already do well, excel; while those who struggle, continue to do poorly or fall further behind. No Child Left Behind becomes a hollow promise. Yet reduce each class size by 10, and teachers are then responsible for anywhere from 40 to

60 fewer students. This quantitative decrease in the number of students in a class has a qualitative pedagogical impact. Teachers are able to be more creative, instruction can be tailored to the individual needs of students, and, most important, teachers can identify struggling students *and* invest time and energy in mentoring them, increasing these students' chances of success. These lower teacher–student ratios are what wealthy parents seek to purchase when they choose to send their own children to private schools or move to communities where the ratio of teachers to students is low.

When reductions occurred in elementary classrooms, as happened in the Tennessee STAR study, the extra individualized attention and instruction apparently made it more likely for those public school students to graduate at higher rates from high school. This produces huge savings to society, making class size reductions cost-effective over the long run, but requiring additional costs to districts and states in the short run.

The apparent paradox that exists in the arguments from some quarters that class size doesn't matter, seems not to matter. The paradox is this: Fiscal conservatives contend, in the face of overwhelming evidence to the contrary, that students learn as well in large classes as in small. And yet, the very constituency whose taxes they are trying to reduce, namely, the affluent families, consistently opt for public and private schools that have small classes, often paying handsomely for them. Furthermore, they report that class size is often the reason they make a choice to enroll their child in private, charter, or other schools that are not their neighborhood public school (Walford, 2011). So, for which students are large classes okay? Only the children of the poor?

References

Black, P., & Wiliam, D. (1998). Assessment and classroom learning. *Assessment in Education, 5*(1), 7–74.

Blatchford, P., Bassett, P., & Brown, P. (2011). Examining the effect of class size on classroom engagement and teacher–pupil interaction: Differences in relation to pupil prior attainment and primary vs. secondary schools. *Learning and Instruction, 21,* 715–730.

Glass, G. V., Cahen, L. S., Smith, M. L., & Filby, N. N. (1982). *School class size: Research and policy.* Beverly Hills, CA: SAGE.

Hanushek, E. (1999). The evidence on class size. In S. Mayer & P. Peterson (Eds.), *Earning and learning: How schools matter* (pp. 131–168). Washington, DC: Brookings Institution Press.

Molnar, A., Smith, P., Zahorik, J., Palmer, A., Halbach, A., & Ehrle, K. (2000). Wisconsin's student achievement guarantee in education (SAGE) class size reduction program: Achievement effects, teaching, and classroom implications. In M. C. Wang & J. D. Finn (Eds.), *How small classes help teachers do their best* (pp. 227–277). Philadelphia, PA: Laboratory for Student Success at Temple University Center for Research in Human Development and Education.

Mosteller, F. (1995). The Tennessee study of class size in the early school grades. *The Future of Children: Critical Issues for Children and Youths, 5*(2), 113–127.

Nye, B., Hedges, L., & Konstantopolous, S. (2000). The effects of small classes on academic achievement: The results of the Tennessee class size experiment. *American Educational Research Journal, 37*(1), 123–151.

Slavin, R. (1989). Class size and student achievement: Small effects of small classes. *Educational Psychologist, 24*(1), 99–110.

Walford, G. (2011). *Privatization and privilege in education* (Vol. 205). Abingdon, United Kingdom: Routledge.

⤚ MYTH 18 ⤙

Retaining children in grade—"flunking" them—helps struggling students catch up and promotes better classroom instruction for all.

Suppose you have children and you dream about their success in life, as do most parents. Imagine also that they like school a lot, although they struggle a bit. Then one day, perhaps in 1st or 3rd grade, your child's teacher informs you that your child is to be "left back" or, as it is euphemistically known, "retained in grade." You are likely to feel pressured to accept the opinions of the professionals—the caring teacher, the authoritative principal, and perhaps an earnest guidance counselor. All of them tell you that your child is "slow," has difficulty learning, cannot keep up, or lacks maturity. They may speak of giving your child "the gift of time." They recommend that it would be better to keep your child back now, so that your son or daughter will have the opportunity to master reading, or mathematics, or to mature as a student. You're told that by repeating a grade your child will be better prepared for more demanding work to come. You also may be told that the teachers in the next grade will find it easier to instruct their class if they do not have to provide extra time and special attention to children promoted without the appropriate grade-level skills.

In this scenario your love for your child may be unchanged, but your relationship with your child easily could be changed forever. After learning that your child cannot keep up with the class, you may, quite naturally, come to expect less from your child in and out of school. It will be hard to mask that belief over the ensuing years.

There are several things worth noting about this common scenario now affecting millions of American families. The recommendation to retain a student in grade (1) is almost always ineffective, (2) is often biased, (3) is likely to be a waste of money, (4) may end up hurting the local economy, and (5) also may be meanspirited!

The decision to have children repeat a grade shows enormous variation by state and district, as well as across nations. In fact, some high-performing countries ban retention in grade altogether. Back in the mid-1980s, Florida made more than 10% of all kindergartners repeat, while Mississippi failed about 1% of its kindergartners. In the United States, a recent estimate is that between 1 in 20 and 1 in 30 students are retained each year in grades 1–8. This adds up to about 450,000 students annually (Warren & Saliba, 2012). But this number does not include the unusually high numbers of school children retained at the end of kindergarten and 9th grade, as well as those left back in other high school grades. Cumulatively, it is likely that at least 10% of all the students in the nation have been "flunked" at least once, a policy affecting more than 5 million of our nations' public school children. This is happening despite extensive, if not always consistent, research demonstrating that this policy is usually ineffective or harmful.

In 1975, 44 studies of retaining children in grade were reviewed, and the evidence failed to support the claim that retention was sound educational policy. Ten years later, in a review that included an additional set of studies, researchers studied students who were about equal in performance, some of whom were promoted, and some of whom were not. The *promoted* students had higher academic achievement, better personal adjustment, and more positive attitudes toward school than did the retained students. Seventeen years after that study, yet another researcher reviewed the evidence, old and new, and concluded that most of the comparisons showed no significant differences between promoted and retained students on measures of achievement or personal and social adjustment (Jimerson, 2001; Jimerson & Renshaw, 2012). However, in those studies that did show a difference, the results favored the promoted students, especially on measures of academic achievement.

Why would so many sensible educators favor retention when the research data are seldom supportive? The answer is faulty logic! If children are left back, and repeat the same material they had the year before, it is likely that they will do better on that material and do better on the tests at that grade level, impressing their teachers with their growth. Thus, teachers and school administrators usually do see improvement in test scores after a child is left back, and the child may appear to be more mature, which is what usually happens when a child grows a year older.

Here is the catch: What school personnel don't know is how well that child would have done if promoted. That's where research usually tells a different story. When comparing two statistically similar children, one retained and one promoted, the promoted one usually does better on the tests given in the next higher grade, or the two children perform at about the same level, indicating no discernible academic advantages to retention. In addition, an immature child left back to spend a year with children who are younger than himself may seem more mature than his peers. But an immature child who is promoted will be with classmates more mature than she is, and likely to learn a great deal more about age-appropriate behavior. There is still another way that those who retain children are fooled by what they see. Some research has documented short-term academic gains for young students who are left back. But those gains appear to fade over time. Because that fade in achievement takes place over time, it may not be readily noticed by those who had left the child back originally and claimed success in the year following retention.

The research findings, while certainly not unanimous, show consistency: The decision to retain a student subsequently results in that student having more negative outcomes in all areas of academic achievement, and in social and emotional areas of development such as peer relationships, self-esteem, and classroom behavior. We also can expect a retained student, compared with a promoted student with comparable levels of maturity or achievement, to have a more negative attitude toward school (wouldn't you?), and higher absenteeism rates over time, making it even harder for that child to catch up in achievement (Brophy, 2006; Dennis et al., n.d.; Shepard & Smith, 1989). The most recent of the many studies showing negative effects looked at the "Just Read, Florida" program, legislation proudly supported by then governor Jeb Bush, now a possible presidential candidate (Ozek, 2013). The law resulted in thousands of 3rd-graders being left back. The research found that grade retention significantly increased the likelihood of disciplinary incidents and suspensions in the years that followed for both boys and girls. These negative outcomes affected the poor more than the wealthy. And it is poor minorities who make up the majority of those ordinarily left back. Defenders of this program point out that Florida has made considerable progress on state reading tests. That is true, but other educational programs were put into place at the same time, so there is no way of knowing whether "Just Read" helped in lifting state achievement levels. If it did help, then it was by sacrificing poor and minority children—those left back—when other alternatives exist to help children who are slow to learn to read. And forgotten in the praise for the Florida "miracle," is this: Older school children do better on tests than younger school children. So the more children you leave back in 3rd grade, the better your test scores in subsequent grades will look.

Retention simply does not solve the quite real problems that have been identified by teachers looking for a solution to a child's immaturity or learning problems. Other programs appear to do better. Targeted summer programs and tutoring, high-quality preschool, and small class size in the first few grades, are more likely to help struggling or immature students than are the more than 5 million decisions to hold a child back.

Is there bias in decisions to retain a student in grade? When looking at retained students, we find that they are much more likely to be male than female, English language learners than native speakers of English, Black or Hispanic, from a poor household, from a single-parent household, from a household with low educational attainment, and to have made frequent school changes. Retained students also are more likely to have a record of chronic absences, show delayed development or attention problems, have more conflict with their teachers and peers, and hold low perceptions of their ability and social competence. Although there are many characteristics of children who are retained in grade that would argue against bias in identification, it is also true that retention is what happens most frequently to poor minority males, and not to others. Children of middle-class parents with higher social and intellectual skills, as well as financial resources, are rarely left back in school. When presenting many of the same problems that lower class and minority children display, more-advantaged children get attention: They are spared retention with its negative outcomes.

A recommendation to retain a child may seem rational, even kind, with some policymakers arguing that the child they want to leave back is getting "the gift of time." And it is true that some support for retention in grade can be found in the literature. But it is also possible that a decision to retain a child is a way of punishing disadvantaged male students for not having received the same quality of instruction and care in their home as their more advantaged peers. Retention policies, therefore, could be a form of double jeopardy.

Safe to say, few children consider repeating a grade to be a "gift." Researcher Kaoru Yamamoto discovered that children considered being held back the emotional equal of wetting their pants in school or being caught stealing. Only two events were more distressing to them: the death of a parent and going blind. The gift of time indeed (Yamamoto & Byrnes, 1987)!

Does flunking students waste money? Yes. Retention in grade is not optional in about 13 states and in many school districts. Many jurisdictions have mandated retention for children not reading at grade level, usually based on a test given at 3rd grade. States and districts with this policy, therefore, have agreed to spend an extra year's cost of schooling on a child not performing well on standardized tests. This currently averages out to about $11,000 per child annually in our nation's public schools. With at least 5 million children in the system who have been left back at least once, and the commitment of American schools to an average of $11,000 per child per extra year of schooling, the United States could be spending $55 billion annually on a policy that doesn't work well for most children. We may be wasting a great deal of money!

Could that $11,000 per year be used in a better way by capitalizing on the good intentions of those who made a policy to do something to help children now not doing well in school? Probably. Let's say you used $5,500 per year for tutoring services and/or individual counseling, over 2 years, for students currently identified to be retained in grade. Would the results be better? Probably. Research informs us that tutoring is a powerful treatment. And with good training and program management, older students or community volunteers can be taught to tutor, thus reducing the costs of the program substantially. Or suppose that the money now allocated for retention were used instead to fund high-quality summer programs targeted to children who otherwise might be retained. Would that work better? Probably. There is evidence that such programs can work. So billions are spent currently on a policy that usually does not accomplish its goals, and programs that might genuinely help children who are in need of intervention go unfunded. This is maddening.

Can retention in grade hurt the local economy? Probably. Researchers have estimated that students who have repeated a grade once are 20–30% more likely to drop out of school than students of equal ability who were promoted along with their age mates. There is almost a 100% chance that students retained twice will drop out before completing high school (Shepard & Smith, 1990). And the estimates of these researchers are quite plausible. Look at it this way. A 16-year-old who failed 3rd grade and has some difficulty with school looks ahead and sees 3 more years of high school before graduation. That student's "twin," who was never retained, sees 2 more years. Which one is more likely to drop out? And which one of these two students, the high school graduate or the dropout, is likely to go on to postsecondary training, end up with a better paying job, ultimately pay more in local and state taxes, and have fewer problems with law enforcement? For students retained in grade, who do drop out of school much more frequently, the chances of personal and economic success in later life are not great. Thus there are costs to the local economy when harsh retention policies result in increased rates of dropping out.

Is retention in grade meanspirited? It seems clear that there are no easy or inexpensive answers for working with students who are not keeping up with their classmates. But the research data tell us that leaving these children back usually does not work out to the children's, the school's, or the community's advantage. So why do it?

Holding back children who cannot keep up with their age mates also doesn't reduce by much the diversity a teacher in the next grade has to deal with. In any classroom of around 25 to 30 children, the individual differences among the students are huge. The range of academic ability in any classroom spans many grade levels, and the levels of motivation and maturity will vary as widely. So bequeathing a more homogeneous class of students to next year's teacher cannot justify high rates of retention in grade.

Since retention in grade costs a lot of money, paid either through the school budget or eventually through the social services budget, we might expect retention to be infrequently recommended, perhaps even avoided. Retention policies, however, are embraced by both individuals and states, which are ordinarily loath to spend money on school and social services. Why?

Finland and Korea are both countries the United States may want to emulate because they do so well on international tests of achievement. But both have prohibitions against retention in grade, using that approach quite sparingly. So this policy of ours is clearly not necessary to obtain high levels of school achievement.

If we want to end "social promotion," that is, promotion of students who do not meet the standards for achievement at a particular grade, we might more wisely invest in tutoring or summer school. In communities that have high rates of disadvantaged children, we might want to invest in early childhood programs of high quality, programs known to have long-range benefits to individuals and communities alike. So why does retention in grade remain so popular?

Well-meaning upholders of standards, strongly against social promotion, may continue to find some reason for clinging to the myth that retention in grade is good policy. But they are wrong. Even though retention ultimately may work out well for some students, it doesn't work out well for most students. We simply do not know how to identify in advance which students, and under what conditions, this policy might benefit. But we do know that retention in grade usually affects students and their families adversely. To uphold this policy in the face of research that has documented its numerous failures, along with this policy's clear bias against poor and minority students, seems meanspirited. Retention policies in the United States appear to be just another barrier that the least advantaged among us must clear to obtain the benefits our society frequently offers to its more advantaged citizens.

References

Brophy, J. (2006). *Grade repetition* (Education Policy Series #6). International Academy of Education, Brussels, Belgium, & International Institute for Educational Planning, UNESCO, Paris, France. Retrieved from tinyurl.com/qcdaxxr

Dennis, D. V., Kroeger, D. C. , O'Byrne, W. I., Meyer, C. K., Kletzein, S. B., Huddlesston, A., & Gilrane, C. (n.d.). *Test-based grade retention* (Policy brief). Literacy Research Association. Retrieved from tinyurl.com/qddmfo7

Jimerson, S. (2001). Meta-analysis of grade retention research: Implications for practice in the 21st century. *School Psychology Review, 30,* 420–437.

Jimerson, S. R., & Renshaw, T. L. (2012). Retention and social promotion. *Principal Leadership, 13*(1), 12–16.

Ozek, U. (2013, April). *Hold back to move forward? Early grade retention and student misbehavior* (Working Paper 100). Washington, DC: American Institutes for Research, National Center for Analysis of Longitudinal Data in Education Research.

Shepard, L. A., & Smith, M. L. (1989). *Flunking grades: Research and policies on grade retention.* New York, NY: Falmer Press.

Shepard, L. A., & Smith, M. L. (1990). Synthesis of research on grade retention. *Educational Leadership, 47,* 84–88.

Warren, J. R., & Saliba, J. (2012). First- through eighth-grade retention rates for all 50 states: A new method and initial results. *Educational Researcher, 41*(8), 320–329.

Yamamoto, K., & Byrnes, D. (1987). Primary children's ratings of the stressfulness of experiences. *Journal of Research in Childhood Education, 2,* 117–121.

᪥MYTH 19 ᪥

Tracking, or separating slow and fast learners, is an efficient and productive way to organize teaching. Gifted classes and special schools for our most talented students benefit individuals and society.

The practice of grouping students by ability, also known as "tracking," is common in schools. Classes often are divided into fast track, average track, and slow track, although never publicly referred to by such names. It starts early, on the 8th day of kindergarten in one inner-city school (Rist, 1973).

Children typically are placed in reading groups in elementary school: the bluebirds, the cardinals, and the robins. Some students take honors and AP courses as part of a college-prep education in high school, and others take a vocational or remedial track. The hope is that grouping students by ability will benefit both teachers and students. Teaching becomes easier because the range of abilities in a single classroom is limited. For students, those who are doing well in a subject are less likely to be bored because the teacher will not need to devote as much time to lower performing students, and those students who are not doing well are less likely to fall further behind if the teacher gives attention to advanced students. Tracking would appear to be a "win" for everyone involved.

Unfortunately, the reality of tracking is much different. Studies show that tracking provides little to no benefit for low-achieving students and, at best, modest academic benefits for high-achieving students (Carbonaro, 2005; Oakes, 1992). We should note, however, that special accommodations probably should be made for the profoundly gifted—students who display unique talents in a curriculum area, or test at 180 or thereabouts on an IQ test (Winner, 1997). But for the vast majority of those that are labeled in our schools as gifted and talented, or high-achieving, ability grouping by such attributes appears not to work as well as commonly thought.

For teachers, grouping students by ability—sometimes determined by a single IQ test—limits only one of the many characteristics that they must take into account when teaching students. Any group of students, whether high- or low-achieving, will be diverse in learning styles, the speed at which they pick up the course material, and disposition. To make matters worse, academic ability does not seem to be the only characteristic that is "tracked" when schools and teachers group students by ability. Tracking separates students by race and social class. Students who are White and wealthy tend to fill the fast tracks, and students who are non-White and poor fill the slower tracks. However this sorting is done, ability is not easily disentangled from other influences on student achievement. As a result, tracking invariably segregates students by race and class. The segregation that results from tracking affects students' classroom experiences. Teachers in lower track classes tend to have less experience than those in higher tracks. Tracking as it is currently carried out results in increased inequality. It groups the disadvantaged together and then, through administrative decisions, provides them with inferior resources (Gamoran, 1992; Oakes, 1985).

Perhaps this would be an acceptable trade-off if there was enough benefit from tracking for the students who received the better resources. Some will argue that it is worth ensuring that those who show promise receive the best chance to achieve at the highest levels. It is their achievement, those people argue, that will provide benefits for everyone in society. However, this logical-sounding payoff for society never actually comes about because there is little evidence that students in the higher tracks receive significant benefits from tracking itself, as opposed to factors associated with tracking, such as higher quality teaching and resources.

Schools and programs that are targeted at gifted students have the same issues. Inequality abounds, and the programs tend to sort students along racial and socioeconomic lines. The gifted and talented program in New York City provides a telling example. Students are tracked into these programs and schools based on a standardized test given to students at age 4. In 2006–07, most of the students in the gifted and talented programs were admitted based on privately administered tests that cost approximately $100 and recommendations from preschool teachers (for those families who could afford preschool). Students from wealthier families are more likely to have the resources to afford the tests and send their children to preschool. Although there are ways for poorer families to access the tests at lower costs, and low-cost and free preschool is sometimes available, the poor face greater barriers to entering the program. Because of the relationship between poverty and race, this state of affairs has racial implications as well. For example, 18% of the kindergarten and 1st-grade students in New York City schools are White, but White students represent 52% of the students in gifted and talented programs in those grades. It is not hard to figure out the reasons for this. Admission to gifted and talented programs does not just reflect giftedness. Admission is strongly related to the fiscal resources available to families, and to a related factor, the educational levels of the parents.

Tracking separates students by race and class. This means that schools that track students are less likely to provide meaningful opportunities for these students to interact with a broad range of people in society. Thus, tracking makes it more difficult to achieve the democratic goals held for schools. Opportunities for stereotypes to be challenged are lost.

There is evidence that social benefits accrue to disadvantaged students from being in classes with high-achieving students. Tracking influences the formation of friendships in school (Kubitschek & Hallinan, 1998). Students who come from families where parents did not attend college have the opportunity to interact with students whose families have passed on knowledge about college. Being around conversations about colleges and college planning can provide valuable information to students who may not get this information from other sources. This is sometimes called social capital, which is often less available in the homes of the poor and readily available in the homes of more-advantaged students, and the social capital available from friends positively impacts the chance the students will complete college (Cherng, Calarco, & Kao, 2013).

There are also potential negative psychological consequences to tracking (Ansalone, 2003; Chiu et al., 2008). Students are aware of their placement in a particular track. Being in a low track can communicate to students that they lack academic potential. Students may then perceive themselves as bad students for whom school holds little promise. This can decrease their motivation and result in greater disengagement from school. English language learners, in particular, often are placed in low-ability tracks (Callahan, 2005). Language rather than cognitive ability may be their difficulty, but once they are tracked, their academic skills and aspirations may suffer.

It is possible that the negative consequences from tracking could be eliminated if only it was implemented better. This may be true, but the current reality of tracking shows that there are significant drawbacks to the practice, with few benefits. As a result, skepticism about the promises of tracking is warranted, and careful attention should be given to the unintended consequences of ability grouping.

References

Ansalone, G. (2003). Poverty, tracking, and the social construction of failure: International perspectives on tracking. *Journal of Children and Poverty, 9*(1), 3–20.

Callahan, R. M. (2005). Tracking and high school English learners: Limiting opportunity to learn. *American Educational Research Journal, 42,* 305–328.

Carbonaro, W. (2005). Tracking, students' effort, and academic achievement. *Sociology of Education, 78,* 27–49.

Cherng, H. S., Calarco, J. M., & Kao, G. (2013). Along for the ride: Best friends' resources and adolescents' college completion. *American Educational Research Journal, 50,* 76–106.

Chiu, D., Yodit, B., Watley, E., Wubut, S., Simson, E., Kessinger, R., . . . Wigfield, A. (2008). Influences of math tracking on seventh-grade students' self-beliefs and social comparisons. *The Journal of Educational Research, 102*(2), 125–136.

Gamoran, A. (1992). Is ability grouping equitable? *Educational Leadership, 50*(2), 11–17.

Kubitschek, W. N., & Hallinan, M. T. (1998). Tracking and students' friendships. *Social Psychology Quarterly, 61*(1), 1–15.

Oakes, J. (1985). *Keeping track: How schools structure inequality.* New Haven, CT: Yale University Press.

Oakes, J. (1992). Can tracking research inform practice? Technical, normative, and political considerations. *Educational Researcher, 21*(4), 12–21.

Rist, R. (1973). *The urban school: A factory for failure.* Cambridge, MA: MIT Press.

Winner, E. (1997). Exceptionally high intelligence and schooling. *American Psychologist, 52*(10), 1070–1081.

~§ MYTH 20 ॐ

Immersion programs ("sink or swim") for English language learners are better than bilingual education programs.

English language immersion programs have been popular in states with large immigrant populations. They are built on the assumption that English language learners (ELLs) learn English better and faster under conditions of total immersion and typically within 1 year's time. All-English instruction in academic subjects then quickly becomes comprehensible to children, preventing the potentially negative consequences of being instructed in a language that they cannot understand. Or so the story goes. However, closer examination reveals that immersion programs are grounded in value-driven notions of language and cultural superiority, and furthermore, they lack research backing. Immersion programs for ELLs in schools are an inappropriate, if not a harmful, choice (Garcia, Lawton, & Diniz de Figueiredo, 2010).

Alternatives to immersion programs are bilingual education programs. But because bilingual education has been blamed for the high dropout rates and low English literacy levels of many immigrant children, proponents of English language immersion programs have been able to curtail or completely eliminate bilingual education programs across the country (e.g., California, Arizona, Massachusetts). The inappropriate assignment of blame has been driving the growth of English-only mandates for schools. This has effectively revoked school districts' discretion to select from a variety of alternative models—including bilingual education—based on the needs of their individual students. The suspension of this local autonomy has prompted bilingual education advocates to contest the effectiveness of English language immersion programs. The "bilingualists" can cite empirical research in the field of second-language acquisition, and they can offer a better theoretical understanding of the cognitive processes undergirding language acquisition for second-language learners (August, Goldenberg, & Rueda, 2010; Wiley, Lee, & Rumberger, 2009). The debate between a pro-bilingual approach and an English-only perspective rages (Gándara & Orfield,

2010; Garcia et al., 2010; Willig, 1985, 1987), but with politics and folk beliefs, not research, usually winning the debate.

Some studies have shown greater achievement for students in bilingual programs; others have found no differences in student performance between English-only and bilingual programs. But one quite important research finding is lacking: evidence to support the claim that ELL students are doing better as a result of English language immersion programs.

On the other hand, studies comparing the achievement outcomes of ELL students in New Mexico and Texas (states that offer bilingual education) versus those in Arizona, Massachusetts, and California (English-only states) on the National Assessment of Educational Progress have found larger gaps in achievement between English learners and native English speakers in those states with English-only instructional policies (Rumberger & Tran, 2010). Similarly, studies examining the developing literacy skills of Spanish-speaking ELLs in immersion classrooms document how teachers using the state-mandated, English-only approach were successful with fewer than one half of their students. For the other half, more instructional resources, more instructional time, and more than a one-size-fits-all instructional approach were needed (Blanchard, Atwill, Jimenez-Silva, & Jimenez-Castellanos, in press).

These findings bring into question the appropriateness of English language immersion programs for ELL children. The research more convincingly supports the claim that immersion programs are *not* better than bilingual education.

In an age of globalization and international competition, and when most other countries recognize more than just one official language, the goal should be to develop both the cognitive talents and linguistic skills in all our communities. We should not, by design, foster policies that appear to stifle and discourage the participation of ELLs and poorer students in educational advancement. Because one cannot effectively separate language, culture, and learning, English language immersion programs have had the unintended effect of devaluing immigrant cultures via language restrictions. These policies perpetuate assimilationist approaches in the education of ELLs. Immersion is designed to foster abandonment of one's heritage language and culture for the dominant language and culture. It is what we call a subtractive approach to integrating speakers of other languages (Valenzuela, 1999). That is, we try to take away their language and culture. Similar efforts were made during the earlier part of the 20th century before *Brown v. Board of Education* (Gándara & Orfield, 2010; Powers, 2008; U.S. Commission on Civil Rights, 1972). Mexican-born children in the Southwest were segregated from their Anglo, English-speaking peers and punished for speaking their native language in the classroom. The parallels between these approaches and contemporary immersion programs lie within their philosophy to abandon the native language and adopt the English-only model. Bilingual education approaches, for these reasons, provide a more *additive* approach to ELL education, allowing students to engage culturally, merging their native language with the learning of a new one, and to maintain more positive adult–peer interactions because they share language and culture with their families.

Those individuals who argue that the use of any of the student's first language is unpatriotic or counterproductive to helping these students achieve academically should consider the following scenario. You go to another country where you do not speak the language. As much as you would want the instruction to center around the new language and move you to a conversational level, would it not be nice if at least the initial instructions could be provided in your language, so that you could ask questions, in your language, and better engage the learning process? Or would you prefer to be tossed into the pool and be told—possibly in a language you don't understand—to sink or swim?

References

August, D., Goldenberg, C., & Rueda, R. (2010). Restrictive state language policies: Are they scientifically based? In P. Gándara & M. Hopkins (Eds.), *Forbidden language: English learners and restrictive language policies* (pp. 139–158). New York, NY: Teachers College Press.

Blanchard, J., Atwill, K., Jimenez-Silva, M., & Jimenez-Castellanos, O. (in press). Beginning English literacy development among Spanish-speaking children in Arizona's English-only classrooms: A four-year successive cohort longitudinal study. *International Multilingual Research Journal.*

Gándara, P., & Orfield, G. (2010). *Segregating Arizona's English learners: A return to the "Mexican room"?* Los Angeles: Civil Rights Project/Proyecto Derechos Civiles at University of California at Los Angeles.

Garcia, E., Lawton, K., & Diniz de Figueiredo, E. (2010). *The education of English language learners in Arizona: A legacy of persisting achievement gaps in a restrictive language policy climate.* Los Angeles: Civil Rights Project/ Proyecto Derechos Civiles at University of California at Los Angeles.

Hakuta, K., Butler, G., & Witt, D. (2000). *How long does it take English learners to attain proficiency?* (Policy Report 2000-1). Santa Barbara: Linguistic Minority Research Institute, University of California, Santa Barbara. Retrieved from escholarship.org/uc/item/13w7m06g?query=Hakuta

Mahoney, K., MacSwan, J., Haladyna, T., & García, D. (2010). Castañeda's third prong: Evaluating the achievement of Arizona's English learners under restrictive language policy. In P. Gándara & M. Hopkins (Eds.), *Forbidden language: English learners and restrictive language policies* (pp. 50–64). New York, NY: Teachers College Press.

Mahoney, K., MacSwan, J., & Thompson, M. (2005). The condition of English language learners in Arizona: 2005. Arizona Education Policy Initiative. Retrieved from www.terpconnect.umd.edu/~macswan/EPSL-0509-110-AEPI.pdf

Powers, J. (2008). Forgotten history: Mexican American school segregation in Arizona from 1900–1951. *Equity & Excellence in Education, 41*(4), 467–481.

Rumberger, R., & Tran, L. (2010). State language policies, school language practices, and the English learner achievement gap. In P. Gándara & M. Hopkins (Eds.), *Forbidden language: English learners and restrictive language policies* (pp. 86–101). New York, NY: Teachers College Press.

U.S. Commission on Civil Rights. (1972). *The excluded student: Educational practices affecting Mexican Americans in the southwest.* Washington, DC: Author.

Valenzuela, A. (1999). *Subtractive schooling: U.S.–Mexican youth and the politics of caring.* New York: State University of New York Press.

Wiley T. G., Lee, J. S., & Rumberger, R. W. (2009). *The education of language minority immigrants in the United States.* Tonawanda, NY: Multilingual Matters.

Willig, A. (1985). A meta-analysis of selected studies on the effectiveness of bilingual education. *Review of Educational Research, 55*(3), 269–317.

Willig, A. (1987). Examining bilingual education research through meta-analysis and narrative review: A response to Baker. *Review of Educational Research, 57*(3), 363–376.

Wright, W., & Choi, D. (2006). The impact of language and high-stakes testing policies on elementary school English language learners in Arizona. *Education Policy Analysis Archives, 14*(13). Retrieved from epaa.asu.edu/epaa/v14n13/

⮜ MYTH 21 ⮞

Preserving heritage language among English language learners is bad for them.

If you sit in a restaurant, wait in line at the grocery store, or walk down the street in any city or community in the United States, from Dearborn to Dallas, it is likely you will hear languages other than English being spoken. This is a part of everyday life for millions of people who live in the United States. Yet, many Americans support English-only laws, stand against bilingual education, and wonder why recent immigrants don't "want" to learn English. The rationales behind these viewpoints are not always based on facts or research.

For example, many argue that preserving their heritage language—the language spoken at home—among English language learners (ELLs) has negative consequences for them. In particular, they claim encouraging heritage language use prevents ELLs from learning English. Debates over how to best educate these students have been raging since the 1970s. A number of approaches have been tried to help children acquire English while simultaneously allowing them to learn all of the other elements of the school curriculum. Advocates of bilingual education—approaches that embrace teaching academic content in two languages—contend that using the native language of the student to teach content is the most beneficial approach in helping ELL students succeed. Opponents favor an immersion method where students are exposed to their heritage language for only a brief time each day, the goal being to move them into a monolingual English classroom as quickly as possible (see Myth 20). Support for immersion approaches has been based on a variety of rationales, including claims that bilingual education causes confusion, makes it more difficult for students to focus on learning English, and makes students less likely to embrace American values. But few opponents of bilingual education provide any credible research for these claims. Most research actually indicates that, rather than causing a deficiency that ELL students must overcome, preserving heritage language yields a great advantage to these students individually and to our broader society. A substantial body of research demonstrates cognitive advantages for those who are balanced bilingual, adept speakers of their heritage and their new language. Those opposed to preserving heritage languages through our public schools are both devaluing ELLs and their families, and taking away the bilingual students' cognitive advantage.

Why would teaching students to maintain their heritage language while learning English be considered a bad approach for working with ELL students? The believers in immersion hold that bilingual education causes the brain to be confused—a zero-sum game where learning one language necessarily trades off with the capacity to learn another. Many against bilingual education also hold the mistaken belief that the academic skills a child learns in one language, like multiplication tables, will not transfer, and children must then relearn how to multiply once they are proficient in English. These beliefs may have been based on a crude understanding of how the brain works (Baker, 2011). Many more methodologically sound studies have shown that preserving heritage language holds positive benefits for students. A classic study in the field makes this point well. Researchers examined Puerto Rican students in a bilingual education program in New Haven, Connecticut. The students received half of the day's instruction in English and half in Spanish. Although the program emphasized English language acquisition, students still received a substantial portion of instruction in their heritage language. This study, and others that attempted to develop balanced bilinguals, reveals a positive relationship between bilingualism and the development of students' cognitive abilities (Bialystok, 1991; Hakuta, 1987).

Rather than compromise students' brain power, bilingual education has been found to add to students' cognitive flexibility, allowing them to think about and apply the subtle meanings of different words in two (or more) languages (Baker, 2011). Furthermore, bilingual students, compared with monolingual students, have been found to develop complex skills, including readiness to see structure in patterns and a capacity to reorganize their thoughts according to feedback (Ben-Zeev, 1977). Researchers also have found that bilingual students have an advantage when it comes to solving problems that require higher levels of attention and an understanding of numbers, in part because they have developed the ability to create simultaneous connections among many different symbols more effectively than monolingual students (Bialystok & Codd, 1997). Bilingual students possess an added advantage over their monolingual peers that goes beyond the sum of their parts. The complexity of the distinct structures and concepts of the two languages appears not to be additive, but, instead, multiplicative. Bilinguality multiplies the intellectual dividends that each language bestows on these students (Bialystok & Hakuta, 1994).

What's ultimately at stake? ELL students have the distinction of being the fastest growing segment of the public school population. But simultaneously, they have lower academic achievement and higher dropout rates than their peers (National Education Association, 2008). Many studies make a strong case for promoting educational approaches that preserve students' heritage languages as a way to both increase achievement and reduce dropout rate. Proponents of maintaining heritage language, while simultaneously promoting students' acquisition of the English language, often call their approach English Plus. English Plus advocates argue that knowing more than one language should be viewed as an asset rather than a deficit. A student's first language should be preserved and valued rather than destroyed in an effort to teach the English language and U.S. culture. It is a curious thing that at many high schools, ELL students in one classroom will be actively encouraged to abandon their heritage language, while native English speakers across the hall will struggle to learn French, German, Italian, or Spanish.

Beyond the individual, maintenance of heritage language benefits society in important ways. A multilingual workforce will make us more economically competitive, eliminate the shortage of foreign language teachers, and yield significant political, national security, and diplomatic benefits, as well. As a nation we would be well served if the question about ELLs was reframed, away from, "Why don't they just learn English?" to, "How can we develop a multilingual society to live peacefully and cooperate economically in our highly interdependent world?" Currently, one state seems to understand this: Utah (Healy, 2013). It has developed dual-language schools not only in Spanish, for its large Hispanic population, but also in French, Portuguese, and Mandarin. German and Arabic may be coming. Waiting lists to get into these schools are common as parents have learned the benefits of bilingualism. The teachers, most from other countries, teach the regular subjects like mathematics, reading, and social studies, while speaking only the foreign language. At first, they may have to pantomime and use pictures and videos to communicate, but within a few weeks the students quickly learn to understand them. The students in these dual-language programs are graded normally and have to take the same standardized tests as their peers. Utah is seeing none of the deficits predicted by those that claim bilingualism hurts children. While that is still a common theory, Utah has declared it a bankrupt theory.

References

Baker, C. (2011). *Foundations of bilingual education and bilingualism*. Tonawanda, NY: Multilingual Matters.

Ben-Zeev, S. (1977). The influence of bilingualism on cognitive strategy and cognitive development. *Child Development, 48*, 1009–1018.

Bialystok, E. (1991). *Language processing in bilingual children*. New York, NY: Cambridge University Press.

Bialystok, E., & Codd, J. (1997). Cardinal limits: Evidence from language awareness and bilingualism for developing concepts of number. *Cognitive Development, 12*, 85–106.

Bialystok, E., & Hakuta, K. (1994). *In other words*. New York, NY: Basic Books.

Hakuta, K. (1987). Degree of bilingualism and cognitive ability in mainland Puerto Rican children. *Child Development, 58*, 1372–1388.

Healy, J. (2013, April 19). A state seeks to be heard in a new world economy. *The New York Times*. Retrieved from tinyurl.com/n6sccad

National Education Association. (2008). English language learners face unique challenges. Retrieved from tinyurl.com/nfnnvkh

∽ MYTH 22 ≳

Abstinence-only educational programs work to reduce sexual contact and unwanted pregnancies among school children.

Do abstinence-only educational programs work? Not according to a 9-year, comprehensive, national study commissioned by Congress. Between youth who completed abstinence-only educational programs and those who didn't, there were *no significant differences* in the number of adolescents who chose to be abstinent, their age at the time of first intercourse, the frequency of unprotected sex, or the number of sexual partners (Trenholm et al., 2007). Despite rigorous research attesting to the limitations of abstinence-only education, there is also a small body of supporting research.

Advocates of abstinence-only education point to an investigation that found positive outcomes for an abstinence-only program targeting 6th- and 7th-graders. In that study, only a third of students who attended abstinence-only education classes started having sex within the next 2 years, compared with about half of the students who attended other classes (either classes teaching only safer sex or general health education classes). While this program has had some success, it does not satisfy the federal guidelines, suggesting that stringent federal criteria actually may be hindering the discovery of successful sex education programs (Jemmott, Jemmott, & Fong, 2010).

What makes this successful abstinence-only program different from the federal standards for conducting such studies? The program used in this study was theory-based and tailored to a specific population. It addressed students' beliefs about the consequences of sexual involvement, did not criticize the use of condoms, and was not moralistic. The government's criteria for financing abstinence-only educational programs come from Title V, Section 510, of the Social Security Act passed by Congress in 1996. It will fund only programs that:

- Have the exclusive purpose of teaching the social, psychological, and health gains that come from abstaining from sexual activity.
- Teach abstinence from sexual activity outside marriage as the expected standard for all school-age children.
- Teach that abstinence from sexual activity is the only certain way to avoid out-of-wedlock pregnancy, sexually transmitted diseases, and other associated health problems.

- Teach that a mutually faithful, monogamous relationship in the context of marriage is the expected standard of sexual activity.
- Teach that sexual activity outside marriage is likely to have harmful psychological and physical effects.
- Teach that bearing children out of wedlock is likely to have harmful consequences for the child, the child's parents, and society.
- Teach young people how to reject sexual advances and how alcohol and drug use increases vulnerability to sexual advances.
- Teach the importance of attaining self-sufficiency before engaging in sexual activity.

In fact, however, the typical American adolescent has sex by the age of 17 (Trenholm et al., 2007); 95% of adults have sex before marriage (Finer, 2007); and in the United States more than 40% of children are born out of wedlock (Kochanek, Kirmeyer, Martin, Strobino, & Guyer, 2012). In effect, congressional legislation like Title V, Section 510, of the Social Security Act requires public schools to teach abstinence-only programs that are ineffective, dangerous, value-laden, and a waste of money. Moreover, a 2004 report commissioned by the House of Representatives examined abstinence-only programs supported by the U.S. government. It found that 11 of the 13 most frequently used curricula contained false, misleading, or distorted information about reproductive health—including inaccurate information about contraceptive effectiveness, risks of abortion, and other scientific errors (U.S. House of Representatives, 2004).

Numerous studies confirm that abstinence-only educational programs have limited or no effects on young people's sexual behavior. At best, they delay the start of sexual activity slightly. But what happens when adolescents begin to have sex a few years after their abstinence-only educational program ends? Or what about the students sitting in the class who are being told to abstain, but are already sexually active? If the goal of sex education is to give adolescents the knowledge to make informed and responsible decisions about their reproductive and sexual health, then omitting information about contraceptives, condoms, and healthy relationship skills (outside of marriage) is both dangerous and negligent. (Collins et al., 2002)

What are LGBTQ (lesbian, gay, bisexual, transgender, and queer) students in the class supposed to take away from this abstinence-until-marriage doctrine that may be forced upon them at a public school? And what about the students who don't want to marry? How does this message of abstinence-only education keep these adolescents safe from unintended pregnancy, sexually transmitted diseases, and other health problems associated with sexual activity? It doesn't.

What federally funded abstinence-only educational programs *do* accomplish is to impart an ideology that sexual behavior is safe and morally correct only within the bounds of heterosexual marriage. In the secular education setting of public schools, this message verges on religious interference. Public education would be better served by sticking to the science of sexuality; families should discuss their diverse range of beliefs on sexuality at home.

Just how much money is being wasted teaching abstinence-only to the nation's children in public schools? Over $1.5 billion in state and federal funds have been dedicated to abstinence-only programs since 1996 (Howell & Keefe, 2007). Currently, $50 million is allocated annually by the federal government through the Social Security Act to continue funding these noneffective programs. However, in order to receive these grants, states are required to match 75% of the federal contribution, meaning that $87.5 million of public funds are spent on ineffective abstinence-only educational programs each year. That is an awful lot of tax dollars being spent on ineffective programming that only 36% of Americans support (Bleakley, Hennessy, & Fishbein, 2006).

What does work? Comprehensive sex education programs encourage abstinence, but also provide age-appropriate, medically accurate information about contraception and sexually transmitted diseases. Studies show that comprehensive, honest sex education programs work. They result in a delay of first intercourse, decrease teen pregnancies, decrease incidences of STDs and HIV, reduce the number of sexual partners, increase monogamy, decrease unprotected sex, and, in sexually active youth, increase the usage of contraceptives and condoms (Kohler, Manhart, & Lafferty, 2008).

Numerous health and education experts support comprehensive sex education: Advocates for Youth, the American Academy of Pediatrics, the American College of Obstetricians and Gynecologists, the American Medical Association, the American Public Health Association, the National Education Association, the National Medical Association, the National School Boards Association, the Society for Adolescent Medicine, and the Sexuality Information and Education Council of the United States. In addition, 82% of Americans favor programs that teach students about both abstinence and other methods of preventing pregnancy and sexually transmitted diseases (Bleakley et al., 2006). Yet, currently there are no dedicated federal funding streams for comprehensive sex education. In 2011, a bill advocating comprehensive sex education was introduced into Congress. The Repealing Ineffective and Incomplete Abstinence-Only Program Funding Act was intended to redirect the $50 million funding in the Social Security Act away from abstinence-only educational programs to comprehensive sex education programs. With little bipartisan support, the legislation died in committee.

References

Bleakley, A., Hennessy, M., & Fishbein, M. (2006). Public opinion on sex education in US schools. *Archives of Pediatrics & Adolescent Medicine, 160*(11), 1151.

Collins, C., Alagiri, M. P., Summers, J. T., & Morin, S. F. (2002). *Abstinence only vs. comprehensive sex education: What are the arguments? What is the evidence?* Retrieved from ari.ucsf.edu/science/reports/abstinence.pdf

Finer, L. B. (2007). Trends in premarital sex in the United States, 1954–2003. *Public Health Reports, 122*(1), 73.

Howell, M., & Keefe, M. (2007). *The history of federal abstinence-only funding.* Washington, DC: Advocates for Youth. Retrieved from tinyurl.com/pszctw8

Jemmott, J. B., III, Jemmott, L. S., & Fong, G. T. (2010). Efficacy of a theory-based abstinence-only intervention over 24 months: A randomized controlled trial with young adolescents. *Archives of Pediatrics & Adolescent Medicine, 164*(2), 152–159.

Kochanek, K. D., Kirmeyer, S. E., Martin, J. A., Strobino, D. M., & Guyer, B. (2012). Annual summary of vital statistics: 2009. *Pediatrics, 129*(2), 338–348.

Kohler, P. K., Manhart, L. E., & Lafferty, W. E. (2008). Abstinence-only and comprehensive sex education and the initiation of sexual activity and teen pregnancy. *Journal of Adolescent Health, 42*(4), 344–351.

Trenholm, C., Devaney, B., Fortson, K., Quay, L., Wheeler, J., & Clark, M. (2007). *Impacts of four Title V, Section 510 abstinence education programs.* Princeton, NJ: Mathematica Policy Research.

U.S. House of Representatives. (2004). *The content of federally funded abstinence-only education programs.* Washington, DC: Committee on Government Reform, Minority Staff, Special Investigations Division. Title V, Section 510 (b)(2)(A–H) of the Social Security Act (P.L. 104-193).

◌ MYTH 23 ◌

Homework boosts achievement.

Let the dog eat it. Homework does not boost achievement.

We have all been there. We open our backpack to find the worksheets our teachers gave us to complete at the kitchen table, a neighbor's house, on the school bus, or under the watchful and enthusiastic eye of our father. To him, the quality of the work submitted to our teacher would be a direct reflection of our family's morality.

Most parents eagerly include "homework time" as part of the daily household routine and act as tutor, even "ghostwriter" if the child struggles to complete her assignments. This is not because parents necessarily enjoy homework. "Homework," as *New Yorker* columnist Louis Menand (2012) put it, "is an institution roundly disliked by all who participate in it. Children hate it for healthy and obvious reasons; parents hate it because it makes their children unhappy; and teachers hate it because they have to grade it." Parents enforce homework because they believe children who study hard make the grade. But is this accurate? Do the extra hours practicing concepts, memorizing facts, and preparing essays at home add to her grades in school or her test scores? Perhaps not! In fact, there is more credible scholarship on the negative effects of homework than on its merits.

The practice of assigning students tasks to complete outside of school hours has evolved. One hundred fifty years ago homework focused on math, spelling, and history facts, but was limited to children who had the privilege to attend secondary grades. Without access to local libraries and photocopying, teachers dictated lessons to children who then had to memorize them to demonstrate proficiency. Homework was rote repetition of math, spelling, geography, science, and history. Today school systems overwhelmingly use homework as a pedagogical staple and a measurement for assessing students' academic growth in the short term. In some schools very young children spend hours each night struggling with rote memorization, the scientific method, reading quotes, and engaging in Internet research.

The debate over the effectiveness of homework is as old as the practice itself. Historically, critics of homework have stressed two points: Homework compromises children's health; and homework does not boost achievement. In 1860, *Scientific American* (2010) published an article decrying extending a child's school day with homework—particularly the ethics behind memorization assignments. They wrote, "By dint of great and painful labor, the child may succeed in repeating a lot of words, like a parrot, but, with the power of its brain all exhausted, it is out of the question for it to really master and comprehend its lessons." In 1900, the *Ladies Home Journal* garnered supporters in a campaign to abolish homework for elementary school students and to limit it for children in secondary classes. Until that point, critics of homework were passionate but ineffective. This was likely because homework was not a widespread practice for young children, and very few older children were enrolled in secondary education.

The progressive education movement, however, fanned the flames of the anti-homework movement. Between 1890 and 1940, progressives developed principles of effective, moral education for all. Borrowing from the growing field of pediatrics for scientific endorsement, education progressives argued that homework prevented children from exercising and developing social skills. Their campaign gained strength and resulted in most school systems outlawing or limiting the practice. In 1930, the movement was robust. The American Child Health Association even argued that, like child labor, homework would contribute to serious health issues such as tuberculosis, heart disease, and even early death. Perhaps the movement was slightly overplaying its hand, but its heart was in the right place.

By the 1950s, progressive education and other more liberal movements fell victim to a paradigm shift. Similar to the years after the Civil War when a culture of fear of Black retaliation compelled southern legislatures to enact Jim Crow sanctions, the United States saw its victory in World War II as an invitation for competition and retaliation from enemy states. Thus, the 1950s set the stage for policies designed to protect U.S. soil (and culture) from enemy invasion. While the military engaged in a Cold War against the Soviet Union, Blacks attempting to migrate away from Jim Crow to the liberal, integrated North were met with a mass exodus of Whites. In large numbers Whites left the urban centers and created suburbs, which were insulated against certain cultural influences. It was during this time that schools evolved away from practices that promoted family and child wellness. Progressive educational ideas were slowly replaced with values based on international competition. American students were expected to maintain a measurable standard of academic excellence. Over the next few decades, schools institutionalized homework as a primary means for determining a student's academic proficiency on almost a daily basis.

Harris Cooper (Cooper, Robinson, & Patall, 2006), the leading scholar in this area, found 69 correlations between homework and achievement, 50 of which were positive. But 19 of those correlations were negative. Thus, almost one-third of the studies reviewed showed negative effects of homework on achievement. Although the average correlation across these studies was positive, it was quite modest, and it was higher for older students than for younger ones. At the elementary grade levels there appears not to be any significant effect of homework on achievement.

The positive relationship that Cooper found was primarily between time spent in homework and the in-class tests given by teachers. That is plausible since teachers often give homework directly related to the tests they will use in class. Thus students get to practice and memorize what is needed to do well in class. But most studies of homework are correlational, meaning we do not know if more time on homework produces better achievement, or if better students spend more time on homework. In the latter case, it is the motivation and drive of the students that produce the effects we see, not the homework, per se.

Furthermore, on the classroom tests, Cooper found hints of a curvilinear relationship between homework and achievement— meaning that after certain modest amounts of homework were completed, more homework resulted in lower test scores. In addition, Cooper also considered the link between homework completion and standardized test scores, not just the in-class tests. The results? There is no convincing connection. Students who spend hours completing homework are likely not to see significant improvements in their scores on standardized tests.

In 1983, David Pierpont Gardner and the Federal Commission on Education Excellence submitted to President Reagan a report on the status of the U.S. education system. The report, ominously titled *A Nation at Risk*, told a story about the downfall of the American economy and fingered the culprit: schools. According to the Commission, the students who were set to graduate high school in the early to mid-1980s would be the most inept and unproductive generation of workers the country had ever seen. Their SAT scores were abysmal, they lacked higher order skills, and they spent less time on schoolwork than other students around the world. One very specific critique of most schools was that high school students were spending less than 60 minutes on homework each night, while students in Asian countries were spending hours each night on science, computing, and math. Without immediate intervention the United States would not stand a chance against foreign economies. A fear similar to that which led to Jim Crow, and the development of suburbs, and the Cold War had generated an indictment of American schooling. Something foreign this way comes!

Schools responded to the pressure, but a commitment to education excellence was not enough. Schools had to enact policies that allowed them to demonstrate this commitment to parents and legislators. An increase in homework for younger grades and other policies such as high-stakes standardized tests would serve as evidence of America's renewed commitment to pre-eminence. Cathy Vatterott (2009) argues that today's parents, educators, and policymakers (most of whom came of age during the 1980s) see homework as a morality barometer. If a teacher assigns homework regularly, he is providing his students with a rigorous course of study. If a child submits a perfectly prepared assignment, her family has a strong work ethic and cares about her studies. The problem with this tradition is that people are less likely to listen to evidence-based arguments about improving schooling when they feel that their values are under attack.

Thirty years after *A Nation at Risk*, homework is facing another challenge. Progressive parents, teachers, and even principals are considering once again the importance of homework in a child's academic career. This is a particularly hot topic given that many policymakers are rethinking the structure of schooling. Must it always be a teacher in a classroom? What about digital course materials? Distance learning? Is a semester system the best way to organize units of learning? Are there ways to measure content competency regardless of how long a student is enrolled in a course?

As educators think harder about what works, aspects of the homework ritual have come under intense scrutiny—again. And many people find that the international comparisons are fanning the flames of the controversy—again. Consider Finland, whose students often are ranked number one. These students appear never to do homework and they also have shorter school days. Meanwhile, students in South Korea do hours of study each night. They recently were ranked number two. In the United States, some progressive educators are advancing a model that is a compromise between the Finland and South Korean models—both of which are highly successful. They argue for balance when it comes to the amount of study time and common sense when it comes to content. Directors of the popular education documentary *Race to Nowhere* (Abeles & Congdon, 2009) promoted the idea that schools should limit homework time to 2 hours each night, schools should re-implement study halls, and children should be encouraged to read for pleasure.

A popular innovation comes from the idea that schoolwork should be project-based and not task-based. Students design and execute a large project that incorporates core skills like computation and literacy and that requires critical thinking, communication, and problem-solving skills. If they choose to work after hours on the project, so be it. This is popular in Illinois and Pennsylvania. In California some schools have replaced homework with "goal work." These are individualized enrichment tasks that children can complete by themselves. In juvenile justice schools, teachers are asked to alternate days for homework assignments so children have to complete only a small amount each night. One private school in Tucson, Arizona, banned homework altogether, and another in Bleckley County, Georgia, made it optional.

References

Abeles, V. & Congdon, J. (Directors) (2009). *Race to nowhere* (Documentary). Retrieved from www.racetonowhere.com

Cooper, H., Robinson, J. G., & Patall, E. A. (2006). Does homework improve academic achievement? A synthesis of research, 1987–2003. *Review of Educational Research,76* (1), 1–62.

Menand, L. (2012, December 17). Today's assignment. *The New Yorker.* Retrieved from tinyurl.com/a63sgff

Scientific American. (2010). Retrieved from www.scientificamerican.com/article.cfm?id=50-100-150-oct-2010

Vatterott, C. (2009). *Rethinking homework: Best practices that support diverse needs.* Alexandria, VA: ASCD.

৵ MYTH 24 ৵

Group projects waste children's time and punish the most talented.

It is common to see students count off—one, two, three, four, five; one, two, three, four, five, . . . —forming the groups they will work with for group activities and projects. Or a teacher may invite students to select their own groups, and they will do so according to interests, friendships, or convenience. A teacher also might designate members of a group in order to strategically place certain students with certain others. Perceived ability and the classroom behavior of particular students are the common attributes teachers think about when forming classroom groups.

After groups are formed and tasks assigned, what happens next? Will the students work together as a seamless unit to develop a great project, or will they socialize and argue, wasting precious class time? Will the most grade-conscious students do all the work, while the slackers do little, thus earning grades for the whole group primarily from the efforts of only a few of its most talented members? The arguments for avoiding assigning group projects are based on numerous bad experiences. They often take this form:

- One or two students in the group always end up doing all the work. Other students in the group are "free riders" and don't contribute.
- One or two students in the group try to take all the credit for a group effort.
- The smartest (or loudest) students take over the project.
- Students struggle with responsibility when working with unclear leadership.

- Some in the group waste time while others do the work.
- Grades are affected by someone else's effort.
- Many students simply do not like working with other students.

It is certainly likely that these statements are true for some students, and they do characterize some group-work assigned at school and at work. In one survey, group project work was voted both the best and worst of a student's school experiences (Gray, 2006). And your "worst nightmare of a group partner" has had his say on YouTube ("Worst Member," n.d.). But it is also true that these negative descriptions might as easily characterize working in congressional committees, putting out a daily news show or newspaper, the interactions of families as they jointly plan summer vacations, and military operations. In these settings a strong dictator, boss, patriarch, general, or teacher makes for efficiency. And certainly working alone on solutions to problems also may be quicker. But neither dictator nor loner is as likely to produce the best outcomes, and better outcomes remain the goal of group projects. Group-work is hard to do well, of that there is no doubt. Thus, many teachers and school districts avoid using this instructional method. But it has been a teaching tool for centuries, and there are good reasons for that kind of longevity.

Individual and group projects first began to be used in architectural and engineering education in Italy during the late 16th century. The project approach gained popularity in the United States, and in other curriculum areas, during the progressive era. John Dewey promoted the group project method as part of his belief that the best preparation for social life was to actually engage in social life. Dewey was also less interested in what a child learned, the official school outcomes, than that the child learned how to learn what it is he or she wanted to learn, particularly in partnership with others. So, in preparation for a changing society, and for living in a democratic society, progressive educators promoted group projects. These reasons for recommending group projects have not changed.

Nevertheless, the project method has waxed and waned as an instructional tool. It has been promoted or avoided in different school districts, despite having strong support from the research community (Blumenfeld et al., 1991). Currently, the design of school-sponsored group projects is experiencing a renaissance. This is because in recent years group projects have been advocated by business leaders as they push schools to teach skills thought to be necessary for success in the 21st-century economy. The ability of graduates of our high schools and colleges to work productively in groups is a skill almost every business leader is now asking schools to promote to ensure economic prosperity.

Despite its difficulty to do well, and all its faults when done badly, many students, parents, teachers, and community leaders value school-sponsored group project work. They do so because they know such projects afford opportunities for collaboration and cooperation among the student body. Cooperation, rather than competition, is more likely to foster a display of mutual respect and kindness. The group project also allows for peer teaching and learning, promoting far more participation than is true of large-group classroom learning. Learning how to do collective problem solving toward shared goals, as required by group projects, is different from life in ordinary classrooms, where individualism is nurtured and a hierarchical authority structure is ever present. Although business did not want these kinds of collaborative skills promoted when the United States was building its factory economy, these kinds of school activities are now seen as crucial for success in educating students for the information economy.

There are a number of factors that help to make group projects successful and that keep the least productive or laziest members of the group from not contributing. One is that students should have some say in the process or outcomes of the project. Buy-in to a project builds motivation. A second factor is that the project should specify a question or problem that helps students to organize their activities and drives their efforts. Another factor is that students must be given enough time to do their projects well. The projects also need some monitoring by the teacher to ensure they are on track to produce the artifacts required, the final product of the project, such as a written paper, a model, a video, or a presentation. Finally, the projects, even if dealing with the same phenomena, should not be expected to have the same outcomes. Each group may take a different route as it tries to solve a common problem. So if grading is to occur, it must be tailored to each group, weighing both its process and its product.

Under these conditions, the negative effects of group projects rarely play out. If the projects are meaningful, are complex, and extend over time, as students investigate and seek solutions to the problems they address, they acquire a deeper understanding of key principles and concepts. If the group project is to measure water pollution in a region, or the group is tasked with writing a play about a train wreck that occurred nearby, or a group studies what to do about bears that are coming into the towns in which they live, or the group studies how to repurpose the newspapers they asked people to recycle, the activities place students in realistic, contextualized problem-solving environments. They are a lot closer to real-world problem solving than usually occurs in schools, and this is just what both business and educational leaders desire. The potential to improve students' competence in other ways that business desires also occurs because the student group has to formulate plans, track progress, and evaluate solutions during the course of the project. These are adult skills, needed at work and at home, but learned as a participant in a group project (Blumenfeld et al., 1991).

Those who value group projects believe that, collectively, the group can create something that is impossible to accomplish alone. In the individualistic country we live in, beliefs like these sound communistic or socialistic to some Americans. So political ideology, more than negative effects, keeps the group project method from flourishing.

References

Blumenfeld, P. C., Soloway, E., Marx, R. W., Krajcik, J. S., Guzdial, M., & Palincsar, A. (1991). Motivating project-based learning: Sustaining the doing, supporting the learning. *Educational Psychologist, 26,* 369–398.

Gray, N. (2006, January). The good, the bad, and the ugly: Students' experiences of group projects. *Teaching at Nottingham.* Retrieved from tinyurl.com/nscc2rg

The worst member of your group project. (n.d). Retrieved from tinyurl.com/pos29jd

◄§ MYTH 25 ᾀ

School uniforms improve achievement and attendance.

Those supporting requirements that public school students wear school uniforms do so because they believe that school uniforms lead to better academic performance, higher attendance rates, lower crime rates, improved discipline, better school climate, and less competition to wear cool, expensive clothes. Uniforms also are expected to increase student pride in their schools and themselves, and reduce gang activity. If they actually worked this way, uniforms would be a powerful way to change schools for the better. But school uniforms have no such dramatic effects.

Support for claims like these is manufactured out of research that finds weak effects, no effects, or even negative effects of uniforms on the outcomes we all desire. There are too many contradictions in the data, and too many other explanations for the effects that occasionally are found, to support the exaggerated claims for school uniform policies.

Although no state requires public school students to wear school uniforms, and one state even forbids such rules, the public schools of our nation increasingly have passed policies requiring school uniforms. Much of today's interest in uniforms stems from President Clinton's having promoted uniforms in his State of the Union Address in 1996. Then he ordered the U.S. Department of Education to issue manuals to help districts implement school uniform policies. He believed that uniforms could put "discipline and learning back in our schools," even though there was no convincing evidence they had ever left.

Discussions about school uniforms grew more frequent after Clinton's speech and the purportedly successful implementation of uniform policies in some high-profile school districts such as Long Beach, California. School uniform policies were passed primarily in districts that were minority, poor, and not achieving well. But school uniform programs also spread elsewhere because they had prestige. They were associated with the British school system, which had a tradition of school uniforms, and the United States has an affinity for all things English. Forgotten, however, was that uniforms in Britain were often a way for the elite school students to be clearly distinguished from those who went to working-class schools. Uniform policies, in England and elsewhere, reinforced the existing social order. Recognizing this, some who oppose uniforms in the United States do so because they believe the practice marks and stigmatizes poorer children, since the wearing of a school uniform is much less likely to occur in wealthier school districts. That argument has some logic to it. On the other hand, before the 1950s, uniforms often were promoted as a way to reduce social class differences in school, providing poorer parents a chance to dress their children the same way as more affluent children were dressed. That argument also has some logic to it. Supporters and opponents of school uniforms also argue over whether a uniform program saves poor parents money. Uniforms may help some poor parents by reducing their school clothing costs. But it is also true that some uniform programs cost families more money than would a regular wardrobe purchased at a discount store. So the debate about school uniforms is also a debate about schooling and social class, and both wealthier and poorer parents can be found on either side of the issue, complicating a search for authoritative answers to questions about the appropriateness and effectiveness of school uniforms.

Contemporary arguments in favor of uniforms also bring into play the belief that Catholic and other religious private schools, along with the secular private schools—especially the much admired elite private schools—are "better" schools than public schools. Since many of those schools require uniforms, a bit of magical thinking seems to occur: If those kinds of school are "better" schools, and many of them require uniforms, then if our school had uniforms, we would be better too. As made clear in our discussion of the purported superiority of private schools (see Myth 2), there is no convincing evidence that private school students, with or without uniforms, do any better than public school children if the social class of the students is taken into account.

Over the decade 2000–2009, the percentage of public schools that required a school uniform increased from 12 to 19%. Similarly, the percentage of public schools with strict dress codes went from 47 to 57% (Robers, Zhang, & Truman, 2012). Clearly there has been increasing concern about what students wear to school. That is understandable in our highly sexualized society where competition in fashion at school is as common as competition in sports and on achievement tests, and where occasional assaults are committed for a fancy jacket or a pair of shoes.

But the evidence supporting the use of school uniforms relies more on anecdote and personal preferences than facts derived from trustworthy research. For example, some religious schools and religious parents find justification for school uniform policies in the Bible, ignoring secular arguments altogether. They argue that "God implemented a dress code for Adam and Eve in the Garden of Eden as He replaced their aprons of fig leaves with coats of skin" (Gen. 3, quoted in Gouge, 2011). Beliefs of this kind probably cannot be swayed by research results.

In most districts, the discussions about requiring school uniforms are interwoven with other discussions about how to improve school achievement, attendance, safety, morale, and the like. If action on all those fronts takes place at once, as is common, and some of the outcomes we desire come about in the ways we hope they will, we are unable to answer questions about the unique effects of school uniforms on those outcomes. For example, in the decade 2000–2009, just as uniform wearing increased, the percentages of public schools reporting new safety and security measures also increased: Control of access to school buildings during school hours increased from 75% to 92%; control of access to school grounds during school hours increased from 34% to 46%; use of one or more security cameras increased from 19% to 61%; the percent of school security guards increased slightly; and many zero-tolerance policies were instituted (see Myth 28) (Robers et al., 2012). Subsequently, when surveys of students, teachers, and parents reveal improvement in perceptions of school safety, attendance rates, and school morale, it is impossible to unravel these possible causes and isolate the effect of school uniforms. A classic case of this confusion of cause and effect may be the Long Beach, California, schools, often held up as a model of the good things that can happen when uniforms are required. At the same time that uniforms were required of students, there was a reassessment of the district's content standards, the receipt of a million-dollar grant to develop alternative pedagogical techniques for low-achieving and minority children, and a new achievement-reporting system (Brunsma & Rockquemore, 1998). Long Beach was doing lots of things to improve its schools and now is considered a much better district than it was. But uniforms were only one of many changes that occurred simultaneously. And if that policy was rescinded tomorrow, it is likely that Long Beach would still be a highly regarded district.

A second problem for uniform advocates is that other research that has examined the benefits of school uniforms is not strongly supportive of the outcomes claimed. For example, one report by the Educational Testing Service examined a large national data set about youth to study serious delinquency (e.g., fighting, being arrested), nonserious delinquency (e.g., skipped classes, lateness for school), and drug use (e.g., use of cocaine, marijuana, or alcohol) in and out of school (Barton, Coley, & Wenglensky, 1998). Information was also available about whether uniforms were required at the schools. The analysis found that school uniforms made no difference in the rates of serious and nonserious delinquency, nor did they influence students' drug use. In another analysis of federal data sets, the following variables were found *not* to be related to a school uniform policy: student perceptions of safety or the academic climate; principal perceptions of safety or the academic climate; parental involvement; attendance; and scores on achievement tests of reading/literacy, mathematics, science, and history (Brunsma & Rockquemore, 1998). This research fails to support the claims for the benefits of uniforms. But this research has been criticized by others. One critic claimed the authors did their analyses incorrectly, perhaps because they had their minds made up first. Noted was that a different analysis yielded a positive correlation between uniform requirements and measures of academic achievement. While that appears to be true, the correlation was extremely low, suggesting only a weak relationship of uniforms to measures of academic performance.

It should be noted that the arguments against requiring school uniforms seem not to have much support either. Those arguments include the belief that uniforms squash creativity and free expression; do not allow students to make decisions about matters that are rightfully theirs; and squelch self-expression and individuality, characteristics to be prized and supported in a democracy.

In sum, the extant research in this area appears to be highly partisan, with strong beliefs held by advocates and detractors that are based on their personal preferences and political philosophies. A reasonable conclusion is that the evidence for the positive outcomes claimed for requiring school uniforms either is unsupported, or is weak and inconsistent at best. And the arguments against the use of uniforms are difficult to test empirically, so their claims are hard to assess. Perhaps a school's implementation of a sensible dress code, worked out with the students, is the best way for parents and teachers to obtain some of the desired controls they want over student behavior. Top-down rules requiring school uniforms to accomplish this have little empirical support.

References

Barton, P., Coley, R., & Wenglensky, H. (1998). *Order in the classroom: Violence, discipline, and student achievement*. Princeton, NJ: Educational Testing Service, Policy Information Center.

Bodine, A. (2003). School uniforms, academic achievement, and uses of research. *The Journal of Educational Research, 97*(2), 67–71.

Brunsma, D. L. (2006, January/February). School uniform policies in public schools. *Principal*, pp. 50–53.

Brunsma, D. L., & Rockquemore, K. A. (1998). Effects of student uniforms on attendance, behavior problems, substance abuse, and academic achievement. *The Journal of Educational Research, 92*(1), 53–92.

Gouge, W. A. (2011, July). *A comparison research study on the use of school uniforms and graduation, attendance, and suspension rates in east Tennessee* (Unpublished doctoral dissertation). Liberty University, Lynchburg, VA.

Robers, S., Zhang, J., & Truman, J. (2012). *Indicators of school crime and safety: 2011* (NCES 2012-002/ NCJ 236021). Washington, DC: National Center for Education Statistics, U.S. Department of Education and Bureau of Justice Statistics, Office of Justice Programs, U.S. Department of Justice.

⮜MYTH 26⮞

Longer school days and weeks have big payoffs for achievement.

In the fall of 2012, in the midst of the first teacher strike in 25 years in Chicago, Mayor Rahm Emanuel took a bold step to move negotiations forward. Having provoked substantial teacher anger and anxiety with his evaluation and merit pay schemes, Emanuel sought to buy back a bit of good will with the Chicago teachers' union. He proposed that the school day for Chicago public schools be lengthened by 30 minutes and the school year by 2 weeks. The proposal was greeted by all concerned with warm approval. After all, teachers were not going to increase their work day and year without additional compensation, and what parent wouldn't appreciate 2 fewer weeks of child-care expense? But Mayor Emanuel couldn't admit to a blatant attempt to polish his tarnished image with the teachers and the public. So he touted the wonderful benefits to learning and achievement that would result from adding the equivalent of about 2 dozen days to the school calendar. Chicago public school students could now be expected to leap ahead of students around the world.

Mayor Emanuel actually was following the lead of his former boss, President Barack Obama, in advancing his proposal. On more than one occasion, Obama has proposed lengthening the school year by as much as a month. That month can make a huge difference, and we have to do it because India and China are leaving us in the dust—such is the view of the Leader of the Free World.

But will longer school days and school years like the ones Emanuel proposed really make a difference in students' achievement? Research says, "No" (Levin, Glass, & Meister, 1987). Admittedly, the answer to this myth can seem somewhat counterintuitive. Suppose the school year was increased from 9 months to 12 months. Would students learn more after 4 or 5 years of attending school the entire year? Most certainly they would; to imagine otherwise is to gainsay the value of attending school at all. Four years of attending school for 12 months of the year most likely would add a whole year of achievement to students' learning. If this were not the case, then we would not have seen the tragic setbacks in students' learning and even their tested IQs when in the 1950s and 1960s some school districts in the South closed their schools rather than comply with the Supreme Court's mandate to integrate them.

In 2013, Secretary of Education Arne Duncan announced that the U.S. Department of Education would fund schools in five states enrolling 20,000 students in 40 schools to experiment with "extended" school calendars. They could choose to lengthen the day or add days to the school year. The 3-year program will be evaluated sometime down the road. Will we learn much? No. The National Center on Time & Learning estimates that 1,000 school districts nationwide have already extended the school year, in most cases adding about 20 days to the calendar. If simply making the school year longer was the panacea for our supposed education ills, those 1,000 districts would already be outperforming Finland or Korea or whatever nation currently is seen as threatening the U.S. economy.

Around the world, school years can differ substantially in length. Children in Australia and Northern Ireland attend school for 200 days a year. In South Korea, school is in session for 220 days a year; in Japan, 175. And in Finland—where everyone was looking in 2012 for the secrets of success—the school year is the same length as in the United States: 180 days. Finland has many fewer hours of schooling per year, has many more breaks per day from academic work, and doesn't even start academic work until children are about 7 years old. So Finland accumulates a lot less time in academic learning, and it still has managed to outperform many other countries in the world. Those who seek a pattern in the relationship between school year length and student achievement will end up with more unanswered questions than they began with.

A 12-month school year is not what Rahm Emanuel or anyone else is talking about. No one seriously proposes increasing the cost of K–12 public education in America from $600 billion to $800 billion annually, or even bumping up the school year to 220 days as in Korea, at an annual increase in cost of $150 billion or so. Why, then, is Mayor Emanuel's proposal unlikely to raise the achievement of Chicago's public school students? Because 30 minutes a day and 2 more weeks in June are just not enough to impact all that would have to change to produce greater learning.

Will the textbooks be rewritten because school now starts at 8 A.M. and ends at 3:30 P.M. instead of 3 P.M.? Not likely. What class will be lengthened by 30 minutes? Math? Science? Music? Would the schools split the difference and add 10 minutes to each of these classes? Will teachers suddenly—or even eventually—adopt an entirely new way of instructing students? If nothing really changes—not the teaching materials, not the methods of teaching, not how students are grouped—why would anyone expect a change in how much students learn?

Increasing the school year, even by 20 days, never yields 20 days more time spent learning. Think of it this way. A 6-hour school day includes time for taking roll, physical education, transitioning into and out of various activities such as art or music (if the kids are lucky enough to have these), lunch and bathroom breaks, and the like. This often reduces the 6 hours per day to less than 4 hours of instruction in subjects like math and reading. So 20 more days works out to 80 hours of instruction, if you are lucky. But not all that is done in the time allocated for students to master a curriculum is about learning what is on the tests used to assess their learning. The teacher may take advantage of something said in class, or note some event in the news that pertains to what students are reading or doing in science—if he or she is a good teacher, that is. Students are certainly learning, but they are not learning much of what they must know to show increased test scores, which is what the bean counters will be looking at. So the 4 additional hours a day may end up being 3 hours a day, overall, yielding only about 60 hours of instructional time. But that is not all. In the average class, the percent of time students are engaged with the curriculum they are supposed to be learning is about 70%, and that's in an excellent, well-managed class (Berliner, 1979). Inattention, daydreaming, texting, and tweeting surreptitiously almost always use up some of the time allocated for learning. So the 60 hours easily may turn out to be about 40 hours of time actually spent on the tasks the students are intended to learn. So 20 days is likely to become about 40 hours, and those 40 hours may well be divided among reading, science, and math. It is unlikely that benefits to student learning will be detected even if we were to add 20 days of schooling to the school year. Although it will be hard to find evidence for increased learning from this relatively large increase in days of schooling, there are reasons to believe it actually might accomplish that if the time allocated actually was used to increase instruction. But it often isn't, and that's reality.

When Karen Lewis, president of the Chicago teachers' union, and Randi Weingarten, president of the American Federation of Teachers, commented approvingly on the mayor's proposal in a *Wall Street Journal* op-ed piece (September 23, 2012), there was not even a hint that a longer school day and school year would be used to deliver more instruction to students: "Additional seat time doesn't constitute a good education. A well-rounded and rich curriculum, regular opportunities for teachers to plan and confer with colleagues, and time to engage students through discussions, group work and project-based learning —all these contribute to a high-quality education, and these should be priorities going forward."

And did Mayor Emanuel check with the Boy Scouts and the Camp Fire Girls and the Little League and the myriad other organizations that would be affected by a longer school year? Those who have attempted to change the school calendar have frequently abandoned their efforts in favor of the much easier task of relocating old cemeteries.

References

Berliner, D. C. (1979). Tempus educare. In P. L. Peterson & H. J. Walberg (Eds.), *Research on teaching:: Concepts, findings, and implications* (pp. 120–135). Berkeley, CA: McCutchan.

Levin, H. M., Glass, G. V, & Meister, G. R. (1987). Different approaches to improving performance at school. *Zeitschrift fur Internationale Erziehungs und Sozial Wissenschaftliche Forschung, 3,* 156–176.

Lewis, K., & Weingarten, R. (2012, September 23). A gold star for the Chicago teachers strike. *Wall Street Journal.* Retrieved from on.wsj.com/1dez9mL

ଶୈMYTH 27ஓ

If a program works well in one school or district, it should be imported and expected to work well elsewhere.

Some educational programs work. They lead to improvements in student learning. Yet, if the program is tried in a different school, it does not always work. Why? Are the school and district staff just not trying hard enough? Isn't it simply a matter of fidelity—doing the same program, the same way, to ensure positive results?

Perhaps that would be true if education was a simple machine where particular inputs led directly to predictable outputs. However, education cannot be captured in a simple equation, no more than love, marriage, or running a business can be. It is a complex, intricate endeavor that entails inputs we can't control (e.g., the wealth of families, parents' education, community support), variables we can't easily identify or measure (e.g., competing initiatives, classroom culture, peer influence, teacher beliefs), and outputs we often can neither predict nor measure (e.g., unintended consequences such as increases in one set of skills at the cost of decreases in others). The equation is unwieldy, and the classification of variables as inputs or outputs can even be difficult to determine. It is this complex nature of education that limits the ability of schools and districts to duplicate programs in one place that yielded positive results in another (Berliner, 2002). Disseminating a successful program is what some researchers have called the problem of "scaling up." Although they have named the problem, no one has produced any satisfactory solution.

Prediction of outcomes in education is problematic, say, in comparison to medicine, which has earned the public's trust because it has provided some predictability about effects. If you are suffering from high blood pressure, your doctor can prescribe a medication that has been proven to reduce blood pressure for most patients, most of the time. If you take this medication as prescribed, regardless of the exact conditions that contributed to your high blood pressure, you probably can expect your condition to improve. But even then individual differences are great, and so medicines known to be effective overall will not work on every patient.

If your child is in a school that is struggling, you may expect that your district or school can implement a program believed to be effective elsewhere. If that program is applied as directed, you may expect test scores to improve. If the intervention does not work, blame usually is placed on the school staff, who are thought not to have exercised fidelity in implementing the new program, or perhaps are thought not to have exerted the effort needed to make the program work. While fidelity is an important consideration, and effective teaching certainly requires hard work, the assumption that staff simply must work harder ignores the impact that the context of schools and districts has on the success of a program. In fact, context can account for much of the variability in program effectiveness from school to school and district to district. Blaming teachers for a failure to replicate effects may be convenient, but it also may be misleading (Weiss, Bloom, & Brock, 2013). It is akin to blaming a patient who does not get better with a drug that is supposed to work. Individual differences in humans and context effects in social settings make it very difficult to be sure that what we do will work as intended.

We have seen the powerful influence of context in several large-scale reform efforts. In the 1960s, the federal government invested millions in Project Follow Through ("following through" on the effects of Head Start) to study which curricular approaches led to an improvement in student achievement in low-income schools. Project Follow Through was one of the largest education experiments ever completed, involving more than 200,000 students and a dozen different educational programs over several years. Each of the different programs had multiple school sites, often in different communities, as each program attempted to institutionalize its educational philosophy and deliver instruction in the way intended. The goal of the project was to identify effective programs for replication and subsequent support by the federal government. The findings of an evaluation of Project Follow Through (Stebbins, St. Pierre, Proper, Anderson, & Cerva, 1977) concluded that direct instruction programs led to the most improvement in student achievement. The validity of this finding was, and continues to be, debated in the education community. However, a second finding was that the effectiveness of each educational program investigated varied enormously from community to community and school to school. In other words, effective results could not be duplicated even from the same program because the local context had such a large influence on the results. This finding has been largely ignored (House, Glass, McLean, & Walker, 1978) by policymakers seeking simple answers to complex questions.

Comprehensive School Reform (CSR) began in the 1990s as a whole-school approach to improvement. As a large-scale reform effort sponsored by the federal government, participating schools selected programs from a list of approved programs that provided research-based approaches to improving student achievement. The models varied in their prescriptiveness, approach, and philosophical perspective on teaching and learning. As was true with Project Follow Through, the effectiveness of CSR programs varied greatly because of how the programs were implemented and how local context impacted them. Local context includes the community, district, school, teacher and student characteristics, resources, policies, values, and behaviors. The quality and nature of program implementation (Aladjem & Borman, 2006) and adaptability of programs to the local context (Martinez & Harvey, 2004) influenced CSR results. As Aladjem and Borman (2006) noted, "In addition to the characteristics of the CSR model itself (e.g., more or less prescriptive; more or less reliant upon teachers' and principals' leadership, etc.), context arguably most affects how reform will be implemented and sustained over time" (p. 3). As was true with Project Follow Through, context and implementation influenced results as much as (and arguably more than) the program model.

Why is this? Implementation matters because a program as planned may be very different from a program as enacted. Is the program clearly articulated? How closely does a school adhere to the ideal prescription of a program or an approach? What supports are necessary to carry out the program? To what extent do districts and schools provide those supports? Local context matters because teaching and learning exist within the particular culture of the community, school, and district, each of which employs different people, can provide different resources, and must deal with different issues.

Teaching and learning are composed of many different exchanges: teacher and student, student and student, student and material, teacher and material, teacher and teacher, teacher and school leader, teacher and family, and others. These exchanges are influenced by the experiences and personal beliefs of both the teacher and student, and cannot (despite many attempts to do so) be written down, packaged, and delivered with completely predictable results. The way students interact with a teacher, or their peers, or any of the many influences on their learning, can greatly influence their achievement, and we usually judge these programs by measures of achievement. The myriad exchanges that make up life in schools build up over time to contribute to the classroom, school, and district context, and these differences, in turn, present unique challenges to school improvement.

Undoubtedly, we want to find what works in education. District and school leaders, teachers, and parents want to ensure that students are offered programs that will contribute to their success. We want to have evidence-based practices that demonstrate results. Yet, because context matters, because implementation matters, the question is not just what works. The question is what works, for whom, and under what conditions. That is a much more complex question, but that is because education is a complex endeavor.

Laocoon, a Trojan priest in Virgil's epic poem *Aeneid*, warned the Trojans to "beware of Greeks bearing gifts" when they were presented with the Trojan Horse. Ultimately, the Trojan Horse led to the destruction of the city of Troy and ended the Trojan War. Parents and educators likewise must beware of anyone bringing them the gift of prepackaged programs that promise "teacher-proof" teaching or guaranteed results for all students in all schools.

References

Aladjem, D. K., & Borman, K. M. (2006). *Examining comprehensive school reform*. Washington, DC: Urban Institute Press.

Berliner, D. C. (2002). Comment: Educational research: The hardest science of all. *Educational Researcher, 31*(8), 18–20.

Honig, M. I. (2006). Complexity and policy implementation: Challenges and opportunities for the field. In M. I. Honig (Ed.), *New directions in education policy implementation: Confronting complexity* (pp. 1–23). Albany: State University of New York Press.

House, E. R., Glass, G. V, McLean, L. D., & Walker, D. F. (1978). No simple answer: Critique of the "Follow Through" evaluation. *Harvard Educational Review, 48*(2), 128–160.

Martinez, M., & Harvey, J. (2004). *From whole school to whole system reform*. Washington, DC: National Clearinghouse for Comprehensive School Reform.

McLaughlin, M. W. (1987). Learning from experience: Lessons from policy implementation. *Educational Evaluation and Policy Analysis, 9*(2), 171–178.

Stebbins, L. B., St. Pierre, R. G., Proper, E. C., Anderson, R. B., & Cerva, T. R. (1977). *Education as experimentation: A planned variation model: Vol. IV-A. An evaluation of Follow Through*. Cambridge, MA: Abt Associates.

Weiss, M., Bloom, H., & Brock, T. (2013). *A conceptual framework for studying the sources of variation in program effects* (MDRC Working Papers on Research Methodology). New York, NY: MDRC.

∽ MYTH 28 ∾

Zero-tolerance policies are making schools safer.

Imagine you receive a call at work. Your 5-year-old is being detained and questioned (without you or an attorney present) for threatening to shoot a classmate with a pink gun that shoots bubbles. After she is remanded to your custody, the principal of the school informs you that although the threat had no intent and your kindergartner has no concept of malice, she would be suspended effective immediately pending a hearing that could result in her expulsion. The district's zero-tolerance policy was designed to protect the other children from your child —a potential "terrorist."

On January 10, 2013, less than a month after the tragedy at Sandy Hook Elementary School in Newtown, Connecticut, Kelly Guarna received this very call. Her 5-year-old daughter, Madison, was suspended from school for making a "terroristic threat" against a classmate. A teacher learned, after a search of the little girl's backpack, that she did not have the bubble gun at the center of the scandal. Nonetheless, the zero-tolerance policy against threats in Pennsylvania education agencies mandated that the Mount Carmel elementary school suspend her pending a permanent ruling on her case (Bohman, 2013).

In Texas, in September 2010, a boy was suspended on suspicion of marijuana use because administrators noticed he had "red, watery eyes." The student defended himself by reminding staff that his father was murdered over the weekend and he had been crying earlier that morning. The school still required that his mother have him tested for drugs (Gordon, 2010).

In October 2009, school officials ordered a 6-year-old to attend a reform school for 45 days because he brought his new Cub Scout eating utensil with his school lunch—the utensil included a fork, knife, and spoon. After an uproar from the family, community, and the media, the school overturned its decision and revised the code of conduct, limiting kindergarten suspensions for weapons to 3–5 days (Urbina, 2009).

Thirteen-year-old Robert Gomez was suspended for tossing a rubber band on his teacher's desk. Rubber bands previously had been deemed weapons under the school's policy. When he tossed the band on her desk, that constituted assault with a weapon ("Florida Boy Accused," 2005).

In February 2012, a middle school girl borrowed a friend's inhaler during an asthma attack. Both girls were suspended, and the girl who used her friend's inhaler was later expelled (Auge, 2012).

Many proponents of zero-tolerance policies stand firm in light of these incidents. Ken Trump, a national advocate of zero-tolerance and a school security consultant, argues that these anecdotes take attention away from existing safety issues in schools, particularly because he believes there has been a deterioration in teenage behavior. But that belief is not easily verified. Some analysts suggest teens today have about the same values and behave quite similarly to how their parents thought and behaved at the same age (Nichols & Good, 2004).

It is no coincidence that zero-tolerance became a national priority in the mid-1990s. During the early part of the decade, the country had become obsessed with reducing urban violence. The idea that urban teens—Black boys in particular—were inherently dangerous was not new, and the more recent Treyvon Martin murder has brought that issue to the surface once a again. The media and literature have long promulgated racist stereotypes (Uncle Tom, tragic mulatto, Sambo, etc.). The 1980s, however, gave way to new tropes, based on Reagan-era indictments of poor, urban Blacks. Welfare queens, crack mothers, and nihilistic thugs furnished personas to embody the idea that Black people living in urban slums did not value work, took free education for granted, and had found a permanent meal ticket in the social welfare system. These controlling images incited legislators and law enforcement against Black people in some of the country's most ghettoized communities and resulted in the passage of three landmark initiatives: the Anti-Drug Abuse Act of 1986—which mandated sentencing disparities that unfairly targeted African Americans; the Gun-Free Schools Act of 1994—which mandated year-long expulsions for possessing any kind of weapon on school grounds; and the Welfare Reform Act of 1996 —which rolled back welfare benefits and distinguished between "deserving poor" and "undeserving poor."

Some of these laws had their roots in the 1991 brutal beating of Rodney King by four Los Angeles Police Department officers. Once the officers were acquitted and Los Angeles erupted in riots, the national discussion that had been taking place about police profiling and brutality quickly devolved to sweeping indictments of "those people." Every night networks broadcast images of Black residents of Los Angeles rioting in the streets, fighting, burning down local businesses, and looting stores. The scenes from the riots provided a backdrop for the actions of legislators and politicians, who too often relied on fictionalized controlling images to promote laws that marginalized the urban poor. Two years later Congress passed the Gun-Free Schools Act of 1994. The federal government mandated states to enact a "law requiring local educational agencies [schools] to expel from school for a period of not less than one year a student who is determined to have brought a weapon to school." Although this was not the first zero-tolerance policy adopted by U.S. schools, it was the first of its kind to be mandated nationwide, and it sparked a national obsession with making schools safer. With the support of the federal government, districts chose not to rely on the law's provision that "State's law also must allow the chief administering officer of the local educational agency (LEA) to modify the expulsion requirement on a case-by-case basis." Instead, most school systems enthusiastically extended and intensified their zero-tolerance of certain behaviors. The rationale behind zero-tolerance policies is that good children will see the rules as deterrents and refrain from bad behavior. And when bad kids break the rules, the school will be able to kick them out and keep them out!

Proponents of zero-tolerance often argue that no measure is too great to protect children from violence. They are correct. Scholar and anti–zero-tolerance advocate Russell Skiba argued in 2008 that "schools and school boards have the right, indeed the responsibility, to take strong action to preserve the safety of students, staff, and parents on school grounds." But Skiba and others have railed against zero-tolerance because even in the early years of the policy, educators, scholars, and parents found several indications that these kinds of school policies are wrongheaded, ineffective and, over time, detrimental to children.

The Gun-Free Schools Act was a bipartisan effort and willingly accepted by almost every school district in the country. Lawmakers believed that schools were rife with the violence so often depicted on TV and in movies. Nonetheless, the Centers for Disease Control (CDC) have found that schools were not at all like the gang-ruled war zones that Hollywood and hip-hop would suggest. Since 1994, an average of 26.2 children died in school-related violence each year. And homicide accounts for only a portion of those deaths. Suicide was the second leading cause of school-related death in the 1990s. Of course, any death of a child at school is a tragedy, but there is very little evidence to suggest overwhelming rates of school violence and no conclusive evidence to suggest that schools are safer when zero-tolerance policies are in place.

In their analysis, the CDC uncovered a disturbing trend in school violence that also points to the ineffectiveness of zero-tolerance. Incidents of violence where a single student was killed on or near campus have declined in the past 20 years. But incidents where two or more students were attacked have increased sharply. Scenes like those from Columbine, Newtown, and Virginia Tech fuel the zero-tolerance advocates' zeal, who point to these tragedies as justification for the policies. Guns were already banned at Columbine high school when two killers decided to open fire on their classmates and teachers. The same can be said for Sandy Hook Elementary School in Newtown. In fact, guns had been banned at every campus where mass shootings took place since 1994. There is little that teachers and administrators can do to protect the school from the calculated intentions of a psychologically ill individual when such people have easy access to weapons throughout the country.

Between birth and 18 years, children spend a mere 10% of their time in school. And while children are entitled to food, education, medical attention, and protection at school, millions of these children return from school to poverty, homelessness, neglect, and abuse. The CDC found that, on average 1,740 children die each year from parental abuse and neglect. This figure represents only cases where the cause of death of a child was established. Because so many instances of neglect and abuse go unreported, or may take months to prove, it stands to reason that the dangers children face at home far outweigh the dangers faced at school. In 2005, more than 53,500 American children died from all causes. Fewer than 27 of those deaths were school-associated, amounting to slightly less than .0005% of that total. If we really want to do something about child safety, we should worry less about telling school officials how to conduct themselves, and ask the greater society in which we live to take more responsibility for the safety of our children.

Suspensions and expulsions have far-reaching implications for a student's academics and can set them up for failure in their personal lives. Some schools opt for in-school suspension—time spent on campus but away from class. Usually students are required to complete self-paced assignments for 2–3 days while under supervision of a school official. Out-of-school suspension, however, is more common. In some cases, students are not allowed to make up work and subsequently fail for the term in which their infraction occurred. In addition, some suspensions are so long that a student is, in effect, forcibly withdrawn from the school and forced to repeat that grade or make up the credits during the summer. In the most severe cases, school boards opt to expel students; this often means the students must attend an alternative school or simply remain out of school until the next year begins. In cases of suspensions and expulsions, the processes often have negative effects on student persistence, and, even when their disciplinary troubles are over, many students become discouraged and choose to drop out rather than make up for so much lost class time. Falling behind is a strong predictor of dropping out (see Myth 18).

Ordinarily, students accused of assault, fighting, or possessing a weapon are processed through the juvenile justice system, and those officials determine whether the student goes to a treatment center or an alternative school. Studies have shown that the prevalence of zero-tolerance has resulted in school officials routing record numbers of students through the juvenile justice system (Teske, 2011). Research also shows that children who spend time in juvenile detention facilities are far more likely to wind up in adult prison (Kim, Losen, & Hewitt, 2010). To make matters worse, the increase in profit-making prisons has provided a well-financed lobbying group to ensure that minor offenders receive sentencing that includes time in jail. This corrupting influence showed up when a judge in Pennsylvania was discovered to be taking kickbacks from a privately operated detention center after he sentenced a 15-year-old for making derogatory comments about her principal on Facebook (Ecenbarger, 2012).

All of the unintended effects associated with the prevalence of zero-tolerance policies in schools are multiplied for non-Whites. The Civil Rights Project recently released a study that concluded that zero-tolerance policies disproportionately target Black students. The study of suspensions and expulsions revealed that Black students are more likely to be questioned, found guilty of an infraction, suspended, and expelled than their White counterparts (Losen, 2011). This also means that Black children are less likely to graduate, more likely to enter juvenile justice programs, and more likely to spend time in adult prison.

Today most school systems recognize that zero-tolerance policies have not lived up to the promise to make schools safer. Even in the wake of the tragic events at Sandy Hook Elementary School, teachers, parents, and administrators are focused on crisis preparedness and the more political gun debate rather than on stricter policing of school children. Districts all over the country are considering proposals for alternatives to mandatory, severe, and inflexible zero-tolerance policies. In 2000, in Rachel Carson Elementary School in Chicago, the principal reformed the academic environment as well as her outreach to parents. That year the suspension rate fell to less than 1% (The Civil Rights Project, 2000). The students have coordinators and teachers who stay with them for 4 years. If students have an infraction, they first speak with the coordinators, whom they trust and with whom they have a history. One program, Safety First, engages parents as the student's first educator about drugs, weapons, and violence. The National Education Association also has published a list of alternative disciplinary models—none of which promote suspensions and expulsions for status offenses or as a first course of action.

The final word in this brief treatment of zero-tolerance goes to syndicated columnist Robert C. Koehler, who, writing in the *Chicago Tribune* on April 5, 2013, opined, "High-stakes testing, in tandem with 'zero tolerance,' militarized security and sadistic underfunding, has succeeded in warping public education beyond recognition, especially in low-income, zero-political-clout neighborhoods. And the result is kids in prison, kids on the streets, kids with no future."

References

Auge, K. (2012, February 19). Zero-tolerance rules forced Colorado school's harsh stand on shared inhaler. *The Denver Post.* Retrieved from tinyurl.com/ozwyrrn

Bohman, D. (2013, January 30). School board erases suspension of 5 year-old with Hello Kitty gun. Retrieved from http://tinyurl.com/pzbp4gl

The Civil Rights Project. (2000) *Opportunities suspended: The devastating consequences of zero tolerance and school discipline policies.* Los Angeles, CA: UCLA. Retrieved from tinyurl.com/mpevc9j

Ecenbarger, W. (2012). *Kids for cash: Two judges, thousands of children, and a $2.6 million kickback scheme.* New York, NY: New Press.

Florida boy accused of assault with rubber band. (2005, February 23). FloridaToday.com. Retrieved from tinyurl.com/pnkv7qk

Gordon, S. (2010, September 10). Local school tells mom bloodshot eyes equals drug use. NBC Dallas–Fort Worth. Retrieved from tinyurl.com/op3n3rf

Kim, Y. K., Losen, D. J., & Hewitt, D. T. (2010). *The school-to-prison pipeline: Structuring legal reform* (1st ed.). New York, NY: New York University Press.

Koehler, R. C. (2013, April 5). The warping of public education. *Chicago Tribune.* Retrieved from tinyurl.com/bmfxfny

Losen, D. J. (2011). *Discipline policies, successful schools, and racial justice.* Boulder, CO: National Education Policy Center. Retrieved from tinyurl.com/6jhmwz5

Nichols, S. L., & Good, T. L. (2004). *America's teenagers—myths and realities: Media images, schooling, and the social costs of careless indifference.* Mahwah, NJ: Erlbaum.

Skiba, R. (2008). Testimony before the Subcommittee on Education Reform Committee on Education and the Workforce United States House of Representatives. Retrieved from tinyurl.com/m4vbmmk

Teske, S. (2011). A study of zero tolerance policies in schools: A multi-integrated systems approach to improve outcomes for adolescents. *Journal of Child and Adolescent Psychiatric Nursing.* Hoboken, NJ: Wiley Periodicals.

Urbina, I. (2009, October 11). It's a fork, it's a spoon . . . it's a weapon? *The New York Times.* Retrieved from tinyurl.com/olrk2qx

✎ MYTH 29 ☜

The benefits of preschool and kindergarten programs are not convincing and thus not worth the investment.

Are the arguments against supporting preschool and kindergarten credible? Darcy Ann Olsen (2006), formerly of the Cato Institute and now president of the Goldwater Institute in Arizona, writes, "For nearly 40 years, local, state, and federal governments and diverse private sources have funded early intervention programs for low-income children, and benefits to the children have been few and fleeting. There is also evidence that middle-class children gain little, if anything, from preschool. . . . Public preschool for younger children is irresponsible, given the failure of the public school system to educate the children currently enrolled" (p. 1). Elsewhere she concludes that kindergarten as well as early education have little to recommend them (Olsen & Snell, 2006). Olsen is not alone. Elizabeth Cascio (2010) wrote, "Kindergarten had no discernible impact on many of the long-term outcomes desired by policymakers, including grade retention, public assistance receipt, employment, and earnings. . . . These findings suggest that even large investments in universal early-childhood education programs do not necessarily yield clear benefits, especially for more disadvantaged students" (p. 68).

A common but misleading argument used by those against kindergarten and preschool education is that the benefits of these programs do not last. The argument drags a red herring across our path! The residue in later performance of students who have taken geometry and algebra, or studied Chaucer and chemistry, is also hard to demonstrate, even when the immediate benefits were easily demonstrable. For low-income students, gains from preschool may fade for another reason, such as attendance at regular public schools with high concentrations of other low-income children, affecting their school academic climate and safety. The schools these children attend also are likely to be staffed with younger and less well-trained teachers, and society spends less money per student on their education. It may not be preschool or kindergarten that has no benefits; rather it may be that preserving these benefits when children attend inadequate schools is hard to do.

Some anti-preschool and anti-kindergarten critics are producing junk science. The report by Olsen and Snell was determined by the National Education Policy Center to be an unreliable source of information, providing an inaccurate view of research on early childhood education (Barnett, 2006). And the blatant bias of some critics against the poor and minorities is as common as it is nasty. For example, Robert Weissberg (2013) wrote, "We cannot assume that low-income parents actually want their children's vocabulary upgraded or exposed to the art and music favored by the upper middle class. For these low-income parents, a physically safe, clean and nurturing environment with flexible hours is probably paramount. Narrowing academic gaps is undoubtedly far down their list for 'quality daycare.'"

Mr. Weissberg must be made to answer to John Dewey (1907): "What the best and wisest parent wants for his own child, that must the community want for all of its children. Any other ideal for our schools is narrow and unlovely; acted upon, it destroys our democracy" (p. 19). Although we are not sure they are the best and wisest parents, it is clear that the wealthiest parents in the United States pay handsomely for preschool and kindergarten. Tuition at the Horace Mann School in New York City (ironically, named for America's greatest proponent of free public education) currently costs $39,100 annually. Would Olsen, Snell, and Weisberg call these parents stupid?

President Obama recently asked Congress to fund early childhood education for all children. The president draws on a large, convincing (although not always a consistent) body of research to support his recommendation. His proposal for a 10-year, $75 billion appropriation for early childhood programs is supported by a group of presumably wise people—350 retired generals and admirals. What convinced these hard-headed decisionmakers, to whom we entrust the safety of our nation, to support these allegedly ineffectual programs?

One recent study by economists in the United Kingdom examined data from the international test called PISA, the Program for International Student Assessment (Mostafa & Green, 2012). They used data from the United Kingdom and Sweden, both of which had extensive programs of early childhood education, but the programs were not universal. That is, among the 15-year-olds tested in 2009, about 30% had not attended preschool. Not surprising, when they were younger, participation in early childhood programs was correlated with social class. The children of wealthier families, throughout the Western world, participate in preschool education at high rates. The researchers asked what the effects would have been on PISA literacy scores if *all* the children had gone to preschool, not predominantly those from the higher social classes. Their conclusion? In the United Kingdom, students in the lowest social class grouping benefited from preschool on average by an increase of 9.2 points on the PISA test, while those in the top social class grouping benefited by 5.5 points. Similarly, in Sweden, individuals in the lowest social class grouping benefited from preschool by an increase of 7.8 points on PISA, while those in the top social class grouping benefited on average by 4.1 points. Universalizing preschool apparently helps all children, but it helps the poorest children the most. These researchers estimate that the United Kingdom would have improved 12 ranks and Sweden would have improved 7 ranks, had their nations had universal preschool.

Green and Mostafa (2011) found that in all of the 34 countries in the European Economic Community, students at 15 years of age who had attended pre-primary education for more than 1 year outperformed those who did not, by an average of 54 points! Even after controlling for social background, attending preschool for more than 1 year increased performance on average by 33 points. These researchers found no strong evidence that early childhood education reduced inequalities in performance between those who were high and those who were low in social class standing. As a function of attending high-quality preschool programs, all students score higher on academic measures over a decade later. These researchers also discovered that in most countries high-quality preschool allowed more people, particularly women, to be employed. From their research they estimate that a 10% increase in availability of high-quality day care leads to a 6.1% increase in female employment, providing both a boost for the economy and a reduction in payments for unemployment.

A U.S. study of the universalization of preschool in Oklahoma supports these international findings (Gormley, Gayer, Phillips, & Dawson, 2004). The Oklahoma preschool programs are housed in public schools; all lead teachers are college educated and certified in early childhood education; and the teachers are paid at the same rate as other public school teachers. The independent evaluation of the program assessed children at entry to kindergarten with three standard readiness tests. It was found that all children benefited substantially from the preschool program, but the poorest children and Hispanic children benefited the most. One analysis used equivalent kinds of children: those whose birthday was just before the cutoff date to enter preschool, and compared them with those whose birthday was just after the cutoff date to enter preschool. For these two groups of children, almost exactly the same age, those who were allowed to attend the preschool program showed advantages amounting to approximately 7 months on a test of letter–word identification, showed 6 months greater gain on a test of spelling, and also showed 4 months greater gain on a test of applied problem solving.

Other high-quality studies examined other high-quality preschool programs (see Barnett, 2008; Pianta, Barnett, Burchinal, & Thornberg, 2009). They all tell the same story, suggesting that preschool critics misrepresent the data. For example, in the Abecedarian study, full-day child care was started at an early age, and more than 100 children were followed through to age 21. Initial gains in IQ at age 4 for those that were in the Abecedarian project were large, and although more modest, the advantages in IQ were still present at age 21. Significant and relatively large gains in mathematics and reading were noted for the attenders as they entered regular public school. These academic advantages were slightly smaller but still present at age 21. Further, the rate of high school graduation, excluding GEDs, was 16% higher for the Abecedarian attenders. Fourteen percent of the control group, the nonattenders, went on to a 4-year college. But 36% of the children who had been enrolled in the Abecedarian preschool went on to a 4-year college.

Another high-quality study of a high-quality program is the Perry Preschool Study. Compared with its control group, those who attended the Perry preschool had many fewer special education needs in public school, had many fewer arrests by age 19, were much more likely to graduate high school, were more likely to attend college, were much more likely to be employed, and at age 27 were earning over 50% more in income.

A third well-controlled study, the Chicago Child-Parent Centers study, found that the attenders of this preschool program, compared with comparable children who had not attended the program, had about half the special education referrals, about a third fewer were retained in grade, and about a third fewer were arrested by age 19. The attenders also completed more courses in high school, graduated at higher rates, and were about one-third more likely to attend college than the children who did not have preschool experience.

The Abbot preschool evaluation in New Jersey tells the same story. This program decreased rates of special education and grade retention, reducing the costs of education quite substantially. Compared with students who had not had the program, the students who were in the preschool program showed large effects on tests of language arts and reading, mathematics, and science. In fact, the magnitude of the test score gains from 1 year in an Abbot program is equivalent to roughly 10–20% of the achievement gap between minority and White students, while the gains from 2 years in the Abbot program are equivalent to 20–40% of that achievement gap.

The studies cited above all have faults, and any one of them alone would not make a powerful case for the positive effects of preschool. But the studies are remarkably consistent and conform to a common-sense idea that when young children get attention, instruction, and affection from a caring adult, benefits will be found.

Three of the programs cited were analyzed to see whether they were cost-effective. In 2002 dollars, what was returned to society was substantial (Temple & Reynolds, 2007). For every dollar invested in enrollment of a child in the Abecedarian preschool program, society gains $2.69 in benefits (higher employment rates, thus more taxes paid by the attenders; lower crime rates, thus lower incarceration rates by the attenders, and so forth). For every dollar invested in the Child–Parent program, society gets back $6.87. And for every dollar spent on tuition at the Perry preschool, society earns $7.16. There are no other programs for disadvantaged youth that have such convincing impact per dollar spent. Nobel Prize–winning economist James Heckman has his own estimates of these effects (see Heckman & Masterov, 2007). He finds that the effects on American society of investments in education at all levels, but especially an investment in preschool education, make such investments one of the wisest policies to implement.

His estimates are that for every dollar invested in the Perry Preschool program and the Child–Parent program, the return to society is $9.19 and $7.77, respectively. In the present fiscal environment, what other investments pay dividends of around 8 or 9%?

Kindergarten data, like the preschool data, also are mixed. The generally negative findings of Cascio, cited earlier, were not entirely negative. For White students, she found a small decrease in dropping out of school as a function of kindergarten, and a large decrease in the rates of incarceration of White students later in life. Some of Cascio's negative findings were confirmed by another economist (Dhuey, 2011), but more positive results also were found: The experience of kindergarten decreased retention in later grades by almost 8%. This effect was most noticeable for students who were male, Hispanic, and poor, the kinds of students we might expect an introductory year of schooling to influence the most. A third economist (DeCicca, 2007) actually found strong positive effects for all students at the end of kindergarten, but then discovered that those results fade quite a bit by the end of 1st grade, a common occurrence when assessing young children, using different tests months apart. Despite conflicting data and fading effects in some studies, as with the preschool data, there still exists a large and convincing body of work about the positive effects of kindergarten. This existing research base garnered support for kindergarten from such diverse nonpartisan groups as the government of British Columbia and other Canadian provinces; TD Bank, second largest in Canada; the Education Commission of the States; the Department of Defense; and even the Department of Education in our own state of Arizona, which is both conservative and among the lowest spending states in the union. At a minimum, kindergarten gives the gift of time in a school environment, a gift especially important for poor and minority children, and those who speak another language. Arguments about the kindergarten experience exist over the appropriateness of half-day and full-day kindergarten, the amount of academic work versus the socialization experiences to be included in the curriculum, and whether children derive any benefit from being red-shirted (starting kindergarten a year late). But evidence of belief in kindergarten's positive educational experience is everywhere: Kindergarten is almost universal in the United States and Canada, and paid for publicly; it is common in other Western nations; and it is extensively subscribed to by wealthy families, willing to pay exorbitant amounts for private providers.

Of course, there are cautions to think about when we work with young children, particularly because not all programs suit all children, and determining what constitutes high-quality programs is not easy. We have learned that preschool and kindergarten probably do not have as many benefits for middle-class children as they do for lower class children. It is also likely that some middle-class preschoolers might be better off socially and emotionally had they not been in preschool for more than 6 hours a day (Loeb, Bridges, Bassoka, Fuller, & Rumberger, 2007). We also should be concerned that an overly academic focus in preschool and kindergarten may harm children's motivation to learn; that the pressure felt by program providers to test young children may too often yield unreliable and invalid results, as well as unnecessary anxiety by parents and their children; and that an increased failure rate for kindergartners, under the pressures for schools to score higher on tests, is unconscionable and may hurt a failed child's life chances (see Myth 18).

Cautions and disagreements about interpreting preschool and kindergarten benefits exist because we are working with young and vulnerable children, and definitive answers to important questions are not easy to come by. But those who simply are against investments in preschool and kindergarten are either not reading the research, deliberately misconstruing the facts, or blowing the cautions and negative effects way out of proportion. The conservative ABC network newsman John Stossel is one of those. He argues that universal public preschool, of the type that president Obama is promoting, is a scam (Stossel, Brosseau, & Kirell, 2009). His major source of information is a private for-profit preschool provider, apparently afraid that if the government provided preschool funding, she would lose her paying customers. Stossel also cites another "authority" who condemns preschools for being ineffectual, but then notes that private preschools can do the job right! Why would some of the private providers of preschool, the parents who support them, and John Stossel not want what they think best for some children to be available to all children? Alfie Kohn (1998) argues that knowledge of this kind is not widely shared because too many parents believe in providing advantages for their own children, and do not think often enough about, or do not want to share those advantages with, other people's children.

References

Barnett, W. (2006). [Review of *Assessing proposals for preschool and kindergarten: Essential information for parents, taxpayers, and policymakers*]. Boulder, CO, & Tempe, AZ: Education and the Public Interest Center & Education Policy Research Unit. Retrieved from tinyurl.com/okpl9xl

Barnett, W. S. (2008). *Preschool education and its lasting effects: Research and policy implications*. Boulder, CO, & Tempe, AZ: Education and the Public Interest Center & Education Policy Research Unit. Retrieved from epicpolicy.org/publication/preschooleducation

Cascio, E. U. (2010, Spring). What happened when kindergarten went universal? *Education Next, 10*(2), 62–69.

DeCicca, P. (2007). Does full-day kindergarten matter? Evidence from the first two years of schooling. *Economics of Education Review, 26*, 67–82.

Dewey, J. (1907). *The school and society.* Chicago, IL: University of Chicago Press.

Dhuey, E. (2011). Who benefits from kindergarten? Evidence from the introduction of state subsidization. *Educational Evaluation and Policy Analysis, 33*(1), 3–22.

Gormley, W., Gayer, T., Phillips, D., & Dawson, B. (2004, November). *The effects of Oklahoma's universal pre-kindergarten program on school readiness.* Washington, DC: Georgetown University, Center for Research on Children in the U.S.

Green, A., & Mostafa, T. (2011). *Pre-school education and care—a "win-win" policy?* London, United Kingdom: Centre for Learning and Life Chances in Knowledge Economies and Societies.

Heckman, J. J., & Masterov, D. V. (2007). *The productivity argument for investing in young children.* National Bureau of Economic Research working paper number 13016. Retrieved from jenni.uchicago.edu/human-inequality/papers/Heckman_final_all_wp_2007-03-22c_jsb.pdf

Kohn, A. (1998, April). Only for my kid. How privileged parents undermine school reform. *Phi Delta Kappan, 80*, 569–577.

Loeb, S., Bridges, M., Bassoka, D., Fuller, B., & Rumberger, R. W. (2007). How much is too much? The influence of preschool centers on children's social and cognitive development. *Economics of Education Review, 26*, 52–66.

Mostafa, T., & Green, A. (2012). *Measuring the impact of universal pre-school education and care on literacy performance scores.* London, United Kingdom: Centre for Learning and Life Chances in Knowledge Economies and Societies.

Olsen, D. A. (2006). *Universal preschool is no golden ticket: Why government should not enter the preschool business.* Washington, DC: Cato Institute.

Olsen, D., & Snell, L. (2006). *Assessing proposals for preschool and kindergarten: Essential information for parents, taxpayers and policymakers.* Los Angeles, CA: Reason Foundation.

Pianta, R. C., Barnett, W. S., Burchinal, M., & Thornberg, K. R. (2009). The effects of preschool education: What we know, how public policy is or is not aligned with the evidence base, and what we need to know. *Psychological Science in the Public Interest, 10*(2), 49–88.

Stossel, J., Brosseau, C., & Kirell, A. (2009, March 13). Universal pre-K: "This whole thing is a scam." *ABC 20/20.* Retrieved from tinyurl.com/pe6zjpd

Temple, J. A., & Reynolds, A. J. (2007). Benefits and costs of investments in preschool education: Evidence for the Child-Parent centers and related programs. *Economics of Education Review, 26*, 126–144.

Weissberg, R. (2013, February 18). The risk of Obama's universal daycare. *American Thinker.* Retrieved from www.americanthinker.com/2013/02/the_risk_of_obamas_universal_daycare.html

❧ MYTH 30 ❧

Character education will save America's youth and strengthen the nation's moral fiber.

It is possible that for as long as our ancestors have been recognizably human, those of the older generation have looked on the behavior of the young and found it rife with signs of moral decay and cultural decline. Plato, quoting Socrates about 2,500 years ago, wrote, "The children now love luxury; they have bad manners, contempt for authority; they show disrespect for elders and love chatter in place of exercise. Children are now tyrants, not the servants of their households. They no longer rise when elders enter the room. They contradict their parents, chatter before company, gobble up dainties at the table, cross their legs, and tyrannize their teachers."

We've all heard it so frequently: The young don't know as much as they did, don't work as hard as they should, and, worst of all, do not properly respect their elders. Today, the remarkable rate of social change, carried along by the development of new technologies and forms of communication, give greater credence to the argument that young Americans are very different from those of the past, and not different in good ways. Differences take on an ominous tinge as violence in schools is featured on the nightly news and becomes a flashpoint for major policy debates, often leading to more frequent and harsher disciplinary measures in schools across the nation (e.g., zero-tolerance; see Myth 28).

In the media, in conversations at water coolers, in the barbershop, and at the school board meeting, perhaps you've heard the common complaints about the declining character of our youth, and of the national decline this is assumed to portend. Of course, in a democracy, concern for the character of youth is important. Since democracy trusts in the people to govern, we all have a legitimate concern for the competence and character of our neighbors and the next generations' values and behavior. Public schooling in the United States is built on the notion that education is a public, not just a private, good, precisely because education helps to make good citizens and a good society (Feinberg, 2012). In this light, character education seems to have received *too little* attention in recent discussions of school reform.

That's not to say official policy discussions haven't broached the question of character development in our schools. On the contrary, many parents, educators, and policymakers have taken action on the idea that our children need more, or perhaps better, character education. The common wisdom is that students need direct instruction in behaving well and reinforcement of positive social skills. Indeed, this push seems to be supported by some important social scientific findings. Developments in cognitive psychology have underlined just how important social and emotional development is to academic achievement and overall life chances. The popularity of what is known among education researchers as social and character development (SACD) programs has grown tremendously over the past decade, and new programs have been implemented in many of the nation's public schools. Character development has become a big selling point in the school choice movement. "Come to this charter school; we require uniforms and have a zero-tolerance discipline rule."

So are these interventions actually helping kids in and out of school? In 2003, the Institute of Education Sciences (IES) entered into collaboration with the Division of Violence Prevention of the Centers for Disease Control and Prevention to begin the SACD Research Program. The goal was to evaluate several school-based SACD programs "in a consistent manner." The researchers studied the seven most popular programs in the nation, as they were implemented in schools in New York, Idaho, North Carolina, Massachusetts, and Washington. As time passed, these programs developed a track record, so that we can now answer with some confidence the question: Do the SACD programs out there work?

Perhaps surprisingly, according to the IES consortium study, the answer is a resounding "No." These programs don't seem to show benefits either on student behavior or academic performance. Across states, districts, and schools, the major SACD programs simply do not seem to work. On 20 measures of social and emotional competence, academics, behavior, and perceptions of school climate, students in schools that implemented these programs did not show outcomes different from students in schools that had no such programs (Social and Character Development Research Consortium, 2010). This was the result each year, as well as after 3 years of the study. Students subjected to PATHS (Promoting Alternative Thinking Strategies), the 4Rs (reading, writing, respect, and resolution), and other typical character education programs failed to show any significant differences from the control group of students on the major measures used to assess the programs.

What are we to make of this? The creator of one of the most popular SACD programs, after the publication of the IES study, returned to graduate school to learn more about how character development instruction might work. One hopes that while there she will discover what researchers have known for a long time, namely, that the behaviors we associate with character do not arise in response to direct instruction. It turns out that character is something that is learned, but not easily taught. Character, it turns out, is very difficult to teach explicitly (Davis, 2003). *Telling* a child to be compassionate or to take responsibility for her- or himself doesn't provide that child much help in actually *becoming* more compassionate or more responsible. Character education boosters—many of them private entrepreneurs who stand to make a profit when a district or school adopts their program—argue that this is because we haven't allowed enough time to see the benefits. Others suggest the negative findings are because we haven't yet found the right approach or discovered the correct instructional formula.

There is reason to think, however, that the results of such programs will always be limited. This is because the causes of behavior are part of the broader context of children's lives, and so the intervention doesn't match the problem. Children spend only a fraction of their time in classrooms; the majority is spent in their homes, their neighborhoods, on the street, or sometimes in undesirable places. The Coleman Report (Coleman et al., 1966) famously determined that about 60% of variation in student performance was attributable to out-of-school influences. That estimate is still considered reasonable by researchers almost 50 years later. Most important, disparities in test scores were found to have more to do with inequalities in income and wealth than the quality of teaching or leadership in a school. This could be the explanation for the IES study finding that the Nashville-based "Love in a Big World" program improved student altruism in the 1st year but, by the 3rd year, was a wash. While an enthusiastic and novel program might have an impact in the short term, the more persistent out-of-school environment usually remains unchanged. If the behavior problems to which character education programs are directed, are the result of inadequate access to health care (vision and hearing screening, dental care, and the like), nutrition, or safety and security, then character education programs seem doomed to fail. The students whose social and academic behavior is thought to need the most improvement are those most strongly influenced by the effects of unequal conditions for living and learning, in and outside of school.

One major policy intervention, in fact, has been found to significantly impact the development of desirable character traits and social skills necessary for good citizenship, along with improving test scores for those who most need it. Desegregation of schools starting in the 1960s led to an increase in achievement for Black students, without harming that of White students (Burton & Jones, 1982; Johnson, 2011). In terms of character development, students *of all races* who attended integrated schools over the decades from 1970 to 1990 are more comfortable in diverse settings and are "more responsive to the rights, needs, and concerns of diverse citizens rather than catering to the interests or perspectives of one or a very few sections of society" (Anderson, 2010, p. 128). While variations in contextual factors make direct instruction less effective for cultivating character, positive and consistent contextual factors can do a great deal to help students learn appropriate behaviors. Unfortunately, serious efforts at creating integrated learning environments have largely been abandoned, and top-down, accountability-driven reforms prevail across the land. The kinds of school environment that promote good character formation are increasingly hard to find.

The IES study was released in October 2010, in the midst of a major economic recession. Since then, because of suspicions about the effects of these programs, and their costs, funding for character education has been substantially curtailed. As better economic times return, we would do better to invest in addressing the issues of social equity and building integrated and adequate schools. SACD programs *misdiagnose* the nature of the problems our children and our schools face. As a result, they offer a pseudo-solution while the real causes of pressing problems go unchecked. But SACD programs are not only ineffectual, they are also dangerous. They distract from the real issues and channel scarce resources into dead-end interventions. Perhaps our children's problems aren't something for which they ought to be personally blamed. Perhaps we ought to instead take greater responsibility for creating a better, more equitable world in which they can learn and grow and develop the strength of character that all wish for.

References

Anderson, E. (2010). *The imperative of integration.* Princeton, NJ: Princeton University Press.

Burton, N. W., & Jones, L. V. (1982). Recent trends in achievement levels of black and white youth. *Educational Researcher, 11*(4), 10–14.

Coleman, J. S., Campbell, E. Q., Hobson, C. J., McPartland, F., Mood, A. M., Weinfeld, F. D., & York, R. L. (1966). *Equality of educational opportunity.* Washington, DC: U.S. Government Printing Office.

Davis, M. (2003). What's wrong with character education? *American Journal of Education, 110,* 32.

Feinberg, W. (2012). The idea of public education. *Review of Research in Education, 36,* 1–22.

Johnson, R. C. (2011). *Long-run impacts of school desegregation and school quality on adult attainments* (NBER Working Paper Series). Cambridge, MA: National Bureau of Economic Research. Retrieved from www.nber.org/papers/w16664/

Social and Character Development Research Consortium. (2010). *Efficacy of schoolwide programs to promote social and character development and reduce problem behavior in elementary school children* (NCER 2011-2001). Washington, DC: National Center for Education Research, Institute of Education Sciences, U.S. Department of Education. Retrieved from ies.ed.gov/ncer/pubs/20112001/pdf/20112001.pdf

ᴥ MYTH 31 ᴥ

Bullying is inevitable; it's just kids. It's a rite of passage. The national effort to eliminate bullying is effectively addressing the problem in our schools.

A student hangs himself after enduring daily anti-gay bullying at school, despite his mother's weekly pleas to the school to address the problem (GLSEN, 2009). Another student jumps off a bridge after his roommate broadcasts the student's intimate encounter with another man via webcam (Foderaro, 2010). Still another hurls herself onto the tracks of an oncoming train after being subjected to relentless bullying for having piercings and living in foster care (Yee, 2012).

Bullying is widespread. It consists of physical, verbal, and social damage to another. Some regard bullying as a rite of childhood passage, a natural part of growing up. But it is not. It is aggressive behavior that is intentional, hurtful, threatening, persistent, and always wrong. More important, it is detrimental to the academic, physical, social, and emotional development of all parties involved—bullies, targets, and the bystanders who witness it (Olweus, 2001; Salmivalli, Lagerspetz, Björkqvist, Osterman, & Kaukiainen, 1996). But this is not the old "boys will be boys" neighborhood bullying we grew up with; it is now much more pervasive because it is also online. The advent of technology, allowing for impulsive, anonymous, and rapid communication, has challenged school officials to respond to this behavior when it occurs, both in and out of the classroom, as well as in cyberspace. Some would say that there is nothing the schools can do to prevent bullying; that teen suicide is a result of serious mental health problems in individuals, and nothing the schools can do will change this. But research begs to differ.

School climate studies have indicated consistently that the perception of a safer school climate is directly related to the availability of school-based resources and support, including student organizations, inclusive curricula, supportive school staff, and comprehensive anti-bullying policies (Kosciw, Greytak, Bartkiewicz, Boesen, & Palmer,

2012). These structures can positively affect students' school experiences. As a matter of fact, schools and districts that are taking these kinds of systemic actions are beginning to make a real difference in improving the lives of students and providing better educational opportunity for all. For example, compared with students at schools with a generic policy that does not include protections based on sexual orientation and gender identity/expression, students attending schools with a comprehensive anti-bullying policy hear fewer homophobic remarks, experience lower levels of victimization related to their sexual orientation, are more likely to report incidents of harassment and assault, and are more likely to report that staff intervened when hearing homophobic remarks (Kosciw et al., 2012).

Despite the positive benefits from these kinds of school interventions, however, few schools have taken an active stand against bullying by adopting comprehensive anti-bullying policies. Far fewer are those that actually provide training for school staff to improve rates of intervention and increase the number of supportive teachers and staff available to students. Because bullying thrives where adults are not present or not observant (Kowalski, Limber, & Agatston, 2008), school administrators, teachers and staff, and parents can play an important role in reporting, stopping, and preventing bullying. Adequate supervision and monitoring of students, including their use of technology, is pertinent to solving this problem. Students need to see and recognize that teachers and staff are in control and that they care about their students.

For these reasons, it is important to have comprehensive anti-bullying/harassment legislation at the state and federal levels that provides clear and effective systems for reporting and addressing incidents that students experience locally. Schools need to be able to educate their faculty, staff, students, and parents about bullying and the policies and procedures in place for confronting it. The national effort to eliminate bullying, solely as an informational campaign, cannot address the problem in our schools. Taken together, however, these efforts can move us toward a future in which all students have the opportunity to learn and succeed in school (Kosciw et al., 2012). It may be difficult to stop all bullying, but it would be wrong to sanction it by doing little to address it.

References

Foderaro, L. W. (2010, September 29). Private moment made public, then a fatal jump. *The New York Times*. Retrieved from tinyurl.com/azv2k8q

GLSEN. (2009, April 10). 11-year-old hangs himself after enduring daily anti-gay bullying: GLSEN calls on schools, nation to embrace solutions to bullying problem. *PRWeb*. Retrieved from tinyurl.com/p7h7p6y

Kosciw, J. G., Greytak, E. A., Bartkiewicz, M. J., Boesen, M. J., & Palmer, N. A. (2012). *The 2011 national school climate survey: The experiences of lesbian, gay, bisexual and transgender youth in our nation's schools*. New York, NY: GLSEN.

Kowalski, R. M., Limber, S. P., & Agatston, P. W. (2008). *Cyber bullying: Bullying in the digital age*. Malden, MA: Blackwell.

Olweus, D. (2001). Peer harassment: A critical analysis and some important issues. In J. Juvonen & S. Graham (Eds.), *Peer harassment in school* (pp. 3–20). New York, NY: Guilford Press.

Salmivalli, C., Lagerspetz, K., Björkqvist, K., Osterman, K., & Kaukiainen, A. (1996). Bullying as a group process: Participant roles and their relations to social status within the group. *Aggressive Behavior, 22*, 1–15.

Yee, V. (2012). On Staten Island, relentless bullying is blamed for a teenage girl's suicide. *The New York Times*. Retrieved from tinyurl.com/nufzo73

◄ MYTH 32 ►

American K–12 education is being dumbed down.

It is not hard to find someone declaring that schooling and, as a direct result, American children are in a precipitous decline, one that has been going on for the past few decades. This is not just the anti-youth tirade voiced long ago by Socrates and repeated ever after by almost every older generation observing the younger generation. The claim is that children "today" are *different* from their predecessors in culturally or morally significant ways, that they are more materialistic, less attentive, even that they are poorly behaved and disrespectful of their elders (see Myth 30). Charles Sykes (1995), for example, went further. He claimed that the younger generation is being "dumbed down," that is, children know less and they aren't as smart as children used to be. The blame for this is laid on our school system and educators themselves, who are responsible for "a flight from high academic standards and expectations" (Sykes, 1995, p. ix). Part of the problem, say critics like these, is a shift in the *culture* of schools, where "self-esteem" has come to be the goal, even when students' skills are poor and when what they think they know is all wrong. "Johnny," Sykes claims, "can't read, write, or add" but nevertheless he "still feels good about himself." The combination of poor performance with a false sense of one's adequacy, Sykes goes on to argue, is the key to understanding why America is "losing the race" in a new global competition for economic success.

The same worry has been asserted concerning students and schools across the education spectrum, from elementary and secondary grades (Hirsch, 1987), through to higher education (Bloom, 1987), providing a repetitive theme in books and articles from the early 1980s through the early 2000s (see Cremin, 1990). The beliefs in a dumber America, based on opinion and anecdote, rather than fact (Berliner & Biddle, 1996), provided the backdrop for the federal government to pass into law an unprecedented reorientation of the nation's schools around "accountability," testing, and standards—the No Child Left Behind Act of 2001. The widely circulated and strongly believed claims made by these critics are not merely the complaints typical of crotchety and misanthropic golden-agers. Indeed, these critics are making an apparently empirical and historical claim that there is a crisis in education. The crisis we face as a nation is that our children are performing worse academically than they used to on the relatively straightforward tasks of reading, writing, and arithmetic, both at the elementary and secondary levels and even at the college level, where remediation of "the basics" is seen as increasingly necessary. As an empirical claim about the performance of students on measurable skills and knowledge, it should be testable through consideration of relevant evidence. Some of the authors mentioned above do cite numbers and studies to support their claims. Yet, a close look at the relevant evidence indicates that these claims are patently false.

Briefly, let's consider two commonly invoked bellwethers of academic decline: college entrance exams and the National Assessment of Education Progress (NAEP). A drop in average college entrance exam scores—scores on the SAT and ACT, in particular—has been cited as evidence of general academic decline. On closer investigation, however, it turns out that declines in average scores, based on the entire pool of all students taking these tests, were not due to any particular group of students performing worse than those like them who had taken the test before. Rather, the decline in the average score was due to the fact that many people who previously would not have attempted to enter college were, in the late 1960s and beyond, finding their way to postsecondary education, in part because of the programs of financial support initiated under the Great Society programs of President Lyndon Johnson. The most recent drop in SAT scores was likely for similar reasons, plus a job market that favors college graduates even if the jobs themselves do not require those degrees. Many students who previously did not take these tests, now were doing so.

In fact, many of these students would not have had access to or been admitted to college in the past, due to their parents' lack of education, attendance at poor and under-resourced schools, and even racist and exclusive admissions policies. So while it is true that the *average score* on these tests went down across the 1970s and 1980s, and again recently, there is no reason to believe it is because our students were dumber than those that had gone to school in previous decades. Indeed, the fact that many who wouldn't have taken the tests before were attempting them indicates, if nothing else, that children were becoming more academically ambitious and, presumably, more adept, such that they decided to take these examinations.

A better source of evidence on academic performance across these decades is the NAEP, a battery of tests of reading, writing, math, science, and civics, administered regularly to a random sample of students from across different social groups. The results of this test often are referred to as the "Nation's Report Card," and while it's not perfect, it is probably the best evidence on trends in student performance that we have (Glass, 2008). So do the NAEP results show the "dumbing down" that critics allege? Here, the facts are even more to the contrary than in the case of the SAT and ACT. The NAEP scores actually show an *increase* in all subjects for *all* students across the decades of the alleged decline that is supposed to now be of crisis proportions! This increase in scores is noticeably more dramatic for minority and low-income students than for their majority, middle-class peers. The difference between the average White students' score and the average Black students' score—what today is often referred to as "the achievement gap"—*decreased* across these decades and probably was narrowest in 1988 (Darling-Hammond, 2013). This wasn't because White children were doing worse, but because Black students were doing significantly better. Certainly, some kinds of students still know a lot more than others, and these differences aren't random, but follow socioeconomic and racial lines. We remain a nation that has yet to deliver on all its promises to all its children. But our children, collectively, actually are doing better in school, not worse.

The efforts to foster education equity that were part of the larger set of programs known as "the Great Society" seem to have addressed inequalities to an impressive degree, although these gains are rarely acknowledged. But as the 20th century became the 21st, the trend was reversed—likely a result of the reduction of support for many of the programs that were making a real difference, the increase in childhood poverty rates, and increased segregation in the housing of our citizenry (Berliner, 2009). These trends have resulted in traditionally disadvantaged children losing ground relative to their more privileged peers. Even so, while the *gap* has once again grown, the NAEP scores show that the absolute level of knowledge in tested subjects has not declined. The notion that "kids don't know what they used to" and "education is being dumbed down" seems to be a myth—at least, if by "dumbed down" we mean schools today produce children who are less proficient in reading, writing, and arithmetic.

This is not to say, however, that there aren't other reasons to worry about an inadequate curriculum and a widespread lack of important, even essential, learning. The complaints and criticism made by the likes of Sykes, Hirsch, and Bloom probably have helped in setting the stage for the Common Core State Standards (CCSS). The faulty belief in a decline in student knowledge and skill, combined with an equally faulty belief that the United States does poorly in international testing (see Myth 1), has led the federal government to demand that states adopt the CCSS. It is thought that curriculum in line with the CCSS will reverse the trends that are believed to have befallen the U.S. education system. The CCSS may or may not promote a richer and deeper curriculum for American youth. Time will tell. But they certainly will homogenize American education, replacing local- and state-adopted curricula with one compatible with the standards promoted by the federal government. Homogenization is sure to reduce the variation in what America's students know. There inevitably will be a national restriction in knowledge, since only some knowledge will be acceptable. Ironically, restricting the knowledge to be learned in our schools is a way to dumb down our students.

In fact, since the No Child Left Behind Act (NCLB) went into effect, education really may have been dumbed down. Kids really may know less than they did. NCLB was inspired largely by concern over lack of standards and accountability and over economic competitiveness fueled by the likes of Sykes, Hirsch, Bloom, and legions of other Jeremiahs. Their rhetoric contributed to a belief in a crisis that NCLB and now the CCSS were to fix. But the heavy testing requirements associated with both programs always results in a narrowing of the curriculum to reflect the tests. In NCLB, increased testing and emphasis on "basic skills" in reading and mathematics drove out many courses and activities that supported creativity, critical thinking, and learning related to civic goals, largely the province of social studies. And because science and the arts were not tested, these curriculum areas also saw reductions in teaching time (Nichols & Berliner, 2007; Ravitch, 2010). So the critics of America's curriculum may well have helped to dumb it down. By attaching the CCSS to particular high-stakes tests, even more narrowing of what is taught and what is learned in schools is likely.

This "dumbing down" in terms of the sorts of skills that make for interesting lives and able, efficacious citizens, doesn't affect all students equally. Tracking programs within schools (see Myth 19) have grown dramatically in recent years. In addition, segregation by housing, as well as the increased concentration of different sorts of students in different kinds of schools, has led to a "dumbed down" curriculum for those who historically have been least well served by public schools (Tienken & Zhao, 2013). In the name of *higher* standards and accountability, some terrible things are being done!

The emphasis on accountability, combined with the favored initiatives of school choice advocates, also has led to an increase in the segregation of students. They are now more likely to be attending schools with other students like themselves in terms of race and class (Miron, Urschel, Mathis, & Tornquist, 2010). Yet one of the main mechanisms whereby children of *all* backgrounds learn to be responsible citizens is by interacting with and learning with others who are different from them in socially significant ways (Howe & Meens, 2012). So contemporary educational policies subvert learning how to live in a multicultural, socially diverse democracy. Failure to provide the necessary skills to live in a multicultural democracy is another form of dumbing down, but this time brought on by the policies of those that claim to be reformers.

In sum, to a great extent, the anxiety expressed by critics of public schools about the "dumbing down" of American education is a myth; to the extent that it is a reality, it has been in large part a *result* of policies implemented in response to worries created by the myth, a kind of self-fulfilling prophecy. This doesn't mean we shouldn't be concerned about making sure that *all* children have access to a curriculum that enriches their personal lives and prepares them to be able employees and good democratic citizens. Quite the contrary is true. Focus on "the basics" just doesn't lead to such a curriculum.

On the other hand, there is a good deal of philosophical and scientific work that shows the way forward. That work suggests that a localized and problem-based curriculum can increase achievement and provide the rich learning experiences that make interesting people, able workers, and competent democratic citizens (Tienken & Zhao, 2013). But to move forward in this way, we first must declare that it is not our schools or our children but rather the anxiety-charged myth of an education crisis that is broken and needs to be fixed.

References

Berliner, D. C. (2009). *Poverty and potential: Out-of-school factors and school success.* Boulder, CO, & Tempe, AZ: Education and the Public Interest Center & Education Policy Research Unit. Retrieved from epicpolicy.org/publication/poverty-and-potential

Berliner, D. C., & Biddle, B. J. (1996). *The manufactured crisis: Myths, fraud, and the attack on America's public schools.* New York, NY: Basic Books.

Bloom, A. (1987). *The closing of the American mind: How higher education has failed democracy and impoverished the souls of today's students.* New York, NY: Simon & Schuster.

Cremin, L. (1990). *Popular education and its discontents.* New York, NY: Harper & Row.

Darling-Hammond, L. (2013). Inequality and school resources: What it will take to close the opportunity gap. In K. Welner & P. Carter (Eds.), *Closing the opportunity gap: What America must do to give every child an even chance* (pp. 77–97). New York, NY: Oxford University Press.

Glass, G. V. (2008). *Fertilizers, pills, and magnetic strips: The fate of public education in America.* Charlotte, NC: Information Age.

Hirsch, E. D. (1987). *Cultural literacy: What every child needs to know.* Boston, MA: Houghton Mifflin.

Howe, K. R., & Meens, D. E. (2012). *Democracy left behind: How recent education reforms undermine local school governance and democratic education.* Boulder, CO: NEPC. Retrieved from tinyurl.com/q6az9vk

Miron, G., Urschel, J., Mathis, W., & Tornquist, E. (2010). *Schools without diversity: Education management organizations, charter schools, and the demographic stratification of the American school system* (EPIC/EPRU). Retrieved from tinyurl.com/3rv436g

Nichols, S. L., & Berliner, D. C. (2007). *Collateral damage: How high-stakes testing corrupts American education.* Cambridge, MA: Harvard Education Press.

Ravitch, D. (2010). *The death and life of the great American school system: How testing and choice are undermining education.* New York, NY: Basic Books.

Sykes, C. J. (1995). *Dumbing our kids down: Why American children feel good about themselves but can't read, write, or add.* New York, NY: St. Martin's Press.

Tienken, C. H., & Zhao, Y. (2013). How common standards and standardized testing widen the opportunity gap. In K. Welner & P. Carter (Eds.), *Closing the opportunity gap: What America must do to give every child an even chance* (pp. 111–122). New York, NY: Oxford University Press.

∽ MYTH 33 ∾

Mayoral control of city schools has paid off in terms of student achievement.

It is hard to call this a myth since it may be true in some cities but not in others, and it may be true on some indicators of achievement, but not others. Because locale seems to determine whether this is a myth or not, that fact alone makes clear that mayoral control is not a panacea for urban schools that are performing poorly.

Mayoral control began only about 20 years ago when the Mayor of Boston, Raymond Flynn, took control of his city's school district. Chicago followed Boston. There Mayor Richard M. Daley appointed both the chief executive officer and the entire school board. Increasingly, throughout the country, mayoral governance of schools has been called a "reform" approach.

The Center for American Progress (Wong & Shen, 2013) recently released a report analyzing the impact of mayoral control, generally lauding this reform strategy. Although the large urban districts get the most attention (Boston, Chicago, New York, Washington, DC, and the like), mayors of some smaller cities also have succeeded in gaining control of their schools (e.g., Hartford, Harrisburg, Trenton, Indianapolis). But since the problems in each city differ, judging the success or failure of mayoral control in each city also differs, and so it is not clear that a simple answer to the question of whether mayoral control works well or not, will ever be forthcoming.

In its report on 11 districts under mayoral control, the Center concluded that five made substantial progress in narrowing the student achievement gaps on state tests; four made some progress, but it was quite variable by subject matter and grade level; and two did not show much progress in reducing achievement gaps. So in this report the results are generally positive, but not always so and often uneven. For example, in New York City the mayor's small schools initiative appears to be graduating a higher percentage of students than do the city's regular public schools. That's good. But the 2013 tests in New York City show that the achievement gap has widened between New York's poorest and its more-advantaged students. That's bad. Amidst all the conflicting data about whether different indices of student achievement showed gains or not, there is one thing that is clear in almost every case of mayoral control: There is a reduction in the democratic processes for governance of the schools. That should be worrisome.

No one we know wants to defend local school boards as the perfect mechanism for school governance, and no one ever said democratically elected local school boards were efficient, or impermeable to corruption. Mark Twain famously remarked, "In the first place, God made idiots. That was for practice. Then he made school boards." But Winston Churchill's views may be closer to the mark: "No one pretends that democracy is perfect or all-wise. Indeed, it has been said that democracy is the worst form of government except all those other forms that have been tried from time to time."

So it is worth thinking about whether we want so much power in the hands of one person, even an elected mayor. The U.S. Constitution wisely required a separation of powers, a system of checks and balances, to ensure that power was never in the hands of one person or one body. Mayoral control generally ignores the reasoning behind this historically successful strategy.

Thus, Mayor Bloomberg of New York could appoint as chancellor of the schools a friend, a successful publisher and businesswoman, who not only knew nothing about the New York City schools, but was a soft-core pornographer as well (Berliner, 2011). Apparently the legendary cronyism characteristic of Tammany Hall never ended. But thankfully she didn't last long on the job. New York, however, is not alone in running a patronage system. Chicago is another system under mayoral control. And current mayor Rahm Emanuel recently substituted a millionaire for a billionaire whom he previously had appointed to the Chicago school board. Millionaire venture capitalist Deborah Quazzo recently was chosen to fill the Chicago public school board vacancy created after billionaire Penny Pritzker resigned to be secretary of commerce. Ms. Pritzker, however, is apparently a heavy supporter of, and investor in, charter schools. Charter schools get their funding directly from the board on which she served. That's usually considered a conflict of interest, but in Chicago that may be merely business as usual!

It is not that Quazzo and Pritzker are bad human beings, unsuccessful businesspersons, or uninterested in education. That's not the point. The point is that they appear to have been picked to help improve education primarily because they are rich and can support the mayor and other favored politicians. In fact, in three of the most notable mayor-controlled school systems, Chicago, New York, and Washington, DC, the mayors' school board choices usually lead to a disconnect between the boards and the population served. For example, in Chicago, the school board is composed primarily of corporate executives. But 92% of the students in the district are of color and 86% of those students are low-income. In mayoral-controlled districts, it is often the case that those served by the schools have little representation on the boards that decide their educational futures.

Where mayoral control is exercised, the mayors usually appoint the majority, or all, of the school board. This results in the mayor having a big say in all major education decisions—the spending of millions or billions of dollars that allow the district to function—and some control over the tens of thousands of jobs the district provides. In such a system, patronage is almost inevitable. Patronage appointments in Chicago, New York, Washington, DC, and elsewhere are not helpful to our schools, nor are they respectful of our ever-fragile democracy.

Nevertheless, if we ignore the inherent loss of democratic governance, the question most citizens want answered about mayoral control is whether it is "successful." Certainly the mayors keep citing their success. But when studying three of the largest mayoral-controlled districts (Chicago, New York City, and Washington, DC), Weiss and Long (2013) inform us that they do not deliver. Their report is used extensively in what follows.

They note that in Washington, "churn" has been enormous. Teachers come and go at rates that are quite high, unsettling the schools and the children and families the schools serve. In Washington, half of all new teachers leave in 2 years, and 80% are gone in 7 years, about the time many teachers peak in competence. They leave because their teaching situations are awful, or they are fired. But a churn strategy for school improvement works only if the teachers who leave the district are replaced by teachers who are better. This does not happen. Instead, the teachers who leave are almost always replaced by novices, sometimes barely trained novices, like those from Teach For America (see Myth 13). Furthermore, aside from the loss of talent and experience, and the disruption of the teachers' relationships with children, the money lost to Washington's schools by their policy of churn is estimated at about 12 million dollars annually. This is substantial. Churn costs. Chicago had similar churn under Superintendent Arne Duncan, the former mayor's choice for school leader and currently U.S. secretary of education. In 100 of that city's low-income minority schools, 25% of the teachers were new each year.

Churn allows mayors to say they are working on the problems of the schools, but the mayors do not address what churn does to student–teacher, parent–teacher, and teacher–teacher relationships. In fact, excessive churn destroys the culture of a school and exacerbates the problems of establishing trust between the residents of a neighborhood and the schools in low-income neighborhoods.

Michelle Rhee, the mayor's choice for chancellor of the Washington schools, not only fired 1,000 teachers in her short tenure, but she hired 90 new principals, over half of whom left while she still ran the schools. She also closed 24 public schools, allowing charter schools to gain a bigger share of the money spent on public education. New York also closed public schools, 140 of them, and helped promote 100 new charter schools as replacements. Chicago closed approximately 50 schools in 2013 alone as it also promotes charter schools. But as made clear in Myth 3, charters are not magical answers to serious problems. Even though they often have easier-to-teach children, charters do not do any better than ordinary public schools in promoting student achievement.

It seems odd for mayoral-controlled districts to keep up the school-closing strategy since school closures lead to increased dropouts and, of course, higher enrollments at other schools, some of which cannot handle the influx of new enrollees. Of the 32,961 students in 21 high schools that were closed in New York City, 5,612 dropped out of school and 9,668 were "discharged." The latter category is for those who leave the district, but it is a catch-all category and probably contains at least 15% of students who actually were dropouts. Thus, roughly 20% of the students whose schools were closed dropped out of school at that time. School closures, therefore, add to the ordinarily high dropout problem experienced by urban schools that serve the poor. This makes costs to these communities, later in the lives of these youngsters, enormous. That is because of the likelihood that those dropouts will end up with lower job skills and thus pay the cities they live in less in taxes. They are likely to have a higher need for welfare (including unemployment insurance), a higher incarceration rate, and so forth. So any policy that increases school dropouts eventually will be costly for the cities.

School closings are a preferred strategy in all three mayoral-controlled districts. But in Chicago it was discovered that only 6% of the students from closed schools moved into schools that were performing better than their old school, the one that was closed! Thus, most students who were forced to move did not improve their performance. Churn just makes it look like mayors are doing something, but what they are doing may not be any good.

One other aspect of the closures in each city is worth noting. When a public school is closed and a charter school that can skim and cream students is opened, the neighborhood often becomes gentrified. Housing prices go up, the new schools are selective and safe, low-income people are driven out, and the community changes character. Substantial real estate gains have been realized as a function of the "educational" decisions that are made about where and when to close schools. Chicago also has another scheme that relies on education to make money for some of its citizens. Sometimes, when a public school is closed, the empty building is offered to a charter operator for $1 per year. Thirty-three charter schools currently benefit from this form of sweetheart leasing.

In both Chicago and New York, many of the charter schools that were promoted were co-located, that is, given a piece of an existing school building to use. These charter schools often received more money per pupil because they had wealthy donors supporting them, and in some cases the cities actually were supplying them with more money than they did their regular public schools. Imagine being a student in the public school part of the building, and down the hallway from your classroom is a charter school classroom with resources you do not have and your teacher dreams about!

Worse, in one school building in New York City, there exists a small school of choice, a magnet school for the gifted, of the kind Mayor Bloomberg promoted when he took over the city's public schools. The building also houses a small neighborhood public school. To get into the magnet school requires high scores on a standardized test. Its students are mostly White and middle class or above. The regular neighborhood school serves mostly poor Latino and Black children. The two schools not only have vastly different resources and curricula, but the mostly White children in the magnet school come in through the front door, and the neighborhood kids, mostly of color, go in through the back door (Thrasher, 2010). "Outrageous" is both the first and the only word that comes to mind. But charters and magnets are known to segregate children (see Myth 3); so when mayors who control education promote charter schools, they are not helping their cities to meet our country's democratic ideals.

In these three districts, the effects of mayoral control on student achievement are in dispute. And to be fair, it is very hard to attribute an entire district's gains and losses in achievement to a single influence such as mayoral control, or anything else. If more wealthy families or more Asian families move into a district, or the local unemployment rate goes down, scores on tests usually will go up. If a recession hits, if jobs are lost, or if crime rates increase, scores on tests usually go down. In these cases it doesn't matter who is running the district.

Despite this caveat, a recent report from the Civic Committee of the Commercial Club of Chicago asserts that most of Chicago's students are expected to drop out or fail. The report says that the vast majority of Chicago's elementary and high schools simply do not prepare students for success in college or for employment. The Consortium for Chicago School Research, at the University of Chicago, agrees with this assessment.

Many of the initiatives now seen as failures were begun under mayoral control and administered by Arne Duncan, now Obama's secretary of education. If the Duncan-era reforms produced gains, it was not with Chicago's Black students, who actually lost ground under mayoral control. Latino scores merely stagnated. But during Duncan's tenure, Asian and White students did show achievement gains. And despite enrolling easier-to-teach children, and promotion by successor mayors, the city's charter schools performed no better than did the city's comparable public schools. And what is the verdict on student achievement under mayoral control of the schools in Chicago? Nothing special appears to be gained.

In Washington, Chancellor Rhee and Mayor Fenty, who controlled the city's schools for a few years, claimed major gains in achievement for all the subgroups of students served by public schools. But some of those claims were based on the city tests, for which children were drilled, and both teachers and principals were fired if they could not get their students' scores higher. There apparently was cheating, as uncovered in recent scandals involving Chancellor Rhee. An outside test, the National Assessment of Educational Progress, suggests that some modest gains did occur, and that is good. But while some gains occurred, the test also revealed that the gap between low-income children and others in the city increased quite a bit in both 4th and 8th grades. And this was true for both math and reading achievement. Overall, when looking at urban 8th-graders from 2005 to 2011, Washington, DC, students lost ground. And what is the verdict on student achievement under mayoral control of the schools in Washington DC? Nothing special appears to be gained.

In New York City, Mayor Bloomberg keeps insisting that the achievement gap between White and Asian students, on the one hand, and Black and Latino students, on the other, in public schools was halved between 2003 and 2011. But the analysis of Weiss and Long (2013) contradicts His Honor. Averaged across state reading and math test scores in 4th and 8th grades, the achievement gap that His Honor likes to cite has stagnated. In 2003 the gap was 26.2 percentage points but in 2011 it was 25.8 percentage points. There really was no statistically significantly difference between the two, and the mayor appears to be wrong, very wrong. The verdict on student achievement under mayoral control of the schools in New York City? Nothing special appears to be gained.

Mayoral control does seem to pry loose some extra funds, as it has the attention of the mayors, and their budget authority can help them move money around a city. Their reputations are on the line, and so their attention is focused. And that is good. But it looks as if the increased funding and their increased attention have not improved the schools much, at least in the three school systems examined by Weiss and Long. Even in the more positive report on mayoral control by Wong and Shen (2013), there is not much to support the idea that mayoral control is a panacea for urban school problems. Furthermore, almost all of the mayor's education decisions and spending are done with very little community input, since the school boards in mayoral-controlled districts are captive. Perhaps with little evidence of success and too much power in the hands of a single politician, we should learn to work harder at making local democratically elected school boards work as they should.

References

Berliner, D. C. (2011, January 25). Soft-core porn and the crisis of school leadership. *Truthout.* Retrieved from tinyurl.com/q2th6y7

Thrasher, S. (2010, February 23). Inside a divided upper east side public school: Whites in the front door, blacks in the back door. *The Village Voice.* Retrieved from tinyurl.com/ok8nqc7

Weiss, E., & Long, D. (2013). *Market-oriented education reforms' rhetoric trumps reality: The impacts of test-based teacher evaluations, school closures, and increased charter school access on student outcomes in Chicago, New York City, and Washington, D.C.* Retrieved from tinyurl.com/njzqdvm

Wong, K. K., & Shen, F. X. (2013). *Mayoral governance and student achievement: How mayor-led districts are improving school and student performance.* Washington, DC: Center for American Progress. Retrieved from tinyurl.com/ppuck26

◦§ MYTH 34 ≳◦

Forced integration has failed.

Racial desegregation of America's public schools is one of the most controversial topics in education; consequently, a wide array of beliefs is associated with the issue. As might be expected of a controversial topic, misunderstandings abound. These misunderstandings have played a role in the public's withdrawal of support from the democratic ideal of integrated schools.

Unless you are inclined to follow education court cases, it likely has been some time since you have heard news in the media about school desegregation. One very significant case was the 2007 *Parents Involved* U.S. Supreme Court ruling on the use of race-based student assignment policies to create and preserve integrated schools. The ruling affirmed racial diversity as important in schools but banned the common ways in which schools achieve diverse populations. Another popular case was the more recent 2010 Wake County School Board's vote to eliminate the busing policy it had used to achieve once racial, and now socioeconomic-based, diversity (Khadaroo, 2010). Although school desegregation once was often discussed, rarely does it arise today in social or political conversations. In a country ostensibly dedicated to equal opportunity, the lack of attention to this issue is regrettable, and it may be in part why so many citizens have come to believe that school desegregation has failed.

The 1954 *Brown v. Board of Education* U.S. Supreme Court decision brought an end to roughly 60 years of legal racial segregation in the southern United States, and it outlawed similar programs across the entire country. The case, preceded by earlier successful desegregation cases in the lower courts filed by African American and Mexican American groups, did little initially to spur desegregation efforts of segregated public schools. The South dug in its heels and fiercely resisted integration efforts. Arkansas governor Orval Faubus defied the court by stationing National Guard troops outside Little Rock High School to prevent the entry of nine African American students. It would take a series of later legal decisions and the 1964 Civil Rights Act for school desegregation efforts to commence. While the public often takes *Brown v. Board* to have "solved" the issue of racial segregation, de facto segregation continues to this day as a pressing concern.

Perhaps the most common misconception is the belief that racially segregated schools no longer exist. While such schools no longer are referred to as "legally" segregated schools, "racially concentrated" schools (i.e., segregated schools) are widespread throughout the nation. Despite increases in integrated schools between the 1960s and 1980s, school demographic enrollments since then show continual signs of resegregation. This has resulted in both minority school concentrations (schools with high percentages of students of color such as Black students or Latino students) and also majority concentrated schools (those with high percentages of White students). Although often overlooked, White students are more racially isolated than other groups, on average attending schools where 77% of the student body is White (Orfield & Lee, 2007). Black and Latino students, despite their lower proportions of the enrollment population, often attend schools where more than half of students are Black or Latino. In fact, about 40% of Black and Latino students attend schools that are composed of over 90% students of color. Similarly, about 20% of American Indian students attend schools where the majority, upwards of 90%, of the student population consists of students of color (Orfield, 2009). This state of affairs prompted the writer Jonathan Kozol to describe the United States as a country supporting apartheid-lite.

Currently popular "school choice" policies and programs (charter schools, online schools, home schooling, tuition tax credits, and the like) are contributing substantially to the resegregation of our nation's public education system. Some critics even see the desire to resegregate schools as the primary motive underlying these movements.

Seattle Public School District provides an example of a district that at one time pushed for integrated schools but now, having abandoned those practices, is experiencing resegregation. The Seattle district desegregated schools nearly 30 years ago, but it has slowly resegregated as a result of school choice and other district policies. As of 2008, previously integrated schools have become both White concentrated schools and minority concentrated schools. The enrollment of students of color exceeds 90% in 20 Seattle schools (Shaw, 2008).

Racially isolated schools, both White and minority, threaten to undermine the diverse social interaction necessary for responsible democratic decisionmaking. Complicating the matter is the connection between race and poverty, with many high-percentage minority schools simultaneously concentrating low-income students. The double bind of racial and poverty concentration restricts educational opportunities for these students as well as constrains later participation in civic life. Isolated schooling experiences intuitively do not bode well for cultivating the respect necessary for living in a pluralistic society.

A common misunderstanding is that desegregation efforts were altogether unsuccessful in generating integrated enrollment patterns among Black and White students. This misunderstanding overlooks demographic patterns in the South, a region that achieved integration to a greater extent than any other. The South, with stringent segregation laws, fiercely fought against desegregation. Where explicit segregation laws were present, federal courts were able to substantially enforce desegregation orders and to create genuinely desegregated schools. This is unlike the North, whose history of segregation resulted primarily from housing discrimination and other inequitable mechanisms, where desegregation has been largely unofficial. Following several court decisions and intense enforcement of desegregation orders, the South, from the mid-1960s to the 1970s, arguably became the most integrated area of the country. For the most part, where the court enforced desegregation, racially mixed schools resulted.

Where integration was achieved, the benefits to students have been significant. Desegregated schools appear to slightly improve African American achievement, with the greatest impact in earlier grades, while desegregated settings have little impact on White achievement scores (Linn & Welner, 2007). Although the benefits of integrated schools for Black children have been highlighted frequently, little attention has been paid to the fact that there were no declines in achievement for White children, who were often of higher income levels. In fact, many Whites often have opposed integration on the belief that it would harm the education of their children. This belief sometimes stemmed from newspaper articles that showed the total school standardized test average dropping after poor African American students entered the school population. Of course that would happen. It would also happen if poor White students suddenly were added to the population of a school that served upper-income White families.

A striking demonstration of the benefits of school desegregation was provided by two researchers working with data from the National Assessment of Education Progress (NAEP) in the early 1980s (Burton & Jones, 1982). The most remarkable change in NAEP data they found was a large increase in the reading scores of young African American students in the southeast United States. And this was precisely during the time period when that region—unlike the rest of the country—experienced significant court-ordered racial desegregation.

But testing and achievement outcomes should not automatically take precedence over what is arguably an even more important desegregation-related outcome. Although often overlooked, desegregation has had a positive impact on one's choice for integrated social relations and environments later in life. Early desegregated experiences lead our children to more integrated adult experiences, including participation in more integrated workplace settings and more racially diverse postsecondary choices. Conversely, early school segregation leads to continued segregation across the life span and across institutional contexts. Early segregated experiences too often teach the lesson that children of other racial or social class backgrounds are inferior, while one's own race or class is seen as superior. The impact of desegregation on later life preferences for more diverse social environments points to the importance of racial integration as a way of supporting diverse social institutions. Diversity in these institutions appears to be fundamental in a multicultural democracy.

Of course, desegregation was not all rosy. Serious implementation issues continued to burden African American communities with the responsibility of integrating into White schools; many Black teachers and administrators were laid off; and minority students in their everyday lives were forced to come face to face with many White students and teachers who had little regard for their physical, emotional, or academic well-being. It is hard to undertake big social changes such as this without a considerable amount of turmoil occurring for all involved.

The promotion of racial desegregation has been hampered by a series of conservative legal decisions and market reform policies, such as the expansion in school choice. Throughout the 1990s the U.S. Supreme Court made several decisions that undermined the practical ways in which race-conscious assignment policies could be implemented (*Freeman v. Pitts*, 1992; *Missouri v. Jenkins*, 1995; *Oklahoma v. Dowell*, 1991; *Parents Involved*, 2007). These cases set an oppositional legal and public tone on the ideal of racial desegregation, have permitted desegregation mandates to end despite the likelihood of resegregated schools, and have drastically limited the tools available to districts that want to support desegregated schools.

Today, despite the continued prevalence of racially concentrated schools, desegregation nearly has been abandoned as a policy option. With rare exception, desegregation-related cases garner little media attention despite the slow unraveling of mandatory desegregation orders. The release of desegregation orders often occurs out of the public eye but has been ongoing across the country. For example, in several southern states alone, 89 school districts have been released from desegregation orders since 2004 (Holley-Walker, 2010). Abandoning desegregation policies is returning us to a past when segregated schools were seen as normal and acceptable.

The issue of racial segregation in schools is closely tied to American beliefs about democracy. Racially segregated schools—both White and minority concentrated—undermine the opportunities and social experiences necessary to live up to democratic ideals. Segregated settings constrain the development of an appreciation of democratic processes by narrowing the range of perspectives students encounter. Decisionmaking bodies arrive at broader and more creative solutions when those involved come from a diversity of experiences and when decisions are made with empathic understanding of other people's lives. Racially integrated institutions are integral to democratic decisionmaking. A key way to support democracy is to encourage efforts to desegregate public schools. However, we must find new, creative ways, as previously used legal routes have been constrained.

There is a strong attraction to the myth that school segregation is no longer a problem, the myth that desegregation never worked, and the myth that desegregation efforts resulted in no benefits to minority or majority children. To accept this set of interrelated myths as true lessens responsibility for parents and policymakers to act at the local and federal levels. Acceptance of the myths will have a negative impact on both student achievement and the development of empathic, multicultural students—the kinds of students necessary to maintain a healthy democracy.

References

Burton, N. W., & Jones, L. V. (1982). Recent trends in achievement levels of black and white youth. *Educational Researcher, 11*(4), 10–14.

Freeman v. Pitts, 503 U.S. 467 (1992).

Holley-Walker, D. (2010). After unitary status: Examining voluntary integration strategies for southern school districts. *North Carolina Law Review, 88*, 877–910.

Khadaroo, S. (2010, March 24). Busing to end in Wake County, NC: Good-bye, school diversity? *Christian Science Monitor.* Retrieved from tinyurl.com/24tlx6m

Linn, R., & Welner, K. (2007). *Race-conscious policies for assigning students to schools: Social science research and the Supreme Court cases.* Washington, DC: National Academy of Education, Committee on Social Research Evidence on Racial Diversity in Schools. Retrieved from tinyurl.com/qbxfwpb

Missouri v. Jenkins, 115 S. Ct. 2038 (1995).

Oklahoma v. Dowell, 498 U.S. 237 (1991).

Orfield, G. (2009). *Reviving the goal of an integrated society: A 21st century challenge.* Los Angeles: Civil Rights Project/ Proyecto Derechos Civiles at University of California at Los Angeles.

Orfield, G., & Lee, C. (2007). *Historic reversals, accelerating resegregation, and the need for new integration strategies.* Los Angeles: Civil Rights Project/ Proyecto Derechos Civiles at University of California at Los Angeles.

Parents Involved in Community Schools v. Seattle School District No. 1, 551 U.S. 701 (2007).

Shaw, L. (2008, June 1). The resegregation of Seattle's schools. *Seattle Times.* Retrieved from tinyurl.com/dypyuds

V

Myths and Lies About How Our Nation's Schools Are Paid For: All Schools Are Equal, but Some Are More Equal Than Others

In this part, we present myths about the money to support education in the United States. Not surprisingly, one of the most regularly occurring of these myths is that money, or funding for the public schools beyond some minimum level, doesn't matter. We note, of course, that these statements often are made by those to whom money matters so much that they will do whatever they can to keep it; and, worse, they will try hard to have others possess less of it than they do. But as we note from a court case about school finance, in the opinion of that judge, the testimony by "experts" that money doesn't matter defies both evidence and logic! It really does make us believe that those who argue otherwise must have less than commendable motives driving their beliefs.

Some public school critics also promulgate the idea that society should pay only for basic education, say, through grade 6 or 8. That may have been worth arguing in the early 20th century, but seems to be plainly out of touch with the education needs of the 21st century. We argue that there are public, not just private, benefits from a sound and as nearly free as possible public education system.

In this part we also deal with the favorite policy of both the political and religious Right, the promotion of tuition tax credits as a way to partially fund private and private religious schools. As we make clear, their policy ploy is a brazen, although thus far legal, way to use public money to subsidize the children of the rich and the religious. Despite all the rhetoric by supporters of these programs about opening opportunities for the poor, these policies do no such thing. In fact, because they starve the public schools of funding, they actually may hurt the poor.

We also contend that the current attempt to have portfolio models of school governance in cities (a set of public, private, and charter schools to administer) is both difficult to manage and detrimental to furthering the democratic goals that underlie our nation's public school system. As with all parts of this book, in the end there appear to be many dubious beliefs shaping U.S. educational policy in the area of finance. Some policies are not working correctly and can be fixed; some are destructive of public education and should be opposed.

⊰ MYTH 35 ⊱

Money doesn't matter!
We're spending more money than ever, but test scores are stagnant.

According to a number of very vocal politicians and business leaders, we Americans are pouring vast sums of money down the drain of a broken public education system. Backed by researchers in conservative think tanks, these individuals have long argued that while the cost of running schools is increasing at an alarming rate, we have little to show for it when we look at our test scores. The logical conclusion seems to be that money doesn't matter. What does matter? Better teachers. Better curriculum. Better parents. More motivated students. Most of the suggestions on how to improve schools involve more standardized testing, supposedly a cost-effective way of keeping teachers, parents, and students accountable and motivated. The frequency and fervency of this argument have escalated in recent years—accompanied by deeper and deeper cuts to state education budgets.

There are a number of commonsense reasons to reject the "money doesn't matter" argument. Linda Darling-Hammond, one of the most perceptive analysts on the state of U.S. education, once remarked that if money doesn't matter, then why are the rich trying so hard to hold onto it? Anyone who has ever wished to move the family to the suburbs, or send their children to a private school, knows that money matters in education. Anyone who has seen her young child struggle for the teacher's attention in a class of more than 30 students knows that money matters in education. Anyone who has seen the stark contrast in school facilities, course offerings, and support services in affluent neighborhoods versus inner cities knows that money matters in education. It *is* common sense. But it is also well documented by credible research. For very good reason, one school finance expert calls the recent political clamor "a rhetorical war against an otherwise overwhelming body of empirical evidence" (Baker, 2012).

This chapter highlights three aspects of that empirical evidence about money and education: the misleading and often blatantly false claims about how much we are spending and what test scores we are getting; the strength of the research demonstrating both that money matters generally and that money spent on specific resources also matters; and the ironic fact that school choice, despite being embraced by proponents of the "money doesn't matter" argument, demonstrates that money actually does matter.

To highlight the factual inaccuracies of this myth, we can begin with Bill Gates's (2011) claim in a *Washington Post* op-ed that "over the past four decades, the per-student cost of running our K–12 schools has more than doubled, while our student achievement has remained virtually flat." As Richard Rothstein (2011) explained, both parts of this claim are inaccurate. The part about student achievement is actually just blatantly not true. According to long-term trend data from the National Assessment of Educational Progress (NAEP), our only source of longitudinal data on U.S. student achievement, all subgroups of American students have shown substantial improvement over time. Those who claim that achievement is flat are citing either the NAEP data that are cross-sectional (that part of the testing program that is not concerned with national trends) or other data sources. These cross-sectional snapshots of American achievement almost always ignore the fact that the percentages of poor and minority children included in the average scores have been increasing for decades, so a drop in average score is to be expected. But even then, some subgroups, such as African Americans, have demonstrated extraordinary improvement over time. Beyond the NAEP test, we also know that the percentage of college graduates in the United States has nearly doubled over the past 4 decades. There is simply no evidence to support the claim that academic achievement has been flat.

Rothstein describes Gates's claim about the rising cost of running our K–12 schools as misleading rather than blatantly untrue, since spending has approximately doubled over the past 4 decades. The problem is that without context it is too easy to conclude that all that money has been poured into the general education system. In fact, less than half of that money has gone to regular education. Instead, a very large portion of the increased funding has gone into special education. Rather than institutionalizing children with disabilities, we are now supporting them as students in our public schools, and we are remarkably successful in educating many of these children so that after finishing school they become contributing members of society. This is a meaningful accomplishment, but it does not affect the test scores of children in regular education. It is unfair and misleading to expect that the rising expenditures for education over the past 40 years, during which we have completely revised our ideas about the rights of children with disabilities, should have led to greater academic gains for children in regular education.

Clearly, the rhetoric about how much we are spending and what we are getting is deeply flawed. Just as there is ample evidence to disprove these claims, there is also ample evidence to prove that money really does matter in education. Decades of high-quality, peer-reviewed studies have come to that conclusion. One of the few researchers who have not come to that conclusion is Erik Hanushek (1986), who often is quoted by proponents of the "money doesn't matter" argument. Hanushek compiled the findings of a large set of studies investigating this question and concluded that there was no consistent relationship between expenditures and performance. Researchers who have reexamined the studies included in Hanushek's meta-analysis, however, have found that many of those studies were of poor quality; when they included only the strong and peer-reviewed studies, the results showed that resources actually do strongly predict outcomes (Baker, 2012). And yet Hanushek continues to testify in court case after court case that money for education doesn't matter. In a recent Colorado school finance case (*Lobato v. State of Colorado*) he did so once again. Only this time, a Colorado judge had little sympathy for counterintuitive social science data. In her 189-page ruling deciding in favor of the plaintiffs, Judge Sheila Rappaport (Hoover, 2011) lucidly commented on Hanushek's testimony: "Dr. Hanushek's analysis that there is not much relationship in Colorado between spending and achievement contradicts testimony and documentary evidence from dozens of well-respected educators in the State, defies logic, and is statistically flawed." Conservative economists might enter courtrooms more cautiously if the likes of Judge Rappaport become more widespread.

The big picture is clear: When we compare school districts that have sufficient resources with those that do not, we see that achievement outcomes are definitively higher in the former. We can gain further confidence about this finding by looking at the specific ways in which districts that have money, spend it. Does it make a difference in terms of student achievement to hire teachers that cost more because they are more experienced and better educated? More specifically, does it make a difference in schools that serve the poor to spend more money on teachers so that they will continue to teach despite challenging circumstances? Does it make a difference to hire more teachers so that class sizes can be reduced and kept low? Does it make a difference to provide social supports so that high-needs students can learn to the best of their ability? We know with a good deal of certainty that the answer to these questions is a resounding "Yes." Studies consistently show that more experienced teachers—who command higher salaries —are more effective. Studies also show consistently that higher salaries attract better candidates to the teaching profession, help keep them in the profession, and reduce teacher turnover rates in high-poverty schools. New research from Finland, Singapore, and other countries also provides striking evidence that spending more, and targeting that spending at students who come to school with the fewest resources, can have a dramatic impact on a nation's overall education outcomes (Darling-Hammond, 2010).

But it is not necessary to look abroad for evidence that spending more on high-impact educational resources affects student achievement. As Julian Vasquez Heilig (2013) points out, the school choice movement right here in the United States provides plentiful evidence that money matters in education. There are some obvious examples, such as that parents who choose to live in expensive suburbs with well-supported schools or to send their children to expensive private schools do so because they believe those costs are what it takes to achieve high-quality schools. There are also some less obvious examples, such as the fact that school districts with high-performing magnet schools spend considerably more on these schools of choice than they do on their regular neighborhood public schools. Or that highly acclaimed charter school networks like KIPP spend several thousand dollars more per pupil than do the other public schools in their districts. Some urban charter schools, aiming not only to recruit excellent teachers but also to keep them beyond the typical burnout period, are advertising teacher salaries above $100,000. Administrators in these schools of choice know that successful schools need resources to produce successful students.

Simply put, providing 13 years of quality education for every student in the country costs a lot of money. It makes sense to be astonished when faced with the figures, as it makes sense to be angry and to demand action when there are reports of wasted education funds. It does not make sense, however, to argue that because we are spending a lot, we are spending too much. That claim is heavily value-laden and would require a good deal of additional data to support it—data that never seem to materialize. And just because some administrators and teachers make bad decisions about how to use resources, it is also illogical to conclude that our education system, in general, is inefficient or our educators, in general, are unmotivated. Despite the rants of some politicians and business leaders, we have ample evidence that money matters in education. What we do not have is evidence that the alternatives offered by these folks, particularly the extensive use of high-stakes standardized testing, do anything to produce more successful teachers or students. In fact, the most educationally successful countries are substantially limiting the amount and uses of standardized testing.

We should continue to strive for more efficient uses of our education funds, and for more innovative ways to motivate students, involve parents, and support teachers. At the same time, we should be wary of the misinformation and rhetoric coming from the "money doesn't matter" brigade, especially because they and their children benefit immensely from their own ability or their community's willingness to spend generously on their children's education.

References

Baker, B. D. (2012). *Revisiting that age-old question: Does money matter in education?* Washington, DC: Albert Shanker Institute. Retrieved from www.shankerinstitute.org/images/doesmoneymatter_final.pdf

Darling-Hammond, L. (2010). *The flat world and education: How America's commitment to equity will determine our future.* New York, NY: Teachers College Press.

Gates, B. (2011, February 28). How teacher development could revolutionize our schools. *The Washington Post.* Retrieved from tinyurl.com/47mxu7e

Hanushek, E. (1986). Economics of schooling: Production and efficiency in public schools. *Journal of Economic Literature, 24*(3), 1141–1177.

Heilig, J. V. (2013). *Top ten list: Why "choice" demonstrates that money matters.* Retrieved from tinyurl.com/qadz3rn

Hoover, T. (2011, December 11). Denver judge's ruling on school funding levels blisters state's witnesses. *The Denver Post.* Retrieved November 17, 2013 from www.denverpost.com/ci_19520710

Lobato v. State of Colorado. Retrieved from www.coloradoattorneygeneral.gov/departments/state_services/education/lobato

Rothstein, R. (2011, March 11). *Fact-challenged policy.* Washington, DC: Economic Policy Institute. Retrieved from tinyurl.com/4zwkrsb

❧ MYTH 36 ❧

The money available to school districts is spread equally across their schools.

Despite our many disagreements about education, Americans are unified in embracing the ideal of equal educational opportunity. Education is one hallmark of our nation's promise that anyone who is willing to work hard can be successful here. This ideal is codified in nearly every state constitution, with the promise that all children are entitled to an adequately and equitably funded K–12 education. In practice, however, the principle of equal funding is almost universally violated. Beyond the huge variations in spending that exist between states, similar gaps exist between districts within states and even between schools in the same district. Why do these disparities exist? How do they affect different subgroups of students?

First, it is important to note that, on average, school districts get about 48% of their funds from the state, about 44% from local sources, and about 8% from the federal government. Decisions about how schools should be funded take place at the state and district levels; the federal government distributes primarily "categorical" funds, to be used for mandated programs such as special education and free and reduced-price meals. This is one reason that there is resentment by many school districts about the greater role the federal government has had in school politics over the past 20 or so years. In addition to the widespread philosophical belief that the federal government should have little to do with education, which is a state and local responsibility, is the clear fact that the federal government does not pay for much of the costs of education.

Some variations in spending between states are caused by simple differences in wealth. Others occur because of more nuanced factors, like differences in public will to support other people's children. Political pressure to slash school funding seems to be particularly strong in areas where the population is aging and fewer families have children in public schools. There is similar political pressure in places where public school students are increasingly "minorities." Some argue that it is only natural that residents would be primarily interested in supporting their own children and grandchildren, rather than being concerned about the education of all children. But it would be only "natural" to curtail public education for all citizens if education was seen as a private good, a possession of an individual, and not a public good, something that serves the broader community (see Myth 38).

State-to-state funding differences also reflect often-ignored factors like population density. Since the bulk of educational funding goes for teachers, highly rural states with many small classes have to spend considerably more than highly urban states, with populations that allow for full classrooms. Demographic differences like these usually are overlooked in the battles raging between progressives and conservatives over school funding. Teachers' unions in urban states often point to states like North Dakota as examples of places that "truly care" about education. In truth, more education funding simply may reflect inconvenient necessities rather than admirable values.

Perhaps the most important variations in funding exist between districts in the same state. Because child poverty rates are so high (nearly half of our nation's children qualify for free or reduced-price meals because their families live dangerously close to the national poverty line) and because poverty is so concentrated within particular districts, states face a significant challenge when it comes to figuring out how to provide adequate and equitable funds across highly segregated districts. Facing the additional challenge of strong political pressure to balance budgets by cutting school funding, state lawmakers typically pass legislation giving all schools a very low baseline level of per-pupil funding and then allowing districts to supplement those funds through voter-approved local taxes or bond sales. Inevitably, "have-not" districts end up with far fewer per-pupil funds than "have" districts.

Across the country, this approach to fulfilling the promise encoded in state constitutions has resulted in a now predictable outcome, with what have come to be known as "school finance" court cases. Only five states have never had a school finance court case, and in 2010, 13 states had such cases pending. Court decisions on equitable funding have favored plaintiffs 3-to-2 when systems of unequal funding were challenged. But change, even in these states, has come slowly if at all. Rather than wholeheartedly seeking equitable systems of funding, if for no other reason than to avoid lawsuits, nearly all states instead have found ways to both legislate equity and then allow exceptions that promote inequities once again.

The resulting funding disparities play out in a number of ways that have a high level of impact: Wealthy districts can attract and retain more highly trained and experienced teachers, reduce class sizes, and provide students with support to learn English as a second language, deal with family-related challenges, and access future educational opportunities and scholarships. Poor districts find themselves with fewer and fewer resources to serve increasingly high-needs student populations. The educational opportunities, outcomes, and future prospects of students in these two types of districts are decidedly unequal.

While state-level funding plans have at least come under some scrutiny, disparities between schools in the same district are seldom discussed. The most striking source of these inequalities is district allocations of federal and state categorical funds. The federal government requires per-student expenditures at Title I schools to be at least 90% (not 100%) of those at non–Title I schools. Districts thus have some discretion on how to allocate Title I funds between schools and can allow some of those funds to actually exacerbate rather than remedy funding disparities. Moreover, districts can demonstrate "equality" by allocating an equal number of teachers to each school of a certain size. But the "value" of these teachers can be highly unequal. That is because experienced teachers tend to go to low-poverty schools, and novice teachers tend to go to schools that serve the poor. Since experienced teachers cost far more than new teachers, the amount of funding allocated to schools can be vastly different.

Beyond these district-level decisions, local inequities also stem from differences in wealth between school communities. School foundations, which allow parents and other community members to make tax-deductible donations to a particular school, often can raise enough funds to buy iPads and other technology; support athletic teams, debating clubs, and college scholarships; and provide peer counseling or career readiness programs. For example, through its foundation, one small Marin County, California, elementary school of approximately 250 students supplements state and local funding generously. Over $1 million a year in "extra" funds come from the parents of students attending that public school. California will provide about $8,500 per child to this and every other school in the state. But this particular school actually is spending about $12,500 per child. Such sources of funding are obviously unavailable to schools located in poorer neighborhoods.

All this matters not only because it demonstrates a disturbing breach of our national ideal of equal educational opportunity, but because it is inextricably linked to our country's educational and economic success. Countries like Finland, South Korea, and Singapore have demonstrated great educational progress and economic growth by addressing educational inequalities head-on (Darling-Hammond, 2010). As Joseph Stiglitz (2013) recently wrote in *The New York Times*, "Singapore realized that an economy could not succeed if most of its citizens were not participating in its growth. . . . By understanding that children cannot choose their parents—and that all children have the right to develop their innate capacities—it created a more dynamic society."

Our nation was built on that same aspiration of a dynamic society, where social mobility is the rule rather than the exception. Yet sadly, it is now known that social mobility is greater in many other countries than in our own. The great American faith that you can be anything you want to be, and that your parents' income is not your destiny, may always have been more mythical than real, but it seems less true now than it may have been previously (Berliner, 2012). If our national aspirations are to be promoted, we must develop an equitable approach to school finance. No matter what reforms we propose, whether new standards or charter schools or merit pay, schools simply cannot succeed unless they have adequate funds to meet the promise we keep making and breaking: high-quality educational opportunities for all students.

References

Berliner, D. C. (2012). Effects of inequality and poverty vs. teachers and school-ing on America's youth. *Teachers College Record, 116*(1). Retrieved from www.tcrecord.org/content.asp?contentid=16889

Darling-Hammond, L. (2010). *The flat world and education: How America's commitment to equity will determine our future.* New York, NY: Teach-ers College Press.

Stiglitz, J. E. (2013, March 18). Singapore's lessons for an unequal America. *The New York Times.* Retrieved from tinyurl.com/ph7folb

⤙ MYTH 37 ⤚

In America, public money is not used to support religious schools.

Religious schools actually are receiving large amounts of government money. Or, they receive money that should be the government's, such as the money that flows to religious schools in the form of tax credits (see Myth 39). A little history is needed to understand why.

As the Union was formed, one of the lessons learned from its ties to Europe was that government and religion should be kept separate. This was enshrined in the First Amendment to the Constitution, in language known as the establishment clause. It states simply that "Congress shall make no law respecting an establishment of reli-gion." It is followed immediately by the free exercise clause: "or pro-hibit the free exercise thereof." Through more than 200 years of court interpretation, these statements have come to mean that government should not fund or provide other support for religious activities, but it also must not interfere with them, and should always try to accom-modate them, remain neutral toward them, and avoid endorsement or coercion.

In the first century and a half of our nation, the establishment clause was largely ignored, since the country increasingly saw itself as a Protestant Christian nation. Public Protestant prayers and public support for Protestant groups were common. Public schools frequent-ly were run by ministers and their families, often the most literate citizens in small-town America. Ties between churches and public schools were strong, in part because the Protestant revolution was also about literacy, so that teaching everyone to read was both a secular and a national goal.

But America changed. The immigration pattern shifted from Protestant England and the Nordic countries, to Catholic Ireland, Poland, and Italy, with a rise, as well, in Jewish immigrants. These new arrivals to the country came at about the same time the public school movement also took off. It was not long before the Catholics in particular rebelled against the distinct Protestant bias of the public schools. They began to establish their own schools and tried to obtain public monies. Anti-Catholic sentiment was strong, and their attempts were vigorously rejected.

President Ulysses S. Grant, among others, attacked those (mainly Catholics) who wanted government support for schools run by religious organizations. Coming from a perspective where Protestant teaching was the unquestioned norm, he called for the defense of public education "unmixed with sectarian, pagan or atheistical dogmas." Grant declared that "Church and State" should be "forever separate." Religion, he said, should be left to families, churches, and private schools devoid of public funds.

These sentiments were widely shared. But Protestants were still scared that Catholic schools would receive some public money. So individual states began crafting their own legislation to prevent this. These efforts usually took the form of so-called Blaine amendments to state constitutions, named for Congressman James Blaine who tried and failed to get a federal constitutional amendment specifying more clearly the meaning of the First Amendment. Thirty-nine states have their own, rather clearly stated Blaine amendments in their constitutions, supplementing the U.S. Constitution. In these state constitutional amendments, public money simply was forbidden from being used by religious schools, and the legislation usually specified that there would be no funding for private nonreligious schools as well.

Over time, Protestant teaching decreased in public schools, and the federal Constitution's establishment clause and state constitutions' Blaine language became more consistent with a neutral, hands-off approach to religious teaching. Almost a century of adherence to these laws is the basis for the myth that in the United States public money does not support religious schools.

In recent decades these "establishment laws" have come under attack by some powerful Catholic and Protestant religious leaders, now joined together in their attempt to get public money for their schools. They also have the support of many conservative legislators. The result of this alliance is that a great deal of money that is, or should be, public money is diverted to sectarian purposes.

An example of a Blaine amendment is in the Arizona constitution. It declares, "No tax shall be laid or appropriation of public money made in aid of any church, or private or sectarian school." As is true in most states, the law appears to be quite clear. Yet in 2012, Arizona provided more $11 million in tuition tax credits for the people and corporations who donated to the Arizona Christian School Tuition Organization (STO). The Episcopal STO received more than $1 million in donations for which additional tax credits were handed out. Two Catholic STOs received about $9 million combined. And a Jewish STO received about $1.5 million in tax credit eligible donations ("Private School Tuition," 2013). Nonsecular private school STOs also received many millions of dollars that would have been included in taxes paid to the state if the intent of the state's constitution had been followed.

But ways to circumvent the laws have been found and upheld by various courts and legislatures (Welner, 2008). In the short time this Arizona program has existed to support private (mostly religious) schools, the money *not* paid as taxes has totaled more than a half-billion dollars. To add to the concern the public might have with this circumvention of the state and federal constitutions, the leaders of two Christian and one secular STO earned about $100,000 each in salaries to administer these funds. Furthermore, although the selling point of these STOs is to provide scholarships to private schools for children who are poor (family incomes under 185% of the federal poverty level), the vast majority of scholarships offered did not go to poor children. In fact, a large percentage of scholarship support went to families earning more than 340% above the poverty level. During the first 3 years of Arizona's program, most of the scholarships went to children who already were enrolled in private schools (Wilson, 2002); thus, money collected by Arizona's STOs was subsidizing parents already able to afford private schools.

Arizona's experience is not unique. The Supreme Court ruled that the Cleveland, Ohio, vouchers (direct payments to parents for their children's religious schooling) did not violate the federal establishment clause (*Zelman v. Simmons-Harris*, 2002). Given friendly courts, no STOs were even needed as a work-around to state and federal constitutional prohibitions on such expenditures. Government funds in Ohio now pay directly for tuition at private schools. Ninety-six percent of the students who initially received these vouchers in Cleveland were already in private religious schools.

Legislation in Indiana that allows for religious school support has been upheld by the Indiana Supreme Court, despite the Indiana constitution's ban on tax aid to religion. In New Jersey, the authority for school bonding has allowed its governor to allocate around $11 million to two religious schools. The Princeton Theological Seminary is to receive a small allotment, with the lion's share of the money going to Beth Medrash Govoha, an all-male, ultra-Orthodox religious institution that discriminates in its admissions policy and provides a narrow curriculum based on Talmudic scholarship.

In addition to an increasing number of states using voucher and tax credit policies to support religious education with public funds, or with funds that should have gone into public coffers, longstanding policies have provided state aid for religious institutions. Title I teachers and assistance for students' special needs are provided in many states to religious schools. Public support is also provided because the government exempts religious organizations from property taxes and other taxes; as with any charitable donation, it provides tax subsidies (deductions) for donated money that supports these schools. When all this aid is added together, the myth is dispelled: Religious schools do in fact receive quite a bit of government financial support.

Why worry? One reason is that the diversion of existing public school resources to private schools results in taxpayer support for all kinds of religious instruction at all kinds of religious schools, with little or no oversight by states or the public. When taxpayer money goes to public schools, we tie that funding to standards, protections, and accountability. But there are few, if any, strings attached when taxpayer money goes to private schools. These institutions are, for example, free to choose textbooks that provide instruction on subjects such as biology, chemistry, history, and economics that are not just religiously influenced, but factually incorrect. The curriculum materials, supported in part with public money, may reject evolutionary theory or teach Christian dominionism, a belief that America was meant to be a Christian theocracy.

Exclusionary practices at private religious schools are also a concern. Parents who wish to enroll their child in an admired religious school may not be able to do so. Children of gay or lesbian parents also may be rejected. At the most basic level, religious schools often mandate religious curricula and prayer, making them unsuitable for students who might want to attend a school but do not share the school's religious beliefs. Nonreligious children are simply not welcome at such schools. Even the short history of support for religious schools teaches us that they need not, and usually do not, provide services to students with disabilities or who require English language instruction. As a result, many students effectively will be unable to participate in publicly supported religious schools, even though these programs often are sold to the public as a way to increase "parental choice."

The transfer of taxpayer dollars from public schools to religious schools comes with minimal transparency and oversight. Thus, many of the approved voucher- and STO-supported religious schools are exempt from requirements to report on, and be accountable for, student performance. Private schools that would be considered "failing" under public school accountability plans often continue to receive taxpayer dollars.

The trend is clear. Despite the intent of the federal Constitution and state constitutions, America is increasing its legislative and fiscal support of religious schools.

References

Private school tuition organization income tax credits in Arizona: A summary of activity fy 2012. (2013). Phoenix: Arizona Department of Revenue. Retrieved from tinyurl.com/ps9pz4b

Welner, K. G. (2008). *Neo vouchers: The emergence of tuition tax credits for private schooling*. Lanham, MD: Rowman & Littlefield.

Wilson, G. Y. (2002). *The equity impact of Arizona's education tax credit program: A review of the first three years*. Tempe, AZ: Education Policy Studies Laboratory, Arizona State University. Retrieved from epsl.asu.edu/epru/documents/EPRU%202002-110/epru-0203-110.htm

Zelman v. Simmons-Harris. (2002). Retrieved from tinyurl.com/p8s9pts

⇜ MYTH 38 ⇝

Education benefits children individually, not the public in general; so supporting education for all past a minimal level— 8th grade or 12th grade, say—is hardly justifiable.

The myth of education as a private not a public benefit is one of the most pervasive and influential myths about public education in the United States, and one of the least often discussed. Its invisibility is especially dangerous, since it has to do with the most fundamental questions: What is public education for? Whom does it serve? Who gains from a public education?

Debates about the adequacy of public schooling in the United States today assume many things about the purposes of education, two of which are discussed here. One is that education is important mainly to make children more employable. That is, education is primarily to enable students to make a living by teaching work-related skills. Thus, education benefits society as a whole by helping to sustain or grow the economy.

A second and even more deeply held assumption is that parents have the primary responsibility for shaping their children's character and instilling values (e.g., moral and religious ideals), and to do so as they see fit. Within certain limits we think it is appropriate for parents to teach their children about right and wrong, how they should treat others, what they should believe about God, and how to define personal success.

Leaving aside discussions of other assumptions about education, these two alone combine to form the prevailing picture of the purposes of public education in this nation. *If* it is *inappropriate* for schools to teach values that are more properly the prerogative of parents, *and* the main goal of schooling is to prepare children for employment, *then* it seems fairly obvious that the focus of schooling should be basic skills—the three Rs—early on, with perhaps a focus on more technical skills in later grades. Carl Bereiter, for example, argued something along these lines in his 1973 book *Must We Educate?* Apart from teaching basic skills and providing affordable child care for working parents, Bereiter suggested that it is morally problematic and practically dangerous for schools to try to influence children such that they become adult citizens of a particular sort. He also takes this to mean that schooling beyond a certain minimal threshold (perhaps 6th or 8th grade) is unnecessary, at least at any cost to taxpayers.

The views Bereiter expressed in *Must We Educate?* (which most likely have changed in the decades since the book appeared) are perhaps more extreme than those held by most Americans, who are quite used to the idea of compulsory schooling up to age 16, fully funded schooling through high school, and publicly subsidized postsecondary education. Yet Bereiter's assumptions about the purposes of public education have grown more common. They are now part of a widespread shift in the perception of public education as serving private individual interests rather than the public good.

When we refer to schools as *public,* we mean that they are funded through taxes and that all children may attend them, regardless of wealth, disability, and so on. This notion of public is very different from what was in the heads of those who helped established compulsory public schooling through much of U.S. history. After the Revolutionary War, when public education was supported by leaders such as Thomas Jefferson and John Adams, and later, with such advocates as Horace Mann and Booker T. Washington, public education was regarded as an integral part of the American experiment in political democracy. Drawing on a notion of the *public good* with roots in the works of Rousseau, and in the ancient world in the works of Aristotle, Jefferson and others conceived of a public good *that is more than the sum of the interests of individuals.* Public education was promoted as an essential venue where citizens learned solidarity with others, as well as the skills and dispositions that enable them to reason across differences to discern what is in the interest of the community as a whole.

In the 20th century, a major shift occurred in the understanding of democracy prevailing in academic circles and in the general public. The shift was from a vision of members of the public deliberating together and coming to decisions about the common good, to democracy as a means whereby private preferences of individual citizens compete to determine policy for all. The contemporary U.S. political system seems less about compromise and cooperation, and more like a winner-take-all game. This has influenced educational thinking as well. Today, perhaps a majority of those on the political and cultural Right, with support from many on the Left, share the view that the primary purpose of public schools is to benefit individuals irrespective of the well-being of the community. Insofar as the benefits of schooling exceed those that accrue primarily to the individual (e.g., employability, emotional well-being, or self-actualization), these benefits often are talked about by economists as "neighborhood benefits" (Friedman, 1955). When the politicians speak of the risk that our "failing" education system poses for our economic competitiveness, this appears to be a conception of the common good being upheld. But that belief by many politicians and economists is embedded in an economic theory that a failing education system hurts my neighbor's private interests, not that it hurts something ephemeral like the common good. My being employable is obviously good for *me* in an individual way—yet, if you are an employer, then my employability also benefits *you* (in your own individual way). We all benefit, but we all "do so separately" (Feinberg, 2012, p. 10). This is a subtle, but nevertheless pernicious, undermining of what we mean by the public good.

A *public good* is a very different sort of thing from having neighborhood effects. Public goods benefit us all together, as a collective rather than as private individuals or private companies. What is in the public interest is what serves the American people as a political entity in its own right. The idea that "we're in this together" means not only that each individual's welfare is bound up with the welfare of others (which is to a large extent true, of course) but that there is a "we" that can be helped or harmed by our various policies and practices. This "we" is greater than the sum of private interests.

The myth that schooling is primarily (or exclusively) an individual good is dangerous. It ignores the essential role of public schooling in our still-young experiment in political democracy, (almost) unprecedented in the history of human societies. The loss of a sense of the public as more than the collection of interests of its constituent members leads some citizens to worry about the "nanny state," a bloated and overly bureaucratic government attempting to make the lives of citizens better at others citizens' expense. The loss of the sense of "we-ness" that comes with some common identity and a sense of our shared fate supports competitive individualism as the driving force for policy (Glass & Rud, 2012).

What justifies taking from one to benefit another? Why should I be taxed to support the private interests of "other people's children"? What right does the government have to try to influence my children to become people of a particular sort? Consideration of neighborhood effects will justify only a very limited amount of schooling. This is a problem because it ignores the fact that, in a democracy, our survival and well-being very much depend on our ability to respond *together* to the challenges we face as a society.

If we reject the myth of public education serving only private interests, we stand a chance to return to America's "deep democratic tradition" (West, 2004). Education in the service of the public good is what enables effective participation of citizens in the activities of self-governance. This requisite level of education is what Amy Gutmann (1987/1999), in her book *Democratic Education*, refers to as the "democratic threshold." In a democracy, the public interest involves having *all* citizens capable of participating meaningfully in politics—in Gutmann's phrase, "the *conscious* social reproduction of society" (p. 287, emphasis added). The educational threshold for the nation that our founding fathers envisioned is whatever skills, dispositions, and knowledge are necessary for meaningful participation in democratic decisionmaking. Such a threshold almost certainly will include training in "basic skills" of the sort emphasized by Bereiter (1973) and mandated by the No Child Left Behind Act of 2001, but it will go much further, as did Scardamalia and Bereiter (1994) in their creation of classroom-based, computer-assisted learning communities involving a high level of dialogue, conversation, discussion, and collaboration about the *group's* goals, values, and the quality of its work. Their computer-supported intentional learning environments project promotes both deep and democratic learning.

Aristotle thought that the ability to *reason* well was the basis of participation in democratic life—an ability he thought not all people were likely to develop. The Roman philosopher and statesman Cicero, some centuries later, argued by contrast that this was a capacity available to *all* citizens (Feinberg, 2012). Today, scientific inquiry and expertise have replaced to some extent the role that Aristotle and Cicero saw for reason in public deliberation. This leads to a sense that the average citizen must know an awful lot to form an opinion and participate fully in the life of the political community. A democratic education clearly must go far beyond "basic skills"; indeed, some college education may be essential for reaching the democratic education threshold in a modern, pluralistic society like our own.

The myth that public education in the United States is primarily a private good (even one that benefits others through "neighborhood effects") leads to policies that undermine the nation's still-young experiment in political democracy. The extent to which the ideal of a public has been realized is debatable—some read U.S. history as consistently moving in this direction, despite frequent setbacks and a long road remaining (West, 2004). Increasingly individualistic pictures of the aims of education, however, and the lack of imagination that a genuinely public good can be identified and promoted, pose a major threat to the viability of the experiment. In our emphasis on basic skills to the exclusion of dispositions, knowledge, and skills necessary to participate in democratic life, we have gotten things quite backwards. Until we put the "public" back in "public education" in a meaningful way, we very likely will continue down a road that diminishes not only our children and their future, but all of us who are in this historic political project together.

References

Bereiter, C. (1973). *Must we educate?* Englewood Cliffs, NJ: Prentice-Hall.

Feinberg, W. (2012). The idea of public education. *Review of Research in Education, 36*, 1–22.

Friedman, M. (1955). The role of government in education. In R. A. Solo (Ed.), *Economics and the public interest* (pp. 123–144). New Brunswick, NJ: Rutgers University Press.

Glass, G. V., & Rud, A. G. (2012). The struggle between competitive individualism and communitarianism: The pressure of population, prejudice, and the purse. *Review of Research in Education, 36*(1), 95–112.

Gutmann, A. (1987/1999). *Democratic education.* Princeton, NJ: Princeton University Press.

Scardamalia, M., & Bereiter, C. (1994). Computer support for knowledge-building communities. *The Journal of the Learning Sciences, 3*(3), 265–283. Retrieved from tinyurl.com/o225z5w

West, C. (2004). *Democracy matters.* New York, NY: Penguin.

◄§ MYTH 39 ≈►

Tuition tax credits for families that choose private schools are appropriate, since they are spending their own money to educate their children.

There are *tax credits* and then there are *tax deductions*. They are very different things. Suppose you and your spouse have an income of $100,000—and we hope you do. And suppose that the federal income taxes you owe to the IRS amount to about $25,000 a year. If you take a tax deduction for your contribution of $1,000 to the Red Cross, that will reduce your tax indebtedness by about $250.

Not so with tax credits, an increasingly popular tool of state legislatures being used to fund pet projects. If you and your spouse live in a state with a state income tax—all states except for Texas, Alaska, Florida, Nevada, South Dakota, Washington, and Wyoming—then you can direct $1,000, say, of your state income tax to the My-Pet-Project fund and your state income tax indebtedness will be reduced by the full $1,000. That's the equivalent tax reduction of having given $4,000 to a charity and taken a *tax deduction*. Some states give that full 100% tax credit for tuition; some give "only" a credit of 90% or 65%—but always much higher than the benefit of a deduction. Tax credits have proved to be very powerful tools in the funding of politicians' favorite programs (Datta & Grasso, 1998).

Tax credits to fund "scholarships" for private schools, even religious private schools, are spreading across the country. Pushed by the American Legislative Exchange Council, school tuition organizations (STOs) are pulling in tens and hundreds of millions of dollars that are being parceled back out to selected recipients to help with private school tuition. Advocates' rhetoric surrounding the introduction and passage of the bills in legislatures is overwhelmingly about poor and minority children trapped in underperforming schools longing to escape to wonderful private schools. The reality of how these STOs function is quite different (see Myth 40).

While some voucher advocates continue to strive for conventional voucher programs, others see these tuition tax credit programs as just as good an approach, if not better, to achieving their goals. In fact, policy researcher Kevin Welner (2008) has called these school tuition tax credit programs "neovouchers."

Eleven states ended the 2012–13 school year with some 14 different tuition tax credit programs: Arizona, Florida, Georgia, Indiana, Iowa,

Louisiana, New Hampshire, Oklahoma, Pennsylvania, Rhode Island, and Virginia. Take Arizona as a prime example. Couples can direct up to $1,000 of their state income tax obligation to a nonprofit STO. (A lesser amount, $200 for individuals, can be directed to a public school for "extra-curricular activities or character education.") Since the inception of this program in 1998, STOs have collected more than half a billion dollars in state income tax monies. For fiscal year 2012, the take was more than $71 million. STO administrators are allowed a 2% administration fee for their efforts to find worthy students and award scholarships. That the worthiest students usually have proven to be those closely connected to the most generous contributors was not unexpected. One legislator who was instrumental in passage of the enabling legislation, and who also heads an STO, was discovered to have been paying himself a handsome salary in his post and to have bought two high-priced SUVs to help with the duties of his organization. STOs are growing in popularity in Arizona; currently there are 57 of them.

Large amounts of the money flowing into the STOs are sent back out to religious schools (see Myth 37). A sampling of the names of the STOs operating in Arizona reveals the close ties between these organizations and religious schools: Arizona Adventist Scholarships; Arizona Christian School Tuition Organization; Jewish Education Tax Credit Organization; Jewish Tuition Organization; Arizona Episcopal Schools Foundation; Lutheran Education Foundation; Arizona Lutheran Scholarship Organization; Catholic Education Arizona; Catholic Tuition Support Organization; Chabad Tuition Organization; Christ Lutheran School Foundation; Christian Scholarship Foundation; Christian Scholarship Fund of Arizona; Valley Lutheran Scholarship Organization; Cochise Christian School Tuition Organization.

In April 2011, the U.S. Supreme Court threw out a challenge to an Arizona tax credit scholarship program. Arguments before the court and among the justices were bitter. The court's majority ruling essentially prevented legal challenges to neovoucher laws because, it concluded, taxpayers cannot sue when the money going to the private school never makes its way into state coffers. This makes challenges to such programs, alleging a violation of the constitutional separation of church and state, much more difficult. Rev. Barry Lynn, executive director of Americans United for Separation of Church and State, was sharply critical of the ruling: "This misguided ruling betrays the public school system by directing tax dollars to religious schools. The court, with the full support of the Obama administration, has slammed the courthouse door in the face of Americans who don't want their tax dollars to subsidize religion."

Other efforts, based on state constitutions, may be more successful. In January 2013, three civil rights organizations, Americans United for Separation of Church and State, the New Hampshire Civil Liberties Union, and the American Civil Liberties Union, filed suit to block the New Hampshire tuition tax credit program, on the grounds that it violates the constitutional provision of separation of church and state. The trial court ruled in favor of these plaintiffs. Similar challenges are expected in other states. While liberal organizations are seeking to dismantle these tax credit programs, conservative politicians are working to expand them and lessen requirements for accountability.

References

Datta, L-E., & Grasso, P. G. (Eds.). (1998). *Evaluating tax expenditures: Tools and techniques for assessing outcomes.* San Francisco, CA: Jossey-Bass/Wiley.

Welner, K. G. (2008). *Neovouchers: The emergence of tuition tax credits for private schooling.* Lanham, MD: Rowman & Littlefield.

⪪ MYTH 40 ⪫

Tuition tax credits and education savings accounts are helping many poor children escape failing public schools and enroll in excellent private schools.

Full-fledged school voucher bills have failed to pass in virtually every legislature in which they have been introduced. With the exception of very limited "experimental" voucher programs in places like Milwaukee and Cleveland, the public has staunchly opposed turning a state's public school system over to a voucher system. Rebuffed and bloodied, conservative politicians have had to settle for "vouchers-light," or, as some have called them, "neovouchers": tuition tax credits, education savings accounts, and various state-funded scholarship programs (Welner, 2008).

Tuition tax credits started in Arizona in 1997 and quickly spread to 10 other states. In Arizona, taxpayers filing jointly can direct up to $1,000 to an intermediate, nongovernmental organization that then hands out scholarships to students who redeem them at private schools (see Myth 39). The amount directly reduces their tax liability, money that otherwise would have been available for roads, teachers, firefighters, police, and the like.

Education savings accounts are actual bank accounts into which the state deposits money that is withdrawn by parents of certain eligible students and spent for tuition at private schools, for tutors, and for other education services. The state gives parents the right to spend the money as they want. As should be obvious, true believers in free-market solutions to society's problems consider programs like these to be even better than full-fledged voucher programs. In fact, in 2011, it is estimated that only 70,000 vouchers were issued, but about 170,000 neo-vouchers were issued (Miron & Welner, 2013).

The school tuition tax credit movement is education's prime example of the old bait-and-switch. To get the bills passed in state legislatures, proponents of this neo-voucher had to sell the program as a way to rescue poor and minority children from failing public schools: "Get rid of $1,000 of your state income tax debt by donating to a school tuition organization (STO) so that poor children in miserable public schools can use their scholarships to choose an outstanding private education." Of course, it hasn't really worked out that way. What was sold was a hoax.

Consider Arizona, the poster child for states attempting tirelessly to withdraw support from public schools in favor of directing public money to private and religious schools. Incidentally, it is not by accident that Arizona promotes these programs. Its population is approaching "minority/majority" status and is a bellwether for the future of the United States. Currently Arizona has a plurality of old, middle-class, White retired voters. These voters are strongly motivated to slash taxes and cut support of public schools that increasingly are serving the minority population.

In 2010, the state legislature, with the help of the Right-wing Goldwater Institute, created the Arizona Education Savings Account program. In its first 2 years of operation, only students with special needs were eligible. The state deposited the equivalent of an average per-pupil expenditure into the bank account of parents of a special-needs child, and the parents used the money to shop around for an appropriate school for the child. If that school just happened to be private or religious, no problem. Who wouldn't want the best for a child with special educational needs? The program survived challenges in court in its first 2 years. It boldly expanded in 2012 so that starting in 2013 it applied not just to students with special needs but to (1) all children in failing schools, (2) children in active-duty military families, and (3) children adopted from the state's foster care system.

It is difficult to view an approach like that used to promote these neovoucher programs as anything other than a cynical attempt to insert the voucher camel's nose under the public taxpayer tent.

So how has the Arizona tuition tax credit program, for example, worked out for poor children? Have hundreds, thousands, tens of thousands of poor and minority pupils been rescued from those horrible, failing public schools, and—$2,000 or $3,000 scholarship in hand— have they succeeded in enrolling in any of the many outstanding private and religious schools in the state? No one knows.

The STOs are not required to divulge the names or circumstances of the scholarship recipients. Repeated attempts by journalists and researchers to investigate precisely how scholarship recipients are chosen, have run up against stone walls. This has happened in another state with a tax credit program as well. In 2011, the Georgia legislature adopted rules restricting even further the information that the Department of Revenue, which tracks the money going into the state's tuition tax credit program, was allowed to release to the public. In 2012, the Society for Professional Journalists' Black Hole Award was conferred on the Georgia program for the way it disguises the disbursal of funds. Hiding data is what sensible politicians do when state funds flow to those who need them the least.

Suffice it to say, in Arizona the typical $2,000–$3,000 scholarship is going to leave poor families many thousands of dollars short of covering the tuition of any of the elite private schools in the metropolitan areas of the state. Recently, only *five* tuition scholarships of between $10,000 and $20,000 were awarded at a private school in Phoenix, an amount that might cover tuition for a poor student. The many other "scholarships" of about $2,500 each were awarded to students whose families presumably could already afford private school. Small wonder that these tuition tax credit programs have been called "welfare for the rich."

One other tax credit possibility exists for Arizona citizens: a cash donation to a public school. Policy researcher Glen Y. Wilson (2000) examined the tax credit contributions to Arizona public schools stratified by school wealth. A single taxpayer could direct $200 of his or her state income tax debt to a public school for "extra-curricular activities" or character education programs, which do not work (see Myth 30). Married couples filing jointly could give up to $400. This credit also was publicized as a way to help schools that serve the poor. But the wealthiest quarter of schools in the state received more than three times as much money as the quarter of the schools that served the poor. This should be no surprise since the schools that serve poor and minority children cannot raise as much money from the families in their communities, who have low incomes and owe no income tax. With no tax liability, there is also no incentive to use the tax credit. More than 40% of U.S. families pay no federal income tax because they are too poor. The families in the communities near schools that serve the wealthy have both disposable income and tax liability. Thus there is an incentive to support their local public school, allowing those people to both feel generous and deduct $200–$400 from their tax bill. The policy provides many more benefits for wealthy children than it does for poor children, as is true of all the education tax credit programs we know. To them that have, much is given!

References

Miron, G., & Welner, K. (2013). Introduction. In G. Miron, K. Welner, P. H. Hinchey, & W. J. Mathis (Eds.), *Exploring the schools choice universe: Evidence and recommendations* (pp. 1–16). Charlotte, NC: Information Age.

Welner, K. G. (2008). *Neovouchers: The emergence of tuition tax credits for private schooling.* Lanham, MD: Rowman & Littlefield.

Wilson, G. Y. (2000). Effects on funding equity of the Arizona tax credit law. *Education Policy Analysis Archives, 8*(38). Retrieved from tinyurl.com/nspkt8j

∽ MYTH 41 ∾

Portfolio management models of schooling will increase district performance.

If you search for "portfolio management" online, your search is likely to return "Investopedia." It provides definitions related to financial markets, links to webpages sponsored by for-profit companies that aim to help stock investors make money, and a mixed bag of resources offering words of wisdom on investing. But there is another kind of portfolio management under discussion recently that has very little to do with money . . . at least in theory. That is, "portfolio management" is applied to a type of school district management model. The myth surrounding portfolio management models of schooling is that they increase district performance.

To create a profitable *financial* portfolio, an investor selects different types of stock. Diversity in selection is beneficial, as the failure of a whole sector or industry (dot coms, banks, automobiles) could wipe out a too narrow stock portfolio. This is basic "don't put your eggs in one basket" wisdom. Likewise, companies large and small may experience different shifts in stock value, so variety in company size is important too in selecting differentiated stocks for the portfolio. Investors also must determine the kinds of return they have in mind and the ideal amount of time to be spent on investment ventures. For example, growth stocks may jump in value quickly, but they are more risky than stocks in stable companies that make money and pay dividends over longer periods of time. A volatile portfolio needs more time and attention. The key is to be able to drop problem stocks without much effect on the worth of the portfolio as a whole. The goal, of course, is to make as much money as possible in the end.

Then, there's that other kind of portfolio—the school management portfolio. Some school districts (in Baltimore, Chicago, New Orleans, New York City, Philadelphia, Washington, DC) have adopted a portfolio model of district management to see whether they can cash in on better schools (and get rid of their clunkers) by diversifying school types and sponsors. Philadelphia's management model is illustrative. The district maintains multiple school types—publics, privates, and charters—backed by funding sources that also are diverse—private management, university-sponsored, nonprofit-supported, and the like. In Summer 2013, the intention was to close 23 Philadelphia public schools and lay off thousands of employees, teachers included, and invest in something more needed by the state, a $400 million prison. Mayor Nutter argued that Philadelphia's school system would not suffer from the closures because of the expansion of charter schools in the city, a part of the portfolio. Chicago in the summer of 2013 closed 50 public schools and requested charter school operators to fill the needs of the communities affected by opening charter schools in the neighborhoods.

School value, like stock value, is supposed to be measured in terms of performance, and performance is determined by student test scores. "Good" schools get more investments than not-so-good schools. Schools that fail to perform are dropped from the portfolio, which means they close. The goal in this model is to maintain the fitness of the system's overall design. Other aspects of quality, such as the role of the school in the community, the familiarity of individual students and teachers and their affection for one another, the economic benefit of the school to the community, and so on, are not part of the decisions about what to cut. Just as financial investors might pull money out of underperforming stocks, districts readjust their school portfolios by shutting down low-performing schools and authorizing new schools to replace them. In the spirit of refusing to invest in, protect, or care for schools that produce uncompetitive test scores, they divest themselves of such schools. The venture capital of the portfolio manager goes elsewhere, to charters, privates, or new public schools, in a way similar to the management of a stock portfolio.

Praise and support of a portfolio-based approach to school systems is not uncommon. Big foundations like Gates and the Carnegie Foundation of New York have demonstrated their support in the form of grants to support the portfolio system of school district management. Education consultant Craig T. Jerald believes that the portfolio model will provide "the best possible system of all" (as cited in Robelen, 2006). Bonnie S. Copeland, once known as the chief executive officer (read: CEO) of Baltimore schools, really captured the comparison between money markets and portfolio-managed schools in 2006 when she remarked of Baltimore's 85,000-student system: "This combination of kinds of schools and governance structures is enlightening and enhancing, but it is a lot to mange in terms of governance, in terms of contracts. . . . We just need to be mindful of that in terms of return on investments" (as cited in Robelen, 2006). Copeland stepped down in June of the same year, amid a "mixed picture" (Anderson, 2006) of the success of the portfolio model in Baltimore.

A University of Washington publication from the Center on Reinventing Public Education, founded by Paul Hill, details how a portfolio strategy has the promise of "dramatic student achievement gains at scale" (Portfolio School Districts Project, 2012). The way to success requires implementation of the following seven features: (1) options for families; (2) universal school autonomy; (3) pupil-based funding; (4) performance-based teacher recruitment; (5) data-driven accountability systems; (6) financial support from diverse independent providers; and (7) public engagement.

In principle, people like options and choices, especially with something as important as their children's' education. But what if free parent choice is not free for all, as described in the myths about charter and private schools? Moreover, at the center of the portfolio system is competition for test scores; keep them up and you secure the longevity of the enterprise, the school. In that case, some students are more desirable than others. Schools can ensure themselves more potentially high-scoring students in a number of ways—expulsions based on discipline policies, offering full inclusion only for students who need limited special education services, and upholding admissions preferences by, for instance, admitting students with special talents, or the ability to play musical instruments or speak multiple languages. Scores will go up too if they limit class size. Also, school location largely determines who "chooses" to attend. Finally, different types of social capital are needed to navigate the "choice" process, so parents' ability to choose is really unequal on several fronts.

And not fully explained is that with great organizational autonomy comes a lack of support for individuals who are not at the top of that organization. Remember, the portfolio is a competitive model that regards test scores as the pinnacle of achievement and school success. As individual schools do everything in their power to compete to survive, what role might trained teachers and struggling students play? Do they become expendable? Are teachers easily replaced by nonhuman resources that also *can* get test scores up, such as computer workstations? Would that be good? Or is "good" not the operative word when efficiency is wanted? Universal autonomy suggests that these kinds of decisions are up to each school leader to make. An elected school board that represents a larger and more democratic constituency has no power over such decisions.

Pupil-based funding determined by some average amount of dollars places students who are more expensive to teach at a disadvantage. English language learners and special education students require specialized resources, perhaps placement in classes of smaller size. These are expensive decisions. "Inclusion only," not genuine special education, may be the only form of service that many schools in the portfolio offer. This means portfolio schools are more likely not equipped to serve the special needs of special children. In fact, schools actually might benefit financially from deliberately being ill-equipped to properly teach ELL students or students with autism or even regular students. Thus, as we have seen with some charter operators, if instructional costs can be kept low, it allows higher salaries to be paid to the owner/operators of the charters. The ability to make a lot of money because there is little inspection of the books kept by private and charter school operators often takes precedence over more morally appropriate decisionmaking. We learned this quite clearly from the bankers and stockbrokers who produced the recent worldwide economic downturn.

Pay-for-performance and retention strategies for teachers based on student test scores incentivize teachers to care primarily about the bottom line, just as do the schools in which they work. As mentioned in Myth 11, in this kind of system the teachers soon identify "the money kids," those that can earn them a bonus, as different from those that could cost them their job. The former are sought after; the latter are avoided and resented. The performance-only classroom need not be a place of learning and discovery. Instead, the performance-based classroom can become a place of test preparation, competition, and surveillance; it is yet another marketplace in which only results that are fiscally beneficial to the organization might help a teacher retain his or her job. In short, this portfolio strategy further transforms the desire to teach children into the incentive to help students prepare for tests.

Performance-based accountability for schools has the same effect, but on the school level rather than the classroom level. And both types of performance-based incentives require the abandonment of many wonderful parts of teaching, learning, and education that are not amenable to measurement. In short, high-stakes testing, integral to the accountability plan demanded of a portfolio system of schooling, has remarkable negative effects on curriculum, teaching, and learning (Nichols & Berliner, 2007; Ravitch, 2010).

Free choice of sponsorship also means that any corporation or entity, regardless of how it makes its profits, can fund schools. Moral compromises are likely. For example, Florida Atlantic University recently named its football stadium "GEO Group Stadium." Naming rights were provided after it received a $6 million contribution from a private prison company that holds the same name. Should youth in our *public* schools be tied to Nike, Coke, Verizon, or private prisons? Are educators' sensibilities for sale because public funding is directed elsewhere?

Finally, the seventh component of an effective portfolio system is extensive public engagement. On the surface this is hard to argue against. After all, more transparency and responsibility for management of the organization is good, right? Not necessarily. Schools may be beholden to stakeholders who have financial investments that supersede the organization's obligations to parents, teachers, and children. These groups may have competing social, cultural, or community investments in their schools. In fact, the pay-for-performance part of the strategy discussed above suggests that teachers, students, and their parents must perform their roles in accordance with the mission of the school, namely, achievement of high test scores. Any other parental interests, like the arts, athletics, use of the project method, promotion of democratic and multicultural activities, volunteering in the community, and so forth, may be thwarted by the school's primary mission to which its sponsors subscribe.

Our more typical central bureaucratic model of schooling might seem rigid, uniform, stagnant, or unpromising amid the charms of diversification and competition. Yet, we should question any alternative that further segregates students, measures returns based on the promise of scores alone, and commodifies students and teachers based on the results they are able (or unable) to produce.

Further, portfolio-managed school districts so far have not reflected the amazing returns they have promised. Despite the attraction, our schools are not stocks, student scores are not dividends, and closing public facilities is not good for communities or the children who lose a part of the stability that is good for them. Our nation would be better off investing in the commons, not some Darwinian portfolio that uses narrow outcomes to direct investment or divestiture. Schools that are not working well need fixing, of course, but the market ideology that comes with portfolio management of schools seems to be undemocratic, and at this time unable to meet its own goals for achievement.

References

Anderson, N. (2006, June 20). Baltimore schools chief to step down. *The Washington Post*. Retrieved from tinyurl.com/q2yloyd

Nichols, S. N., & Berliner, D. C. (2007). *Collateral damage: How high-stakes testing corrupts America's schools*. Cambridge, MA: Harvard Education Press.

Portfolio School Districts Project. (2012, April). *The 7 components of a portfolio strategy*. Seattle, WA: University of Washington, Center on Reinventing Public Education. Retrieved November 18, 2013 from www.crpe.org/portfolio/components

Ravitch, D. (2010). *The death and life of the great American school system: How testing and choice are undermining education*. New York, NY: Basic Books.

Robelen, E. W. (2006). "Portfolio" idea gaining favor in some cities. *Education Week, 25*(29), 1–26.

VI

Myths and Lies About Making All Students Career and College Ready

In this part we deal with current education fashions, such as that all children can learn. Anyone who has ever muttered under her breath that so and so was really stupid has put the lie to this myth. It is really a fine aspirational goal. We think all teachers should believe that all children can learn everything we have to teach, until faced with the real possibility that it just isn't so. It is a myth. And because it isn't so, we need to be sure we don't make everyone take advanced algebra, or push everyone into honors English, or suggest that college is for everyone. No other nation we know believes that all of its children can learn all of what we deem important to learn. Instead, other nations, particularly in Europe, frequently provide alternative ways to live a middle-class lifestyle without advanced education credentials. We might learn from their apparent success. The pressure to make every high school graduate "college ready" has more to do with the gradual morphing of our nation's universities into corporations headed by administrators aspiring to half-million-dollar pay packages than it does with the needs of our economy. Currently, proponents of universal higher education turn a blind eye to the fact that millions of sociology and art history graduates leave college with no prospects of contributing more to the nation's economy than waiting tables.

We also find the president and many in the business community refusing to face the fact that we are already producing more STEM (science, technology, engineering, and mathematics) graduates than the nation needs. Their relatively high unemployment rate, along with moves into non-STEM fields by current STEM degree holders, suggests an abundance of American talent, although not always in the right community at the right time. More than a shortage, what we are heading toward is the creation of a glut of such workers, ensuring that the wages of these highly educated, technically able workers will be restrained.

We also deal here with myths concerned with intelligence testing, a sure way to imperfectly predict the futures of many children. We cover, as well, the myth that intelligence is fixed at birth or early in life.

This myth, in turn, generates the belief that the teaching of problem solving, creativity, and general thinking skills is wasted on the general population. This belief is wrong. Such skills are teachable to many of our students who are not now receiving a full education because we believe them to be of lesser ability.

We also cover myths about the quality that is ensured by high school exit exams. Quality assurance through examinations is not working in the ways that politicians and the public think. And for those students who have the talent and the motivation to go to college, the myth of the meritocracy may give them false hope. In many prestigious colleges, the admissions officers search diligently for children from wealthy potential donors more than they do for talented poor students. Frequently a place in the freshman class is offered the child of the wealthy over an equally or better prepared student from a poor family. You can be anything you want to be in the United States, as the Horatio Alger myth once held, but your chances are substantially better if you start out that journey with a good deal of family wealth. This belief that all can enter a good college through hard work is also refuted by data from the study of advanced placement courses—how available they are, who gets them, and how rigorous they may be. The Horatio Alger myth is wrong once again. The advanced placement deck to prepare for college and reduce its costs is actually stacked against some children, and they are usually the children who go to schools that serve the poor. Minority students take AP tests in large numbers, often with the help of "scholarships" subsidizing the testing fee from the College Board that owns the AP testing enterprise. But the catch 22 is that they fail in large numbers because their schools cannot afford to offer training sessions for the AP tests, cannot afford many AP classes, and do not have the quality of instructors that make it easier to pass the tests that accompany AP courses.

Other myths about college and preparedness for life are discussed in this closing part. As should be obvious by now, the search for black and white, true and false, clear and unambiguous findings about important issues in education is not easy. This leaves the way open for some to make statements that are not true, or are half true, or are myths—beliefs that serve a purpose—as often offered by politicians, business leaders, and school boards, and, of course, by those closest to the enterprise—teachers, their unions, and professional associations. Myths serve the purposes of the Right and the Left, the rich and the poor, teachers and parents alike.

Our goal in writing this book is to be sure that these 50 ideas we think of as myths are challenged, and to suggest to our readers that there surely are at least 50 more such ideas floating around that are not quite as simple as they first seem. Educators and other citizens—particularly those who run our schools—need to be vigilant to sort out myth from fact as they do the best they can in running a democratic, public education system, as economically and effectively as possible.

‹§MYTH 42 ᷢ

All kids can learn.
Schools can teach all students to the point of mastery.

The 1960s gave the world tie-dye, bell bottom jeans, and the Summer of Love. They gave education "mastery learning" and *Every Kid a Winner*.

Perhaps it was those heady days of liberation and love that helped disseminate the idea that every child could learn everything the school had to offer to a point of mastery. Instead of fixing the time allotted to "geography of the Middle East," with the result that some students learned a lot and others not so much, why not let the time allotment vary depending on each child's circumstances and ensure that every child master the subject? Some academics, including Benjamin Bloom (1968) and John Carroll (1963), thought it was a good idea; and a bureaucrat, Leon Lessinger, in both the Johnson and Nixon administrations made a splash by embodying the notion in the phrase and book title *Every Kid a Winner* (1970). Regrettably, outside of Alice's Wonderland where the Dodo proclaimed "Everybody has won, and all must have prizes," in the real world not every kid can be a winner.

In the first place, how does one determine the point at which a student has mastered a subject, or even a tiny piece of a subject, like adding two single-digit numbers? What on the surface appears to be a simple question turns out on further examination to be quite complex. Well, simply give the children a list of addition problems, say 20 of them, and tell them to add the numbers: $1 + 3 = ?$; $4 + 7 = ?$; and so on. Not so fast. Does a child have to answer all 20 questions correctly to have "mastered" single-digit addition? Well, no; let's recognize that no one is perfect, even a "master," and that 19 out of 20 is good enough. Why not 18 out of 20, or even 15 out of 20? Academic experts of the 1960s and 1970s actually recommended that 95% correct on a test was evidence of mastery—95% of any test about anything! We are back in Wonderland again.

Where we set the point at which we have a master will make a big difference in how many "masters" we get, and for how long these

202 50 MYTHS AND LIES THAT THREATEN AMERICA'S PUBLIC SCHOOLS

children are subjected to the drudgery of adding digits. And it gets even more complicated as we try to unravel this notion of mastery. It has been shown that among 2nd-graders, 3 + 5 = ? is much more difficult than when the problem is arranged vertically, because most instruction is done vertically. That is,

3 + 5 = ? is a lot harder than 3
                                +5

For an adult, the format with which we test "mastery" appears to be of little consequence. But on a test given in New Jersey, when students who received the same instruction added decimals in the vertical format, 86% passed. Lots of masters there. But when equivalent students added equivalent items in the horizontal format, only 46% passed. A lot of failures there. For subtraction of decimals in the two formats, the passing rates were 78% and 30%, respectively (Shepard, 1988). When slight changes in format result is such big differences in passing rates, something appears to be wrong with the notion of mastery.

Here's the bottom line to mastery learning and every kid a winner. It is immensely difficult, normally bordering on impossible, to create a test that tells us whether a child has "mastered" a subject (Glass, 1978). And even if we had such a test, if we returned a month or a year later and tested the same children, they would be arrayed along a continuum from "I can still do it" to "I haven't the foggiest idea; forgot it all." Individual differences in aptitude, memory, motivation, family support, and the like, are a fact of life that is denied at one's peril.

Why is this myth so pernicious? Because it underlies other myths about teachers and schools. If every child can learn all subjects to the point of mastery, if every child is to be a winner, then who is to blame when children fail, when not every child wins, when some children quit and drop out, when others are rejected by the college of their choice, or when the employer says, "These people are not job ready"? Obviously, the teachers are to blame, and their unions, and the administrators who failed to turn out every child a winner. If this blame game can be pulled off, then certain reformers, with their charter schools and cyberschools and value-added testing schemes, stand a chance of selling the public their extravagant promises. And if the public buys into their promises, then there indeed will be many losers.

Life has winners and losers. And it is not always fair. And there is only so much that the best teachers and schools in the world can do to help each child master something.

References

Bloom, B. S. (1968). *Learning for mastery. Evaluation comment.* Los Angeles: University of California, Center for the Study of Evaluation.

Carroll, J. B. (1963). A model of school learning. *Teachers College Record, 64*(8), 723–733.

Glass, G. V. (1978). Standards and criteria. *Journal of Educational Measurement, 15*(2), 237–261. Retrieved from tinyurl.com/o3eukvu

Lessinger, L. M. (1970). *Every kid a winner: Accountability in education.* New York, NY: Simon & Schuster.

Shepard, L. (1988). *Should instruction be measurement driven? A debate.* Paper given at the meetings of the American Educational Research Association, New Orleans, LA, April 1988.

⤳ MYTH 43 ⤳

Our nation's economy is suffering because our education system is not producing enough scientists, engineers, and mathematicians.

There is an interesting metaphor used by some who want to reform science, technology, engineering, and math (or STEM) education. They mention "pipelines," as if children are like petroleum and can be pumped through a pipe and delivered to prosperity, happiness, and opportunity. But it is not clear that what we need is to strive harder to fill a STEM pipeline. Advocates for STEM reform say our nation is suffering because our education system is not producing enough scientists, engineers, and mathematicians. This story has taken on mythical proportions, but it is founded on suspect evidence and has problematic implications.

Although this story is on the tip of many tongues, it ultimately may be more nonsense than truth. How does one even define "American suffering"? Beyond symbolic implications, how problematic is it that the United States does not hold the number one spot in this or that international competition in achievement? And while it may seem that measuring STEM proficiency and counting the number of STEM graduates and STEM jobs is a simple matter, there are significant difficulties in doing just that. Does the math proficiency of 4th-graders matter most or does the science proficiency of 15-year-olds? Should social science jobs be counted in statistics that determine the size of STEM labor demand? Should cashier jobs at Wal-Mart that require math skills be counted as requiring STEM skills? And should these jobs be counted in STEM employment statistics? Depending on one's cherry-picking skills, statistics that measure various facets of STEM proficiency, STEM worker supply, and STEM jobs can substantiate or contradict the notion that America is in imminent danger of falling behind the rest of the world.

There are also legitimate concerns about the STEM advocates' arguments that need to be confronted. Basic economic theory tells us that an increase in labor supply will decrease wages. So reforming and enlarging STEM potentially would benefit the owners of large corporations by lowering labor costs. These economic and political facets of STEM education reform likely influence some profit-seeking corporations and self-interested organizations to spend significant cash to produce STEM advocacy reports and even television advertisements. Considering the potential power of these reports and advertisements to sway public opinion, a counterargument that adequately takes into account very real definitional problems and ambiguities of the available evidence is unlikely to swing public opinion back into a better reasoned position. It seems clear to us that the science-crisis rhetoric, the claims of America's decline, and the STEM education causes of it appear to go far beyond the available evidence.

Education is considered the panacea to all sorts of real and purported problems like poverty or "moral decay," and, increasingly, the "problem" of not enough students studying science, technology, engineering, and mathematics. And with television commercials, websites, and President Obama advocating more STEM education, the story about the necessity for STEM holds a dominant position. Unfortunately, misinformation and one-sided thinking have given the STEM story undue prominence.

But if the STEM myth is not all it is cracked up to be, why do so many people believe it? One reason is that lots of money is spent broadcasting the STEM-as-solution message. From industrial giants like ExxonMobil and their lobbyists, to politicians on both the Left and Right, the STEM mantra has been preached in various forms since Sputnik launched the space race in the 1950s. Recent reports find that of the approximately $3 billion the federal government spends on STEM education each year, much of it has been used to advertise, market, and otherwise cajole students with financial incentives to study STEM (Government Accountability Office, 2012; Kuenzi, 2008). The justifications for the expenditures to produce more STEM graduates are based on economic arguments that jobs, wages, and international competition hang in the balance.

President Obama and Secretary of Education Duncan repeatedly claim that we need to produce more graduates with STEM degrees to meet labor demand. President Obama (2012) says he hears "from many business leaders who want to hire in the United States but can't find workers with the right skills." And Secretary Duncan goes even further: "The President and I believe that ensuring our nation's children are excelling in the STEM fields is essential for our nation's prosperity, security, health and quality of life" (U.S. Department of Education, 2009). The message: America's future rests on putting more children in STEM education. Thus the Obama administration plans to increase STEM education spending, create 100,000 new STEM teachers, create 1,000,000 new undergraduates with a STEM degree, and hinder STEM majors from changing disciplines through stipulations attached to financial scholarships (National Science and Technology Council, 2013). One of the central premises of the push for more STEM education is the supposed shortfall in STEM-educated workers. Here is a representative "short on STEM workers supply" argument:

> Investing in STEM education is critical to the Nation and its economic future. . . . The jobs of the future are STEM jobs: The demand for professionals in STEM fields is projected to outpace the supply of trained workers and professionals. Additionally, STEM competencies are increasingly required for workers both within and outside specific STEM occupations. A recent report by the President's Council of Advisors on Science and Technology (PCAST) estimates there will be one million fewer STEM graduates over the next decade than U.S. industries will need. (National Science and Technology Council, 2013, p. vi)

To understand the validity of this pervasive argument, we need to know the answers to three questions: Does the United States actually have too few STEM graduates now? Will the country run a shortage in the near future? And, will "shortages" cause America to suffer?

If there actually is a supply problem, it may be one of oversupply rather than undersupply. There is currently unemployment and underemployment for those with STEM degrees (National Science Board, 2012). Yes, unemployment rates for graduates with STEM degrees are lower than for those without STEM degrees. But the prevailing rhetoric is not about how some workers are less employable than other workers; it's about shortages in STEM fields that harm our economy and thus the nation. The fact that there is already some unemployment among STEM degree holders suggests that increasing the supply of STEM graduates will not address unfulfilled needs. Instead, it will decrease or eliminate the current comparative advantage of STEM workers, increasing the likelihood of more unemployment for all STEM workers and simultaneously decreasing their current wage advantage.

Also, there is a much smaller unemployment advantage when the comparison group is not everyone, but just other persons who also have college degrees. In September 2009, in the midst of the most recent recession, the unemployment advantage for STEM workers completely disappeared. "The unemployment rate of college educated S&E [science and engineering] workers rose to 5.5%, approximately the same rate as for all college graduates (5.4%)" (National Science Board, 2012, pp. 3–30).

One more easy-to-understand statistic also suggests that there is not a STEM shortage problem: Millions of graduates with STEM degrees do not currently work in STEM jobs. According to this way of accounting for degrees and jobs, there is a huge oversupply of STEM graduates. An authoritative source on STEM statistics convincingly states, "Only about 38% of college graduates whose highest degree is in an S&E field work in S&E occupations" (National Science Board, 2012, pp. 3–15). In 2008 there were more than 17 million individuals with a STEM bachelor's degree or higher, but even by the highest estimates there were fewer than 7 million STEM jobs (National Science Board, 2012, pp. 3–5). With about 10 million STEM graduates currently without STEM jobs, it is unclear how anyone, particularly our president and secretary of education, could claim that there is now or soon will be a shortage. Why would they participate in a hoax?

Advocates for increasing the supply of STEM graduates cite a different set of numbers. They often refer to a report by Georgetown University's Center on Education and the Workforce. According to this report, America will have 2.8 million STEM job openings between 2008 and 2018 (Carnevale, Smith, & Strohl, 2010, p. 52). About 2 million of these jobs supposedly will require a bachelor's degree or higher. Yet, taking into account the STEM graduates who work outside their field, there would still be approximately 8 million STEM graduates not working in STEM jobs in 2018. The bottom line is the projected shortfall numbers seem to disregard the millions of people who currently have STEM degrees but do not work in STEM jobs. And the bottom line does not even count the fact that without any expansion of the STEM education "pipeline," there still will be new STEM graduates looking for work each year. When you include the fact that in recent years about 700,000 STEM degrees at the bachelor's level or higher have been awarded annually, then concern for an oversupply rather than a shortage appears to be the more reasonable position.

The federal government is one employer that acknowledges this adequate reserve of STEM-educated workers, although those in positions to know this have obviously not communicated with the president and secretary of education. The government employs over 200,000 individuals in STEM occupations—and most of the positions are required to be held by U.S. citizens (National Science Board, 2012, pp. 3–24).

So if there was a shortage of STEM students or workers, the federal government would be hit hard. However, the authors of a government-sponsored report published in 2004 wrote, "Despite recurring concerns about potential shortages of STEM personnel in the U.S. workforce, particularly in engineering and information technology, we did not find evidence that such shortages have existed at least since 1990, nor that they are on the horizon" (Butz et al., 2004, p. xv). Some skeptics might say that 2004 was back "then," and the economy subsequently has changed. But these skeptics seem to disregard the fact that during the period that the 2004 report covered (1990–2004) there were very similar (and equally unfounded) claims about STEM worker shortages. Someone who also might know about this situation is the former director of research and senior vice president for science and technology at IBM, Ralph Gomory (quoted in Myerson, 2011). He says that worry about the shortage of scientists is "nonsense." The shortage he notes is not in applicants for jobs but in jobs for applicants.

Even if there were shortages, it might be best to increase the attractiveness of *working* in the STEM fields before trying to recruit to the field. Increasing the supply of STEM graduates by promoting STEM at the school level instead of the occupational level could induce students to choose educational trajectories that will not be fulfilling. This might account for the large numbers of STEM graduates currently working outside those fields. Managing the STEM workforce directly, via incentives such as changes to working conditions, salary, and benefits, is one possible way to attract and retain workers so that the imagined shortages can be avoided. Of course, these solutions would require businesses to spend more money, and so it is in their financial interests to give this "problem" to the education system.

It sometimes is suggested that Americans suffer from low wages because of a lack of quality education, and particularly STEM education. But because STEM jobs make up such a small percentage of the workforce, it is unclear how STEM education would increase average American wages significantly. While some research suggests that STEM jobs are *growing* fast, the absolute number of jobs is still quite small. Only a very small percentage of the total U.S. labor force, less than 5% of all workers in 2010, had STEM jobs, and this number is not expected to rise much beyond 6% by 2020 (National Science Board, 2012, 3–10). One report suggests that the increase actually will be miniscule: from 5.0% in 2008 to 5.3% in 2018 (Carnevale et al., 2010, p. 52). STEM jobs, currently available and predicted to be available, are dwarfed by sales, office support, blue-collar, and food and personal services jobs. The jobs of the future will be much the same as they are today: low-paid cashiers at big-box stores, retail sales, home health care workers, and servers at your local restaurant. Projections for the next few years suggest that about 63% of job openings will *not* require a bachelor's degree. And only a small percentage of the remaining job openings will require STEM bachelor's degrees or higher. So even if more STEM education led to more graduates with high-paid, consistent, and meaningful work, which is doubtful, there is still the issue of an economy that will continue to contain many low-wage jobs.

Whether there will be more STEM jobs in the future is not just a function of the supply of STEM graduates. If politicians and corporations decide to spend more on R&D, then the demand for STEM graduates will change. And by the simple law of supply and demand, if the STEM graduate supply increases without changes in the demand, then the wages of STEM workers will decrease. If innovation is what Americans want, then paying for more R&D is a much more direct path to this end than trying to overfill the STEM education pipeline.

Is America lacking in STEM skills and thus losing an international race? Evidence from science and math test scores, transcript analyses, and even the international distribution of Nobel prizes suggests that there is not a clear answer to this question. And what evidence currently exists, suggests, once again, that the crisis rhetoric likely exceeds the reality. Just like the supposed supply problem, the framing of the issue as one of low skills in America's graduates shifts the burden from companies to the education system. If the problem is deemed to be one of inferior education, then schools, and not businesses, are given the responsibility to train workers. But schools already seem to be doing significant amounts of training.

More and more U.S. students have spent more and more of their time studying math and science in recent years. By 2009, more than 80% of high school graduates received course credits in *advanced* science, math, and engineering (Nord et al., 2011). And not only do most students already take a significant number of STEM courses, but the trend is continuing to go up. For example, credits earned during high school have increased for science and math faster than for English from 1990 to 2009 (Nord et al., 2011). The percentage of students earning calculus credits in high school has more than doubled, and the percentage of students earning physics, chemistry, and advanced biology credits has increased more than 50% since 1990 (Nord et al., 2011). Out of 12 categories of STEM, only computer science course-taking has decreased—and even then, just slightly.

But some might argue that all this additional course-taking has not increased skill levels. So even though international tests are notoriously ambiguous about what they tell us about schools, an examination of test scores can be somewhat enlightening. Much of the publicity around internationally administered tests such as PISA and TIMSS is about how the United States does not hold the number one spot. But there are quite a few reasons to be skeptical of the claims that America's education system, including its science and mathematics education, is lacking in some significant regard. America's high child poverty rate, both relatively and absolutely, and the idiosyncrasies of each country's education system, make international comparisons difficult. But when the international tests are adjusted for social class differences in different nations, then the rank of the United States among OECD countries increases significantly, in reading from 14th to 6th, and in math from 25th to 13th (on the 2009 PISA test) (Carnoy & Rothstein, 2013). And unadjusted ranks on the other major international test of science and math, the TIMSS, were between 6th and 9th place depending on the grade and subject in 2011 (Martin, Mullis, Foy, & Stanco, 2012; Mullis, Martin, Foy, & Arora, 2012).

Berliner (2011) commented on the release of PISA data in 2006; hardly anyone noticed that the United States had 10% of its 15-year-olds scoring in the top two categories of performance in science, while the OECD average was 9%. Ten percent out of more than 50 million public school children suggests that the economy can expect an ample supply of highly skilled science students. This number is more than enough to meet the needs of the U.S. labor force, which, as noted before, has been unable to absorb all the scientific talent we graduate from our schools now.

It was true, however, that in 2006 Finland had 21% of its 15-year-olds in these top groups, and the United States had only 10%. So we have reasons for wanting to do better. But the numbers involved in the two nations are vastly different. There were then about 1.4 million youth in school in Finland at all levels of education, and 74 million youth in school in the United States at all levels of education. Extrapolating a bit, that means that Finland had about 240,000 scientifically talented youth, while the United States had about 7.4 million scientifically talented youth. And since the United States has been one of the world's leaders in the percentage obtaining a college education over the past 50 years, we can assume that a huge additional pool of scientifically talented people is already in the workforce. All this suggests that we are in no danger of being left without scientific talent. In fact, as noted earlier, we have the opposite problem: finding jobs for all this American scientific talent.

Nevertheless, the United States, while better in math and science than most other countries in the world, does not hold the number one slot on international test comparisons. So critics charge that U.S. schools are not doing enough. To some degree this seems accurate and, of course, schools, just like any institution, can improve. But while the United States is trailing some countries, it seems important to put this ranking in true global perspective in order to understand whether STEM education is causing suffering in America. One way to think that the United States ranks *low* is that it is only in the 6th or the 25th highest scoring spots in international tests (although these would be higher if adjusted for child poverty). One way to think that the United States ranks *high* is that it scores ahead of 168 to 187 other countries (out of about 193). So claims that the United States ranks low are possibly misleading and depend heavily on the definition of "low rank."

While the crisis rhetoric around STEM suggests that student performance has been getting worse over time, some evidence suggests this is not the case. Scores on math tests, and most of the science tests, on the "Nation's Report Card" (the NAEP), TIMSS, and PISA, over the past 20 to 30 years, follow a fairly consistent upward trend. Science trends on *one* of these tests, the NAEP, are more ambiguous. On the NAEP the trends are both up and down and depend on which of the three age groups tested are analyzed and how the differences in cohort composition are accounted for. Nonetheless, there is a lack of evidence that American students have lower levels of math and science knowledge than at some previous time. Of course, evidence for STEM "decline" can be found by cherry-picking one of the many indicators across tests, grades, and disciplines. But there are just as many, if not more, indicators that show improvements over time in science and math.

The evidence discussed above suggests that U.S. math and science test scores and STEM course credits earned have increased over the past few decades. While other countries such as China and Japan also have increased their numbers of STEM graduates, it is unclear how this means that America will suffer. Even advocates for increasing the STEM pipeline argue that America dominates the international STEM scene: "The United States has the most vibrant and productive STEM community in the world" (President's Council of Advisors on Science and Technology, 2010, p. 4).

More anecdotally but very symbolically, America's dominance in STEM is illustrated by Nobel Prizes in science. America thus far has produced more Nobel Prizes than any other country, and by a wide margin (BBC, 2010). Compared with the second-ranked country, the United Kingdom, the United States claims almost three times as many Nobel Prize winners. Interestingly, the only category of Nobel Prizes for which the United States does not rank first is literature. And America's lack of dominance in Nobel Prizes in literature brings us to a question of priorities.

Should expanding the supply of STEM workers be a priority? There are currently incentives for students to study STEM: At present many science jobs pay well, and a mathematician crunching numbers on Wall Street can do quite well financially. Contrast this with the incentives to, say, be a teacher or work for a nonprofit organization that operates a homeless shelter. One apparent shortage in America is in the number of highly qualified people committed to improving the public sphere. It seems more likely that individuals will understand human problems like racism and homelessness if they study literature or social science than if they study differential equations or chemical reactions. But despite the stability and well-being that result from an economically fair and legally just society, businesses typically do not promote the study of literature or social science because this form of knowledge rarely helps to increase their profits.

Picture a famous storyteller, artist, poet, musician, historian, cultural critic, or philosopher. Now imagine schools coaxing this individual into differential calculus or physical chemistry courses instead of literature or art classes. Some advocates of STEM appear to think this is necessary. Instead, we need to weigh that priority against the alternatives. Other forms of education are potentially just as important as STEM, if not more important. Influential citizens and curriculum designers don't have to agree with this value-laden statement. But they should recognize that the promotion of STEM is the demotion of other educational pursuits, and therein lies a dilemma.

Examining the implications of the demotion of humanities and social science, some have begun to push back against the prioritization of STEM. A 2013 report by the American Academy of Arts and Sciences makes the case that the natural sciences alone cannot ensure a thriving economy and democratic society. The report is worth quoting at length:

> The humanities remind us where we have been and help us envision where we are going. Emphasizing critical perspective and imaginative response, the humanities—including the study of languages, literature, history, film, civics, philosophy, religion, and the arts—foster creativity, appreciation of our commonalities and our differences, and knowledge of all kinds. The social sciences reveal patterns in our lives, over time and in the present moment. . . . Together, they help us understand what it means to be human and connect us with our global community. (American Academy of Arts and Sciences, 2013, p. 9)

Note that these non-STEM educational possibilities are about creating understanding and informed action, not about creating workers. Of course, there always have been those who say that liberal arts education is not "practical" or "useful." But there is a powerful response to this idea: Since when is learning what is true, what is good, and what is beautiful of little value? These are the problems with which the humanities grapple. Surely, understanding what characterizes the human condition is worth pursuing. And trying to solve the myriad social problems we have is at least as complex as any knotty scientific problem, requiring the best analytic minds we have. A society that does not stimulate interest in the arts, humanities, and social sciences ultimately will be impoverished. Adequate balance in the curriculum between the liberal arts and other areas such as STEM is desirable.

If children from poorer families had the kinds of education that gave them high-quality STEM expertise, this might, of course, be good financially for those who earned STEM degrees. But even then we learn that 22% of STEM graduates earn less than $30,000 a year (National Science Board, 2012, pp. 3–32). And as stated earlier, STEM education cannot be the only route out of poverty because the numbers of the poor far exceed the projections for the number of STEM jobs being created in the future. America's infatuation with education as the largest lever to ameliorate economic problems provides mostly false hope. Mere education, regardless of whether it is geared toward STEM or humanities, will not solve the structural problems that contribute to unemployment, underemployment, and poverty. STEM, as a solution to poverty, might be just another distraction, a drop in a bucket full of holes rather than a real solution.

We also should think about STEM education this way: When STEM education is envisioned, designed, and justified by its relationship to employment outcomes, it is a form of job training. If the *raison d'etre* for STEM education is to increase wages and increase employment, then it should be called job training, not education. Education, unlike mere job training, provides students the knowledge and skills to, say, critique the structure of the labor market, as opposed to just being grist for the economic mill. Schools should help students think critically, even skeptically, as a good scientist should, about the global economy, the STEM labor market, and STEM education. But instead of this critical consciousness-raising, much of the STEM rhetoric implies that schools should aim to get students to accept the "requirements" of the labor market and should cram the skills "required" by the economy into their heads.

But it does not have to be that way. STEM education and STEM occupations can be reformed to be more attractive to all students. There are no barriers inherent in STEM education and STEM work that keep students from achieving their personal dreams while also promoting economically just outcomes. But creating interest through campaigns that are motivated mostly by economic interests, instead of scientific and democratic interests, may not be the best recruitment policy. STEM work as a cultural activity that promotes democracy and humanity seems a much better platform for recruitment. Targeted reforms in society as well as in STEM recruitment and working conditions seem more justifiable than what is advocated in the crisis rhetoric calling for a wholesale increase in STEM quantity and quality. For instance, removing the structures that lead to disproportionate representation of women and people of color in certain STEM fields could be a priority. Providing some continuity of employment for STEM workers, instead of hiring STEM workers for projects and dismissing them at project's end, could be a worthy goal. Hiring talented STEM instructors to fill full-time positions in America's colleges and universities, instead of employing them as nontenure-track adjuncts, would help as well.

John Dewey argued that education should produce a scientific approach to knowing and changing the world. This scientific way of knowing would likely improve politics, policy, the economy, and life in general. The focus on the technical skills wanted by employers, or the focus on producing work-oriented scientists and mathematicians, is not what Dewey had in mind. So let us not lose sight of the fact that our nation needs to balance STEM education with other pursuits to promote democracy and economic well-being for all.

The oversupply of STEM graduates and the continued improvement of U.S. students' STEM skills suggest that STEM-mania is based on some false premises. The idea that our nation is suffering because our education system is not producing enough scientists and engineers is a myth. And the myth overwhelms the more desirable goal of seeking a balance between STEM education and so many of the other subjects worthy of our study.

References

American Academy of Arts and Sciences. (2013). *The heart of the matter.* doi:10.1002/jhm.2048

BBC. (2010). Which country has the best brains? *BBC News Magazine.* Retrieved from www.bbc.co.uk/news/magazine-11500373

Berliner, D. C. (2011). The context for interpreting PISA results in the USA: Negativism, chauvinism, misunderstanding, and the potential to distort the educational systems of nations. In M. A. Pereyra, H.-G. Kotthoff, & R. Cowan (Eds.), *PISA under examination: Changing knowledge, changing tests, and changing schools* (pp. 77–96). Rotterdam, The Netherlands: Sense Publishers.

Butz, W. P., Kelly, T. K., Adamson, D. M., Bloom, G. A., Fossum, D., & Gross, M. E. (2004). *Will the scientific and technology workforce meet the requirements of the federal government?* Washington, DC: RAND Corporation

Carnevale, A. P., Smith, N., & Strohl, J. (2010). *Help wanted: Projections of jobs and education requirements through 2018.* doi:10.1016/j.nepr.2010.11.020

Carnoy, M., & Rothstein, R. (2013). *What do international tests really show about U.S. student performance?* Washington, DC: Economic Policy Institute.

Government Accountability Office. (2012). *Science, technology, engineering, and mathematics education: Strategic planning needed to better manage overlapping programs across multiple agencies.* Washington, DC: Author.

Kuenzi, J. J. (2008). *Science, technology, engineering, and mathematics (STEM) education: Background, federal policy, and legislative action.* Retrieved from digitalcommons.unl.edu/cgi/viewcontent.cgi?article=1034&context=crsdocs

Martin, M. O., Mullis, I.V.S., Foy, P., & Stanco, G. M. (2012). *TIMSS 2011 international results in science.* Chestnut Hill, MA: International Association for the Evaluation of Educational Achievement.

Mullis, I.V.S., Martin, M. O., Foy, P., & Arora, A. (2012). *TIMSS 2011 international results in mathematics.* Chestnut Hill, MA: International Association for the Evaluation of Educational Achievement.

Myerson, H. (2011). Back from China? *The American Prospect, 22*(10).

National Science and Technology Council. (2013). *Federal science, technology, engineering, and mathematics (STEM) education 5-year strategic plan.* Retrieved from www.whitehouse.gov/sites/default/files/microsites/ostp/stem_stratplan_2013.pdf

National Science Board. (2012). *Science and engineering indicators 2012: Science and engineering labor force.* Arlington, VA: Author. Retrieved from tinyurl.com/osjre44

Nord, C., Roey, S., Perkins, R., Lyons, M., Lemanski, N., Brown, J., & Schuknecht, J. (2011). *America's high school graduates: Results of the 2009 NAEP high school transcript study.* Retrieved from nces.ed.gov/nationsreportcard/pdf/studies/2011462.pdf

Obama, B. (2012). 2012 State of the Union address. Retrieved from www.whitehouse.gov/the-press-office/2012/01/24/remarks-president-state-union-address

President's Council of Advisors on Science and Technology. (2010). *Prepare and inspire: K–12 education in science, technology, engineering, and math (STEM) for America's future.* Retrieved from www.whitehouse.gov/sites/default/files/microsites/ostp/pcast-stemed-execsum.pdf

U.S. Department of Education. (2009). Duncan endorses efforts to improve STEM education. Retrieved from tinyurl.com/ndzycc9

∽ MYTH 44 ∾

The United States has had to create special passport guidelines to import scientists and engineers because our education system cannot produce enough of them.

Rumor has it that many technology-based businesses in the United States face an imminent hiring crisis. Business leaders claim that a severe shortage of highly skilled workers prepared to meet the needs of a growing IT industry looms ahead, threatening economic growth for the next decade and beyond. While this prediction may sound melodramatic, executives at several major corporations poised at the forefront of technological research and innovation have voiced precisely these concerns. They are demanding big reforms in education and immigration policies to avert the crisis. Careful consideration, however, should be given to evaluating these claims before implementing significant changes in K–12 curriculum and immigration laws that ultimately may benefit employers more than foreign workers and our nation's students. Some years back when Bill Gates appeared before the House Education Committee to dispense wisdom about reforming the nation's education system, he spent nearly the entire time allotted to him complaining about immigration policy. It seemed clear that he cared and knew less about our nation's schools than he did about finding a cheap supply of trained workers.

Recently, Microsoft executives signaled their own distress about the purported shortage, claiming that 120,000 jobs would be generated each year until 2020 that require a bachelor's degree in computer science (Microsoft, 2012). Noting that only one-third of the needed degrees are conferred each year in the United States, Microsoft predicted that the majority of these new positions would go unfilled. In reality, Microsoft projected a purported shortage by simply comparing the graduation rate of STEM (science, technology, engineering, and math) students with the anticipated job openings in the field, incorrectly assuming that only computer science degree holders can satisfy requirements for the new positions (Costa, 2012). However, more than half of workers in these occupations do *not* hold a bachelor's degree in this area, or even a 4-year degree!

Citing government estimates that there are 3.7 million jobs open in the United States today, including 6,000 vacancies at Microsoft, executives also have cited the unemployment rate of college-educated IT workers as evidence that a shortage exists (Microsoft, 2012). Reality, however, appears to be different. Microsoft determined that a shortage exists by comparing the unemployment rates of workers in computer-related occupations (3.4% in 2011) relative to the overall unemployment rate in the economy when under full employment (4% according to Microsoft) (Costa, 2012). Using this calculation as evidence for the shortage claimed, Microsoft relied on the unemployment rate for all workers under full employment rather than the more accurate unemployment rate for college-educated workers in computer-related occupations under these conditions (approximately 2%) (Costa, 2012). In this regard, the unemployment rate of college-educated IT workers is actually higher than would be expected under full employment and certainly much higher than prerecession rates (1.4% in 2007) (Costa, 2012). Claims of a worker shortage in certain occupations are becoming increasingly doubtful, especially as Microsoft and other corporate giants in the IT industry have laid off thousands of workers over the past few years or announced plans to do so in the near future.

The data on wage trends also indicate that a shortage is unlikely. In the past decade, the average hourly wage for those holding at least a bachelor's degree in computer and math occupations increased less than half a percent per year. Given stagnancy in wages, a flood of new foreign workers would only exacerbate the situation, in all likelihood increasing unemployment for American workers and preventing a rise in wages—circumstances that would be welcomed by high-tech corporations, but few other Americans.

In response to this manufactured crisis, Microsoft has proposed a series of education and immigration reforms, namely, an increase in the number of H-1B visas for foreign workers in "specialty occupations" that require at least a bachelor's degree or the equivalent, and the recapturing of an additional 20,000 unused employment-based permanent resident or green cards. They also proposed that corporations should be charged a substantially higher rate to obtain one of the visas than would have been assessed in the past. Microsoft claims that $5 billion could be generated this way over the next decade and suggests that the additional revenue could be redirected to fund increased opportunities for students, especially those at the secondary level, to develop their skills and explore potential careers in STEM. While these proposals would seem to provide the IT industry with a much-needed foreign workforce while also improving educational opportunities for U.S. students, the plan merits careful attention from educators, students interested in working in the IT industry, and the general public.

Corporations in the technology areas claim that a pipeline shortage exists because U.S. college students are either uninterested or unprepared to pursue STEM degrees. Thus the tech industry concludes that employers should be encouraged to hire "the best and the brightest" workers from abroad through an increase in available visas. But the claims of shortage and thus the need to hire from abroad are suspect, at best, and perhaps a hoax (see Myth 43) (Matloff, 2012).

The current guest worker visa program has evolved over time in response to demands from employers, politicians, and lobbyists seeking to influence the labor supply, wages and working conditions, and economic growth in various fields. While corporate support of an increase in the number of available visas seems legitimate at first glance, it is also possible that corporate motives include the ability to decrease worker salaries by manipulating the labor supply. These manipulations advantage the tech employers who have been hiring foreign workers through contract agencies. And that is a whole different story: Many of these agencies recruit young, talented foreign workers and lure them into paying exorbitant fees for their visas to work in the United States. Once arrived, the workers discover that they will be required to work long hours for below-market pay and live in cramped quarters with other workers, if there is a job waiting for them at all (Dorning & Fanning, 2012).

Claiming that the United States is not producing enough STEM graduates and that those who undertake bachelor's degrees in these areas are underprepared when leaving high school, Microsoft and other IT industry leaders blame public schools for the presumably low supply of domestic workers. In reality, graduation rates from postsecondary institutions do not support these claims (see Myth 43). Degrees in science and engineering among all U.S. citizens and permanent residents increased 29% from 2001 to 2009. And this does not include 2-year programs and technical training certificates (Dorning & Fanning, 2012). The supply of graduates remains strong, keeping pace with demand, as evidenced by stagnant wages and massive layoffs at several leading IT corporations (Dorning & Fanning, 2012). Given these circumstances, many students graduating with STEM degrees are choosing not to pursue employment in that field.

Insisting that most American students do not leave high school with the knowledge and skills necessary for success in a STEM undergraduate program, Microsoft has proposed a series of education-related reforms to be funded by increasing the visa fees paid by employers. Based on the testimony and influence of funders like the Bill and Melinda Gates Foundation, the federal government, states, and school districts around the nation are investing enormous amounts of money in STEM education at all levels. While proposals to train and recruit more highly qualified science and math teachers and to increase access to computer science courses in U.S. high schools seem rational, the use of incentives to prompt states to adopt these reforms, and the encouragement of competition among states for the necessary funding to support these initiatives, will neglect the needs of many students whose states do not receive funding. If we need more of this kind of training for our nation to thrive, and that is debatable, then it should be available to all students in all states, not just those that private corporations and the government favor. Moreover, we will be preparing these STEM students for a tech-based industry that, in reality, already faces a surplus of workers and, thus, stagnant pay levels. Nevertheless, by denying that the pipeline is full enough, and promoting ever more STEM graduates, IT corporations still seek a short-term influx of foreign workers. This can reduce the wages of U.S. scientists, engineers, and other tech industry employees (Costa, 2012). By demanding an ever fuller STEM pipeline to nowhere for our nation's students, corporations can lay off or drive down wages of current employees, many of whom are required to train their foreign replacements in order to receive their severance pay. One view of the demand for more visas for foreign STEM workers sees this as an unethical, un-American business practice, a conscious choice made by American corporations to benefit the bottom line at the expense of American workers.

Rather than demand additional visas, IT industry leaders should focus on filling vacancies with some of the 141,000 unemployed workers in computer-related occupations who are actively seeking work nationwide (Costa, 2012). An increase in domestic hiring and rising wages would serve as a market signal to U.S. students considering a career in the STEM fields (Costa, 2012). While few would argue against additional training for teachers in computer science or increased access to related courses at the secondary school level, to promote these goals under the pretense that graduates will find jobs waiting in the STEM fields is unfair at best, and manipulative at worst.

References

Costa, D. (2012). *STEM labor shortages? Microsoft report distorts reality about computing occupations* (Policy Memorandum No.195). Retrieved from tinyurl.com/cldycku

Dorning, J., & Fanning, C. (2012). *Gaming the system 2012: Guest worker visa programs and professional and technical workers in the U.S.* Washington, DC: Department for Professional Employees, AFL-CIO. Retrieved from tinyurl.com/7dg5v9g

Matloff, N. (2012). *Immigration and the tech industry: As a labor shortage remedy for innovation, or for cost savings?* Davis, CA: University of California, Davis. Retrieved from tinyurl.com/mrmmulk

Microsoft. (2012). *A national talent strategy: Ideas for securing U.S. competitiveness and economic growth.* Redmond, WA: Microsoft Corporation. Retrieved from tinyurl.com/qbpy8gy

⋖ MYTH 45 ⋗

High school exit exams guarantee that our graduates will be "college ready" and prepared to succeed as workers in a global economy.

After the launch of Sputnik in the 1950s, amid panic that the United States was losing ground to the Soviet Union, the federal government began requiring high school students to pass basic math and reading tests to graduate. This marked the onset of the high-stakes testing movement. It gained momentum in 1983 with the release of *A Nation at Risk.* This report claimed U.S. public schools were failing and blamed them for the lagging economy of the late 1970s and early 1980s. A number of states adopted more rigorous high school exit exams in response. Currently, 26 states require students to pass a test, or series of tests, to graduate. Nearly three out of every four high school students in the United States are impacted by these policies. Low-income students, African American students, Latino students, and English language learners are impacted at an even higher rate (Center on Education Policy, 2012).

The high-stakes testing movement continues to be fueled by fears that our system is not adequately preparing students to compete in increasingly global economic markets. The reality is that these fears are based on oversimplified and inaccurate portrayals of education and its relationship to the economy.

Could our system be improved? Absolutely. But these policies are not the way to go about it. High school exit exams are costly, inequitable, and ineffective. They do not positively impact student achievement and they certainly cannot guarantee that our students will be prepared for higher education and the workforce.

It is absurd to think that a high school exit exam or any other high school preparation will stop college professors from complaining about the students being sent to them. Such complaints are universal and perpetual. They reflect the prestige hierarchy of the academic world. College professors claim that high school teachers are sending them incompetent students. High school teachers blame middle school teachers. Middle school teachers blame elementary school teachers. The bottom line is that the freshman class will never be deemed "college ready" by the college professoriate.

It is also absurd to believe we can know exactly what students will need in order to be successful in the workforce of the future. Fifteen years ago, no one could have imagined the degree to which technology and globalization have changed higher education and the economy thus far in the 21st century. The next 15 years probably will be even more unpredictable. It is likely that many of the careers today's high school graduates will have in their lifetimes do not even exist currently. How can we predict all the skills these careers will require, let alone accurately test students on them?

There are, however, some skills you can bet on. Students will need creativity as well as communication and critical thinking skills to adapt to an ever-changing society. Unfortunately, high school exit exam policies and other high-stakes testing mandates force educators to narrow the curriculum, limiting their ability to nurture these skills in their students.

Another problem with high school exit exams, and high-stakes tests in general, is that it is impossible to correctly determine passing scores or "cut-off scores," as they are known in the psychometric world. Researchers have been unable to devise any rational way to analyze a test and accurately select the score that separates the "competent" from the "incompetent." Is 70% passing? Well, 70% of what? Any test builder worth his or her salt can compose a test that even someone with a PhD cannot score 70% on. So instead, states manipulate tests and cut-off scores to maintain an image of high standards but also avoid the public relations nightmare of having too many students fail.

In March 2013, the Providence (RI) Student Union prodded 50 accomplished adults—attorneys, scientists, engineers, reporters, and college professors—into taking the new Rhode Island high school exit exam. Of the 50 test-takers, four scored "proficient with distinction," seven scored "proficient," nine scored "partially proficient," and 30 scored "substantially below proficient"; that is, 60% of these professionals flunked and would not have received a high school diploma (Providence Student Union, 2013). Apparently, the Rhode Island high school exit exam and cut-off score need a little more manipulating. Talk about a public relations nightmare!

Researchers at the University of Texas at Austin recently reviewed the studies conducted on the efficacy of high school exit exam policies. Their findings showed high school exit exams are not associated with increased student achievement. Rather, these tests are linked to decreased achievement and increased dropout rates among female students, students of color, and students from low-income districts (Holme, Richards, Jimerson, & Cohen, 2010).

Despite a lack of evidence that these policies have any redeeming value, states continue to promote and put stock in them. As might be expected, private companies are reaping huge benefits while students are losing out. The publishing industry giant Pearson has a 5-year contract worth nearly $500 million with the state of Texas to create and administer the state's exams. Students who fail these tests participate in state-funded remedial instruction provided by Pearson. Those who drop out of high school and wish to earn their GED can pay to take a prep course offered by Pearson. And then (surprise, surprise) they must pay Pearson to take the newly privatized GED test (Rapoport, 2011).

Legislatures in Arizona and a number of other states recently passed an initiative that allows students who follow a specialized curriculum and pass an exit exam to graduate from high school up to 2 years early. Early graduates are then eligible to receive a modest scholarship to attend community college. The initiative is part of the Excellence for All program run by the conservative National Center for Education and the Economy. It has been promoted as a means of increasing participation in higher education. But it also may increase the gap between the rich and the poor. Many program participants, particularly those from low-income families, are expected to take low-paying jobs instead of going on to college after they graduate early. And, of course, "early graduation" means less money spent by the state to give students the kind of education that might prepare them better for the future.

The idea that 4 years of a high school education can be embodied in a single test, or a series of tests, makes a mockery of an education system that has evolved over more than a century to be one of the greatest in the world. The nation would be much better served if the billions of dollars spent on high school exit exam programs and other high-stakes testing mandates were instead invested in programs that promoted teacher and student development and reduced poverty.

References

Center on Education Policy. (2012). *State high school exit exams: A policy in transition.* Washington, DC: McIntosh. Retrieved from tinyurl.com/qd5tn9f

Holme, J. J., Richards, M. P., Jimerson, J. B., & Cohen, R. W. (2010). Assessing the effects of high school exit examinations. *Review of Educational Research, 80*(4), 476–526.

Providence Student Union. (2013). Students release "take the test" results—super majority of accomplished professionals score below diploma threshold [Press release]. Retrieved from tinyurl.com/p48qona

Rapoport, A. (2011, September 6). Education Inc.: How private companies are profiting from Texas public schools. *The Texas Observer.* Retrieved from tinyurl.com/nvvsz5g

ᵛᵛ MYTH 46 ᵛᵛ

Advanced placement (AP) courses are providing minority students an opportunity to get a head start on a college education.

Many see education as the great equalizer, the opportunity to move beyond the social class you were born into by fate or luck. College, in particular, is regarded as a gateway to opportunity. According to a definition in the *Merriam–Webster Dictionary*, opportunity is "a good chance for advancement or progress." The key phrase in this definition is *a good chance*. Simply stating that the gates are open (i.e., offering access) is not enough to ensure one will pass through the gates. Similarly, access to advanced placement (AP) classes alone does not mean that minority students have an opportunity, or *a good chance*, to earn college credit. There are many barriers to minority student participation and success in AP courses and exams. Chief among these are lack of access to AP courses and insufficient preparation for the exams when the courses are available.

AP courses are designed to provide high-achieving high school students exposure to college-level material. The ultimate goal of these courses is for students to pass a content area exam that can earn college credit. In an era of increasing college costs, AP exams offer a route to earning some college credit at little financial cost to the student and his or her family. The program is popular. During the 2011–12 school year, more than 2 million students from 18,647 schools took an AP exam (College Board, 2012). The enrolled students almost all study diligently, with the hope of earning a score of "3" or above on the exam, the minimum to be accepted for college credit. On the surface, AP courses appear to provide minority students an opportunity to get a head start on a college education. But the AP program does not fully live up to this aspiration.

AP is rooted in a history of elitism. The College Board created the program at the request of elite schools as a way to demonstrate their students' mastery of advanced topics to impress top-tier universities. When the program began in 1955–56, approximately 1,200 students from 104 schools took one or more AP exams (College Board, 2012). The program expanded annually. By 1960, there were more than 10,000 students participating in AP exams. From 1980 to 2000, the program experienced amazing growth. At the start of the 1980s, there were approximately 160,000 students participating; by the year 2000 nearly 1.3 million students took an AP exam. The growth in enrollment and passing rate continued in the 21st century. In fact, in 2012, more high school graduates *passed* an AP exam than the number of graduates who *took* an exam in 2002 (College Board, 2013). Despite the expansion of the AP program, the typical student who participates in AP remains eerily similar to the profile of students in 1956—White, upper middle or middle class, and from a suburban school.

The College Board, the administrator of AP, began actively recruiting low-income and minority students to participate in AP courses and exams in the 1980s and 1990s, demonstrating a commitment to diversifying the population who take and pass AP exams. In fact, the College Board has an equity and access policy, and offers supports such as reduced exam fees for low-income students and specialized training and tools for teachers who teach low-income and underserved (African American, Native American, and Latino) minority students. However, underserved minority students continue to participate and pass AP exams at disproportionately low rates (College Board, 2013; Handwerk et al., 2008; Klopfenstein, 2004). In the graduating class of 2012, 19.5% of students earned a passing AP score while in high school. But of this group that passed the tests, 0.5% were American Indian/Alaskan Natives, 4.4% were African American, 12.5% were Asian/Asian American, 15.9% were Hispanic/Latino, and 61.9% were White (College Board, 2013). White and Asian students were disproportionately represented in the group of successful test-takers, while minorities were under-represented. Why does this opportunity gap exist? Why are fewer minority students taking and passing AP exams?

First, minority students often lack exposure to AP. Although minority students may attend schools with rates of availability of AP *programs* that are similar to, and sometimes even higher than, those for White students, it is the case that schools with more low-income and underserved minority students offer fewer and less varied AP *courses* (College Board, 2013; Handwerk et al., 2008). For example, if a school offers just one AP course, it participates in the AP *program*, even though at a less intense level than a school that offers multiple AP *courses* in multiple subjects. This lack of course availability limits the intensity of student experiences in the AP program. The more varied the offerings, the more potential for students to find a subject in which they would like an AP course. Further, students in more intense AP programs earn passing scores eligible for college credit at a higher rate than those in less intensive AP programs (Handwerk et al., 2008). There appears to be a culture of AP course-taking, and passing, at some schools, but they are mostly affluent schools.

In addition, the quality of the courses and preparation varies across districts. Schools are facing increasing pressure to offer AP courses to bolster their reputation, but teachers are often underprepared to teach these specialized courses and, in fact, may lack extensive training or experience in the subject area. To meet the demand for more AP courses, many teachers have had to add AP courses onto an already demanding teaching load, minimizing the time and attention they can spend on the course content and with students in need of help in regular courses. Although AP courses are designed by committees of high school teachers and college professors, the delivery of a course can vary greatly from teacher to teacher. Unfortunately, for some students, their AP course offers paltry exam preparation. These issues are exacerbated in under-resourced schools serving low-income and minority youth.

In predominantly White, upper-middle-class, and middle-class schools, students often participate in a variety of preparation activities for the AP exam. In addition to AP courses, students attend extra preparation such as "AP Camps" where students sequester themselves in a remote location with their teachers and classmates to cram and practice before the exam. These types of extracurricular opportunities bolster students' confidence and better prepare them for success. Such activities are simply not as available to low-income and minority students.

For AP courses to provide minority students an opportunity to get a head start on a college education, more underserved minority students need access to more and varied AP courses, the courses must increase in rigor to better prepare students for the exam, and teachers need additional training and support to better prepare students. While the College Board demonstrates a commitment to minority student success in the program, these barriers at the local level prevent the realization of the vision. For too many poor students, AP exams represent just another experience in failure.

For low-income and underserved minority students, dual enrollment courses may offer a more practical and cost-effective way to earn college credit than do AP courses and exams. These courses, often given at a high school by a certified teacher, usually are offered at a low cost by a local community college. Rooted in the community college commitment to access, dual enrollment has the potential to reach a more diverse set of students than does AP. By design, dual enrollment courses offer students exposure to college-level curricula and learning approaches to help ease the transition to college. Perhaps most appealing, students can earn college credit by completing and passing the college-level course requirements, not by passing a one-time exam like the AP. Further, these college-level courses may be more widely accepted than AP credit. Some ambitious students have earned an associate's degree while in high school, allowing them to enter 4-year universities with general education requirements completed, essentially shaving 2 years off their time to complete a bachelor's degree.

All students deserve a good chance for advancement. The opportunity gap between White and minority students is a systemic problem that requires systemic solutions. Without more support for under-resourced schools and the students and teachers in those schools, these gaps will persist, if not grow larger.

References

College Board. (2012). *Annual AP program participation 1956–2012*. New York, NY: College Board. Retrieved from tinyurl.com/pxfqmjd

College Board. (2013). *The 9th annual AP report to the nation*. Retrieved from apreport.collegeboard.org

Handwerk, P., Tognatta, N., Coley, R. J., Gitomer, D. H., & Educational Testing Service. (2008). *Access to success: Patterns of advanced placement participation in U.S. high schools* (Policy Information Report). Princeton, NJ: Educational Testing Service.

Klopfenstein, K. (2004). Advanced placement: Do minorities have equal opportunity? *Economics of Education Review, 23*, 115–131.

ᦥ MYTH 47 ᦥ

College admissions are based on students' achievement in grades K–12 and their SAT or ACT scores.

If you type the phrase "college admissions" into Google, a plethora of websites, resources, and services will pop up that promise to explain "how college admissions works" and to "get you into the college of your dreams!" High school seniors spend a great deal of time and money choosing the "right" colleges and universities to apply to each fall. These institutions, so the story goes, evaluate each student applicant on the basis of achievement in grades K–12. In reality, every college has its own set of requirements and standards. These may be only loosely tied to high school GPA.

In reality, many institutions practice *admission by category*, giving preference to a particular group like athletes. For these high-priority categories, the competition is less fierce; hence, it is easier for these students to get in, even above other candidates with higher levels of achievement in K–12. One prominent example of this is *legacy admissions*, the policy followed by some colleges and universities that allows the children of alumni to receive preference in admissions.

Perhaps one of the most well-known beneficiaries of a legacy admission is former president George W. Bush (Karabel, 2004). President Bush was fortunate in that his senior year at Philips Academy in Andover coincided with the year Yale changed its admissions policy to give preference to the sons of their alumni on the basis of their families' contributions to Yale and American society. Although the young George Bush never made the honor roll, had only average SAT scores, and was never exceptional in athletics or in any extracurricular activities, he was admitted to Yale with the class of 1968. As the son of a candidate running for Senate and a prominent oil family, and the grandson of a former senator who recently had served as a member of the Yale Corporation, Bush was admitted to Yale.

Legacy preferences undermine the conventional wisdom that if students do their homework, work hard, and score well on their SATs, they have an equal chance of getting into any college of their choosing, even if one of those colleges is Harvard or Yale. Many admissions officers don't like to talk about legacy admissions, and stress that they are only one of a variety of criteria used to make admissions decisions. Although not highly publicized, the use of legacy admissions is widespread among elite national institutions. Among these, almost 75% of research universities and virtually all liberal arts colleges take legacy into account in their admissions decisions (Kahlenberg, 2010).

Supporters of legacy admissions contend that alumni should be granted special consideration because of their contributions, both financial and social. When a college grants admission to a legacy student, in many instances the admissions officers are hoping that this move on their part will be rewarded by a donation. Indeed, the University of Virginia, after studying one of its "development" campaigns in 2001, found that 65% of legacy alumni had donated an average of $34,800 each, as compared with 41% of other alumni, who averaged only $4,100 (Schmidt, 2007). This generosity is not the rule, however. More comprehensive research found no gain in alumni giving for colleges that practice legacy admissions, once researchers controlled for the wealth of the donors (Coffman, O'Neil, & Starr, 2010).

A new twist on legacy admissions is emerging, whereby some colleges are currying favor with donors who are not themselves alumni by giving preference to their children. These so-called "development admits" are being cultivated to increase funding for institutional endowments. Duke University, in particular, has been identified as one institution utilizing development admits as a fundraising tool (Sacks, 2007). Defenders of legacy admissions contend that wealthy families and elite colleges are interdependent—one cannot exist without the other. Preference policies allow these institutions to discriminate against poorer, nonlegacy students in favor of students from wealthy alumni, who in fact may be less qualified in terms of SATs or high school GPA.

Some critics of legacy admissions argue that it is tantamount to an affirmative action program for affluent White families. Yet, legacy admissions have enjoyed a free pass by lawmakers, the press, and the public. By contrast, race-based affirmative action in college admissions has been under attack by lawmakers and in the courts. There is a strong argument to be made that legacy admits do nothing other than benefit the privileged children of wealthy alumni. On the other hand, affirmative action offers several positive benefits, including remedying past discrimination and promoting diversity in the nation's postsecondary institutions.

So, why do things like legacy and development admissions matter? Although colleges like to say that legacies play only a small role in the admissions process and might be used only as a tie-breaker between two similarly qualified candidates, studies suggest that in fact they are providing a huge leg up to those students who are already among the most advantaged. Princeton scholar Thomas Espenshade and his colleagues found that being the son or daughter of an alumnus is worth the equivalent of scoring 160 points higher on the SAT; 160 points can be the difference between being at the median of the SAT distribution versus being well above the 90th percentile (Espenshade, Chung, & Walling, 2004). These sad facts certainly paint a picture quite different from that of the high school freshman, assiduously working away on homework and studying for the SATs, so that one day that coveted acceptance letter from a prestigious school will arrive in the family mailbox.

A researcher at Harvard University studied the admissions policies at 30 highly selective colleges. He found that if a student was considered to be a primary legacy, that is, the son or daughter of an alumnus who graduated with an undergraduate degree from the institution, that student would have a 60% chance of admission, as compared with another identically qualified student, who would have only a 15% of getting in to that same college (Hurwitz, 2011). Taken together, this research tells us that alumni pass on a great privilege to their beneficiaries simply by their birthright, a privilege that directly disadvantages the majority of students who have the misfortune of being born to Buffaloes—University of Colorado alums—instead of Bulldogs—Yale University alums.

Although legacy admissions have been around for nearly 100 years, recently a group of 16 colleges (including the University of California system, Texas A&M, and the University of Georgia) have abandoned them, joining Cal Tech and Cooper Union, which never used them in the first place (Kahlenberg, 2010). Ironically, the institutions abandoning legacy admissions find themselves on the same side as President Bush, who in the 2004 presidential campaign denounced legacy admissions in favor of those based on merit alone.

References

Coffman, C., O'Neil, T., & Starr, B. (2010). An empirical analysis of the impact of legacy preferences on alumni giving at top universities. In R. Kahlenberg (Ed.), *Affirmative action for the rich: Legacy preferences in college admissions* (pp. 101–121). New York, NY: The Century Foundation.

Espenshade, T., Chung, C., & Walling, J. (2004). Admissions preferences for minority students, athletes, and legacies at elite universities. *Social Sciences Quarterly, 85*(5), 1422–1446.

Hurwitz, M. (2011). The impact of legacy status on undergraduate admissions at elite colleges and universities. *Economics of Education Review, 30*(3), 480–492.

Kahlenberg, R. (Ed.). (2010). *Affirmative action for the rich: Legacy preferences in college admissions.* New York, NY: The Century Foundation.

Karabel, J. (2004, September 13). The legacy of legacies [Op-ed]. *The New York Times.* Retrieved from tinyurl.com/nnnjgd3

Sacks, P. (2007). *Tearing down the gates: Confronting the class divide in American education.* Berkeley: University of California Press.

Schmidt, P. (2007). *Color and money: How rich white kids are winning the war over college affirmative action.* New York, NY: Palgrave Macmillan.

✎ MYTH 48 ✎

Education will lift the poor out of poverty and materially enrich our entire nation.

There are convincing reasons to believe that education can increase wages for some, but there are even more convincing reasons to believe that education by itself will not end poverty. Education can do a lot of things, but it cannot resolve the persistent economic problem of extreme poverty felt by tens of millions of Americans. The longstanding, persistent myth that education alone can cure poverty is dangerous because it has caused schools to become overly focused on economic outcomes that will not be achieved without fundamental social and economic reforms. And the focus on the economic outcomes of education has pushed the democratic, social–emotional, and intellectual aims of education to the side. Sadly, if schools continue to be viewed as the principal path to end poverty, then genuinely beneficial educational, social, and economic reforms are unlikely to materialize and poverty in America will continue.

Ask a high school or college student why she is going to school and she is likely to say something like, "so I can get a good job." Underneath this declaration is the hope that a diploma or degree will elevate her social status, keep her out of poverty, and perhaps help her to make millions. These hopes are based on the story America has long told itself about the economic power of education.

In the 19th century, Horace Mann, known as the father of the common school, believed that public education would eliminate poverty by increasing intelligence. It has done the latter, but not the former. Shortly after Mann's ideas began to catch on, the first public school kindergarten was created—in part to address poverty. Skip ahead a century and you find that America is still trying to address poverty via education, only this time starting even earlier than kindergarten. The federal War on Poverty began implementing prekindergarten programs for poor children—Head Start—in 1964. And just recently, in his 2013 State of the Union Address, President Obama called for universal preschool in hopes that no child will get behind in "the race of life."

The policies implemented in the 1960s increased the quantity of educational resources and programs for the poor. The increase in accountability policies that now accompany these programs is defended to ensure that the economic mission of our schools is recognized. But should it be dominant? President Obama's education agenda calls for some version of making every child "college and career ready." Policymakers and pundits almost all say that schools must make students ready to compete in a global economy, one that requires "21st-century skills." Schools at every level must impart what is necessary for the "new knowledge" economy. Almost everyone seems to know what it takes to be wealthy in today's fast-changing world: education. Education is the means to a high-paying job and financial stability. The story has reached mythic proportions.

There are, of course, legitimate reasons to believe that education benefits the individual and the economy; after all, education and income are correlated. Studies have long demonstrated that people with more years of schooling make more money across their lifetimes. Although it may be less true today than in the past, there is a positive return on an investment in education: The amount of money earned by a person with an additional year of school exceeds the money spent on that year of school and any foregone earnings. Individuals with more schooling also are more likely to be employed than individuals with fewer years of schooling. So there is little doubt that schooling raises incomes and lowers unemployment for some individuals. These two hard facts seem as if they should lower poverty rates. But the correlation between education, income, and employment contributes more to the myth that education is the way out of poverty than actually happens in real life. Education will not end systemic and persistent poverty without contributions from other social and economic reforms. For example, education without capital investment does not create jobs. Education in a society with strong class bias (India), racial bias (United States), or gender bias (South Korea) does not lift all of its citizens out of poverty.

There are at least five good reasons why education is not the answer to a nation's poverty. First, education's influence is too indirect to address today's poverty. Education is largely about what will happen for the next generation, but what about the poverty felt by the current generation? It is quite unclear how the adults who currently live in poverty, say, those ages 18 and up, will have their income and level of subsistence altered by better educating today's children. The education of today's youth will likely produce some economic growth. But estimates of the contribution to economic growth made by the skills and knowledge that schools provide range from only 14% to 30% (Grubb & Lazerson, 2004). Any spillover effects from this growth on those living in poverty would be indirect, which raises many concerns. For example, spillover effects from economic growth might not happen at all: In the United States, since the 1970s, the rich have gotten richer and the poor have gotten poorer. In addition, not only is the size of any overall economic growth due to education not precisely known, but the size of the *spillover* impact is even more difficult to predict. Furthermore, spillover effects will occur only at some unknown future date. And how will that influence the more than 20% of children (17% among Whites, 35% among Blacks, and 33% among Hispanics) *currently* living in poverty today? It seems especially cruel to ask these children to wait until they finish their education to experience things like stable housing and adequate health care.

Second, the advantages and disadvantages experienced by wealthy and poor children are pervasive and all-encompassing, the difference between learning math with a tutor or a toothache. Education or wealth? Which is the chicken, which is the egg? For schools to be a powerful solution to the problems of poverty, it would help if an America absent of poverty already existed. We know that the socioeconomic status of students explains most of the variation in educational outcomes. Although there is evidence that some schools with many low-income students are academically successful, there is much more evidence that most schools do not overcome the barriers that stem from low income and low wealth. Health care, housing stability, and a host of other out-of-school influences greatly affect a child's academic achievement (Berliner, 2009). Much of the achievement gap in test scores and much of the gap in graduation rates between racial and socioeconomic groups are due to *opportunity gaps* such as access to medical care, stable housing, and freedom from discrimination. If schools alone are expected to cure poverty, then there will be lots of head scratching as those who work in schools ask over and over: "What comes first? A society with low rates of poverty so that schools can be effective, or an effective school system so that society will have a low rate of poverty?"

Third, our economy does not reward everyone's education equally. The correlation found between education and income implies (a) that income is influencing educational achievement, and (b) that education is influencing income. But (a) usually is rejected, as politicians and business leaders blithely assert things like, "The more education you get, the more money you will make." They rarely say, "The more income you have, the more education you will get."

But there are other complexities to be found in this well-cited correlation. While average educational attainment is correlated with higher income, the financial benefit from education is lower for women, people of color, and children of parents with lower-than-average socioeconomic status. For instance, in 2008 the annual median income for Asian males with a bachelor's degree was $60,300, but the annual median income for Hispanic females *with the identical level of education* was only $41,000 (Baum, Ma, & Payea, 2010). Education pays, but it pays less for those with less status.

Fourth, the nation's high unemployment rate is not going to be substantially reduced because of education. The economy, now and in previous eras, is typified by a limited number of jobs at the top, so that only a small percentage of workers are well-paid. But the economy also has a large "bottom" made up by the working poor, the underemployed, and the unemployed. To suggest that education alone can flatten this centuries-old labor market pyramid is not just unrealistic, but would be actively fought against by those now at the top of the pyramid.

Unemployment statistics, which count only those who are *actively looking* for work, have not been below about 3% in modern times. And unemployment has exceeded 8% six times since 1900. The unemployment rate during the Great Depression exceeded 20%, and the most recent "Great Recession" saw unemployment rates above 10%.

Schooling did not cause the Great Depression or the Great Recession. In fact, there was relatively no change in the quality or quantity of education between 2007 and 2009, a short period when the unemployment rate more than doubled. The idea that education can prevent the next business cycle's surge in unemployment is to place naïve faith in the power of education.

Fifth, and finally, a well-educated America does not equal an economically prosperous America. Educational inflation, which happens when more people, say, get a college degree and subsequently the value of that degree is reduced, decreases the potential for education alone to create higher incomes for all. When considering the number of Americans with diplomas and the number of jobs requiring a diploma, many Americans are already overqualified for the work available. There is strong evidence that educational attainment significantly exceeds the educational requirements of available jobs. In the 1970s, "scholars with doctorates were driving taxicabs and cooking in restaurants" (Spring, 2008, p. 30). Today, hundreds of thousands of adults with law degrees are unable to find work as lawyers. Even though demand for workers with high-tech skills is rising, there are still engineers, computer programmers, and scientists who cannot find jobs that match their skills (which in some cases were in demand just a few years ago), or cannot find jobs at all (see Myths 43 and 44).

The economy that we have right now, and the one that is likely to exist for some time, has many jobs that pay low wages and require little education. The clerks at Wal-Mart, dishwashers in restaurants near your home, housekeepers, child-care professionals, and fast-food cashiers and cooks make up a large portion of today's workforce. The job category projected "to experience the greatest gain in worker share" by the year 2020 is titled "personal care and service occupations." This includes babysitters, barbers, and bellhops, and these fields pay below poverty wages to more than half of their workers (Thiess, 2012). It is unlikely that increasing college-going rates or test scores or innovation and creativity will drastically lower the number of casual laborers, cashiers, cooks, and cleaners who make up the working poor.

The five reasons given above make it obvious that education alone cannot solve poverty. Belief in this myth is dangerous because it allows schools to lose sight of democratic, social–emotional, and intellectual goals, thereby stopping real progress toward a more equitable society. Poverty can be addressed more directly in many other ways: changing the tax structure, increasing job subsidies, reforming collective bargaining regulations, supporting infrastructure investment, increasing job-search assistance, improving the availability of bank credit to businesses, increasing the minimum wage to a living wage, reforming trade agreements, and changing immigration policy, to name a few. Each of these alternatives has various costs, benefits, efficiencies, and possibilities for success. But these alternatives offer a surer path to address the problems of poverty. In addition to reforms that could change the structure of the economy, a stronger social safety net could directly lessen the negative effects of poverty. These might include larger earned income tax credits, increased unemployment insurance, more subsidies for child care, and expanded food and housing provisions.

In sum, education must not be viewed as the only, or even the primary, solution to poverty. To believe that education will achieve what politicians lack the will to achieve is to make our schools, their teachers, and even our children the scapegoats for society's ills. Teachers alone cannot change the world, but they can care for children and they can raise students' critical consciousness about the myths we tell ourselves—including the myth that education is at the root of poverty. Once the myth of education's omnipotence is put to rest, faster progress will be made toward reducing poverty in one of the richest countries in the world.

References

Baum, S., Ma, J., & Payea, K. (2010). *Education pays 2010.* New York: College Board Advocacy & Policy Center. Retrieved from advocacy.collegeboard.org/sites/default/files/Education_Pays_2010.pdf

Berliner, D. C. (2009). *Poverty and potential. Out-of-school factors and school success.* Boulder, CO, & Tempe, AZ: Education and the Public Interest Center, University of Colorado, & Education Policy Research Unit, Arizona State University. Retrieved from tinyurl.com/pxr4hfw

Grubb, N., & Lazerson, M. (2004). *The education gospel: The economic power of schooling.* Cambridge, MA: Harvard University Press.

Spring, J. (2008). *American education.* Boston, MA: McGraw-Hill.

Thiess, R. (2012). *The future of work: Trends and challenges for low-wage workers.* Washington, DC: Economic Policy Institute.

⤳ MYTH 49 ⤺

IQ tests predict success in life. That's why schools use them to form ability groups and pick students for gifted or special-needs tracks.

Intelligence quotient (IQ) tests have been controversial since the beginning. It is important to recognize and clarify some assumptions and misconceptions surrounding success, intelligence, and IQ tests. First, we must note that there is no universally accepted definition of "success in life." What one may consider success in life, another may not.

Proponents of IQ tests often base their definition of "success" on studies showing a connection between IQ and traditionally valued outcomes like academic performance, years of education, physical health, longevity, and job performance (Duckworth, Quinn, Lynam, Loeber, & Stouthamer-Loeber, 2011). Those who would support these outcomes as indicators of a successful life believe that an IQ score *alone* can predict the trajectory of a child's life.

But it is important to note that intelligence is *not* the same thing as IQ. A good definition of intelligence, which allows for both genetic and environmental influences, is that intelligence involves the ability to reason, plan, solve problems, think abstractly, comprehend complex ideas, learn quickly, and learn from experience. It is not merely book learning, a narrow academic skill, or test-taking smarts. Rather it reflects a broader and deeper capability for comprehending our surroundings—"catching on," "making sense" of things, or "figuring out" what to do (Gottfredson, as cited in Nisbett et al., 2012).

An IQ score attempts to measure intelligence through test performance, while the tests providing IQ scores operate under an imperfect collection of assumptions. The designers of traditional IQ tests typically believe that intelligence is a single construct that can be measured by a standardized test and reduced to a number. Proponents believe that IQ tests objectively measure something real and permanent about competence and potential that can and should be used to sort people, both in school and in life (Herrnstein & Murray, 1994). Critics, however, question whether it is even possible to capture such a complex phenomenon as intelligence with a single test.

Developmental psychologist Howard Gardner views intelligence as multifaceted, with eight or more unique components relating to areas like linguistic intelligence, spatial intelligence, interpersonal intelligence, musical intelligence, and the like. He argues that there is a wide range of cognitive modes, and that very weak correlations exist among them. Thus someone could be a musical "genius," but score quite low on an IQ test because it measures only a small subset of intellectual skills (Gardner, 1983). Also in opposition to traditional IQ testing, Robert Sternberg (1985) developed an alternative theory of intelligence with three components that emphasize the importance of creativity and practical experience, both of which are lacking in traditional IQ testing. In fact, there have been three distinct research traditions working to study the nature of human intelligence over the past

100 years: the original psychometric approach, and later in the 20th century, the information-processing and cognitive approaches (Kaplan & Saccuzzo, 2009). IQ testing represents the efforts of only one of these traditions: psychometrics.

With strong disagreement about the nature of intelligence among psychologists, three questions are worth exploring: (1) Why were IQ tests first developed? (2) What do IQ tests measure, and (3) What do IQ tests not measure? IQ tests first gained prominence as a way to improve education. In 1905, at the request of the French minister of public instruction, Alfred Binet and colleagues developed the first IQ test in order to "identify intellectually limited individuals so they could be removed from the regular classroom and receive special education services" (Kaplan & Saccuzzo, 2009, p. 231). Binet believed that intelligence could be measured by testing judgment, attention, and reasoning, and questions were designed to test word knowledge and numerical skills as well. This is the psychometric approach to defining and measuring IQ.

Today, the Stanford–Binet Intelligence Scale (the American derivative of Binet's scale) is in its fifth edition and is used (along with other IQ tests like the Wechsler Intelligence Scale for Children) to assess a child's general cognitive ability. A child's IQ score is generated from questions measuring cognitive aspects of intelligence such as verbal, visual/spatial, and quantitative reasoning, as well as knowledge and working memory (Kaplan & Saccuzzo, 2009). IQ tests often are used to determine whether a child qualifies for gifted or special education services. Some schools use IQ scores in conjunction with other information, such as a child's performance in class and interactions with peers, to make these kinds of placement decisions. Other schools rely solely on IQ scores to make these decisions because it is believed that IQ tests provide impartial and objective measurement of a student's intellectual ability. However, it is important to acknowledge that traditional IQ tests ignore the diversity that exists among test-takers, and critics convincingly argue that they are biased against the poor and minorities. This reliance on what appear to be biased IQ tests for placement in schools may help to explain why low-income and minority students often are under-represented in gifted and talented programs, and over-represented in special education programs.

When you consider that IQ tests originally were designed for schools, it is not surprising that they are able predict to some degree a student's school achievement (Neisser et al., 1996). Unfortunately, what IQ tests do not measure are additional traits such as character, motivation, social skills, attitude, personality, or membership in social networks, all of which have a huge impact on a person's success in life. Ask the average person what qualities are needed to become successful in the real world, and undoubtedly many of these noncognitive skills will be at the top of the list. Scientists, however, just recently have begun to study the importance of these noncognitive skills for children's development. In his book, *How Children Succeed*, Paul Tough (2012) documents this shift by neuroscientists, economists, psychologists, and educators away from cognitive skills. He reports that scientists are coming to believe that noncognitive skills like self-control, tenacity, and resilience are just as important, if not more so, in determining a child's success. Data from the National Educational Longitudinal Study and from longitudinal studies of the effects of high-quality preschool back up this growing belief. When we look at such outcomes as college completion, earnings, and a host of other outcome variables later in life, it is the "soft skills" that determine success every bit as much as do literacy and numeracy (Deke & Haimson, 2006; Lleras, 2008).

The notion that IQ tests given to children can predict success in life 40 years later is closely related to the belief that intelligence is somehow fixed and unchanging. Malleable intelligence is an opposing idea that views intelligence as dynamic and shaped by both biological and environmental factors throughout a person's life. Neuroplasticity, the science behind this idea, has documented large changes in brain development over time through brain scans, which enable scientists to observe structural changes in neural pathways. Simply put, the theory of neuroplasticity views the brain like a muscle: The more you exercise it, the more developed it becomes. This malleable view of intelligence is hopeful, because it promises that cognitive gains can be made through hard work and practice. Combine this with Tough's view that noncognitive skills like character and social skills can be taught to children, and the deterministic view that IQ tests alone can predict success in life seems almost laughable.

In addition, the impact of social life on intelligence scores has been studied by numerous scholars. Flynn (2009) asserts that peer subculture, at least among Britons and U.S. Blacks, affects IQ test performance. By the teenage years, it is so potent an influence on IQ that it swamps family and school in its influence on what we measure. Even more reason to doubt the stability and invariance of IQ test scores is provided by data showing that there are 12- to 18-point increases in IQ when children are adopted from working-class into middle-class homes. Obviously this would not happen if intelligence were a characteristic expressed only through genes.

The bottom line is that IQ tests are thought to shape the lives of children in real and significant ways. Educators use them to make decisions that have long-lasting consequences for a child. Placement in a separate classroom or school, and the development of individualized educational plans are just two examples of how IQ tests can change the course of child's life. Educators who view this cognitive assessment tool as a crystal ball that can see into a child's future are doing a dangerous disservice to children and their families. No test can measure the full and unique abilities of a child, let alone a test that reduces the complexity of the human mind and personality to a single number. Nor can these tests predict the future. Educators need to exercise caution when using these tests, consider the whole child when making instructional decisions, and maintain the belief that all children can learn to their own unique and undetermined potentials.

References

Deke, J., & Haimson, J. (2006, September). *Expanding beyond academics: Who benefits and how?* (Issue Brief No. 2). Princeton, NJ: Mathematica Policy Research. Retrieved from tinyurl.com/nnq7nhy

Duckworth, A. L., Quinn, P. D., Lynam, D. R., Loeber, R., & Stouthamer-Loeber, M. (2011). Role of test motivation in intelligence testing. *Proceedings of the National Academy of Sciences, 108*(19), 7716–7720.

Flynn, J. R. (2009). *What is intelligence: Beyond the Flynn effect.* Cambridge, United Kingdom: Cambridge University Press.

Gardner, H. (1983). *Frames of mind: The theory of multiple intelligences.* New York, NY: Basic Books.

Herrnstein, R. J., & Murray, C. (1994). *The bell curve: Intelligence and class structure in American life.* New York, NY: Free Press.

Kaplan, R. M., & Saccuzzo, D. P. (2009). *Psychological testing: Principles, applications, and issues.* Belmont, CA: Wadsworth Cengage Learning.

Lleras, C. (2008). Do skills and behaviors in high school matter? The contribution of noncognitive factors in explaining differences in educational attainment and earnings. *Social Science Research, 37,* 888–902.

Neisser, U., Boodoo, G., Bouchard, T. J., Boykin, A. W., Brody, N., Ceci, S. J., . . . Urbina, S. (1996). Intelligence: Knowns and unknowns. *American Psychologist, 51*(2), 77–101.

Nisbett, R. E., Aronson, J., Blair, C., Dickens, W., Flynn, J., Halpern, D. F., & Turkheimer, E. (2012, January 2). Intelligence: New findings and theoretical developments. *American Psychologist.* Advance online publication. doi: 10.1037/a0026699

Sternberg, R. J. (1985). *Beyond IQ: A triarchic theory of human intelligence.* New York, NY: Cambridge University Press.

Tough, P. (2012). *How children succeed: Grit, curiosity, and the hidden power of character.* New York, NY: Houghton Mifflin Harcourt.

◢ MYTH 50 ◣

The schools are wasting their time trying to teach problem solving, creativity, and general thinking skills; they would be better off teaching the facts students need to succeed in school and later in life.

Much like the other ongoing debates about public education and teaching, the myth that problem solving and creativity are not teachable skills has been debunked repeatedly (e.g., Johnson & Johnson, 2009; Sternberg & Williams, 1996). Teaching problem solving and creativity is indeed possible, particularly when the teacher is an engaged teacher who uses culturally relevant pedagogical practices. But the issue lies not in whether it is possible, but in whether the teaching of these skills is disappearing. They probably were never emphasized much, but given the current education system with its ever-increasingly test-based accountability systems, classrooms are becoming more controlled. Thus, environments in which problem solving and creativity are likely to be promoted are less evident (Berliner, 2012). And of course, even when classes engage in activities that promote creativity and problem solving, assessing such higher order thinking remains a difficult enterprise, particularly with our current forms of standardized tests. Yet as the nation continues to push forward in its demand for accountability and high standards, as well as for greater creativity and problem-solving ability by our students, standardized tests are likely to remain the yardstick by which the achievement of our educational goals will be measured. This is not easily done.

It should come as no surprise that when teachers focus on multiple ways of knowing and celebrate the wealth of knowledge their students bring to the classroom, collaborative environments spring up. In these environments, students and teachers participate in meaningful conversations about a variety of topics, including issues that are often of direct concern to their local community. It is just this kind of meaningful conversation and dialogue that remain a necessary component in teaching creativity and problem solving. It is through conversation, not didactic instruction, that students are able to articulate what they know and how they know it, while incorporating the knowledge of their peers and their teacher to further their own understanding.

We now know that students are equipped with the ability to problem solve and think creatively well before they ever enter a classroom. Children are inherently inquisitive beings, eager to learn about the world around them, and they demonstrate creativity and problem-solving skills quite early on in life. As toddlers find creative ways to access out-of-reach, yet highly desired, items or determine the most effective way to get their caregiver's attention, they are demonstrating both creativity and problem solving. Furthermore, the activities children participate in at home, whether seemingly mundane household chores or conversations with caregivers about the world around them, all serve to build children's creative capacity and their ability to solve problems that are of immediate and direct concern. As children encounter problems in their daily lives, they determine useful and appropriate ways to solve these problems through both hands-on learning and meaningful conversations with the adults in their lives.

Unfortunately, what happens in too many classrooms actually can serve to quell the development of creativity and problem-solving skills. Schools too often assume that learning must be incentivized, and issue rewards and punishments to this end. Rather than being motivated by curiosity or the need to address a real problem, students are motivated to perform, either by avoiding sanctions or garnering positive reinforcement from their teachers. School then becomes not a place where creativity can flourish, but a place where creativity is extinguished.

Some hold that education should be the inculcation of "facts." This may stem from an ideology that is threatened by the prospect of generations of young people who can think for themselves. It is a world-view that produces long lists of cherished "knowledges" for every child to acquire. The asserted goal of the recently developed Common Core State Standards (CCSS) is to teach "in depth," to teach students to be "critical thinkers." But the CCSS have enormous lists of what children are to know and be able to do at all grades, along with high-stakes tests attached to the curriculum that flows from the standards. Because of these factors, the CCSS are not likely to accomplish this goal.

If education is about a book of facts, then the role of teachers becomes clearer: Just the facts, Ma'am. At the vanguard of the "core knowledge" movement are people like E. D. Hirsch and Allan Bloom, the latter being the author of the elitist and ultra-conservative *The Closing of the American Mind.* Hirsch founded the Core Knowledge Foundation in 1986 and published *Cultural Literacy: What Every American Needs to Know* in 1988, with support from the Exxon Foundation. The epiphany that shaped Hirsch's career came in the form of a lesson he was teaching to Black community college students in Virginia who, he realized, knew little about Lee's surrender to Grant at Appomattox. Hirsch sees himself as a rescuer of the poor and "underclass." The core knowledge model focuses on facts with right or wrong answers. That these facts are acceptable to conservative political positions is not incidental. The core knowledge movement took root during the Reagan administration and was championed by Reagan acolytes such as William Bennett and Chester Finn. An example of a Hirsch test question to measure a child's "cultural literacy" follows:

> The principal character in Arthur Miller's play *Death of a Salesman* is:
> (a) Willy Loman
> (b) Stanley Spencer
> (c) John Smith
> (d) Babbitt
> (e) Tom Joad

Although a "traveling salesman" is about as obscure to a modern teenager as a rotary dial telephone, the choice of this play as a part of American literary history is not troublesome. That is because Hirsch is right: In order to have a unified citizenry, this big, diverse, multi-everything country of ours needs to share some common historical and cultural knowledge. To have a commons requires sharing our common heritage with all our citizens. That is, in part, what a public education ought to provide. Whether classes should be tested on the name of the protagonist, rather than writing essays about why Willy took a pay cut and then was fired, or why Willy retreated into a fantasy world, is the larger issue associated with the curriculum decision to teach *Death of a Salesman*. Tests of memory or tests of reasoning, that is the larger question the United States must face, for what is tested always predicts what will be taught.

When the focus of teaching is on transmitting facts and on students' performance on standardized tests, conversation and dialogue too often are replaced with rote learning, recitation, and regurgitation. Creative, problem-solving endeavors are abandoned for formulaic instruction. Let's not discuss what is going on in Egypt today; let's memorize the names of a few Pharaohs. Teachers sacrifice lessons that address issues of genuine concern to the children in their classrooms in favor of preparation for high-stakes tests—tests that can determine the child's future in public education, the future of their school, and, more recently, the teacher's tenure in the profession. But teaching children facts that they can memorize and give back does little more than prepare them to be competent test-takers. Some of us want citizens who will question the content and source of their information, or even question why some knowledge is privileged in schools in the first place. This move away from critical thinking and problem solving is exacerbated for students who find themselves in a low-income or urban school district with limited funds, insufficient resources, and teachers who often are inadequately prepared. There what is called education often resembles test preparation.

The Bush administration, with the passing of No Child Left Behind, made standardized tests, and, of course, preparing for them, the hallmark of our nation's education system. And now, under the Obama administration, teachers' salaries and advancement are tied directly to student performance on these high-stakes tests, despite arguments from the majority of the research community that these methods are both unreliable and invalid (see Myth 11).

Teachers can learn techniques for promoting creativity, critical thinking, problem solving, and other higher order cognitive skills in classrooms, in addition to memory (Sternberg & Williams, 1996; Tharp & Gallimore, 1991). But encouraging and facilitating the learning of these skills is of no use unless teachers have the autonomy to create classroom environments that encourage exploration, dialogue, and conversation. Teachers need something in short supply today—license to be unsure where a lesson may go. They need permission to not worry about whether the conversation will directly improve test scores. And they need a class size that is reasonable in order for this kind of teaching and learning to take place, which in some districts is a barrier to teaching and learning these habits of mind.

References

Berliner, D. C. (2012). Narrowing curriculum, assessments, and conceptions of what it means to be smart in the U.S. schools: Creaticide by design. In D. Ambrose & R. J. Sternberg (Eds.), *How dogmatic beliefs harm creativity and higher-level thinking* (pp. 79–93). New York, NY: Routledge/Taylor & Francis.

Bloom, A. (2012). *The closing of the American mind: How higher education has failed democracy and impoverished the souls of today's students.* New York, NY: Simon & Schuster.

Hirsch, E. D. (1988). *Cultural literacy: What every American needs to know.* New York, NY: Vintage Books.

Johnson, D. W., & Johnson, R. T. (2009). Energizing learning: The instructional power of conflict. *Educational Researcher, 38*(1), 37–51.

Sternberg, R. J., & Williams, W. M. (1996). *How to develop student creativity.* Alexandria, VA: Association for Supervision and Curriculum Development.

Tharp, R., & Gallimore, R. (1991). *The instructional conversation: Teaching and learning in social activity.* Santa Cruz: University of California, Center for Research on Education, Diversity & Excellence.

Additional Sources

We purposely did not use many sources that could have been cited to bolster our arguments. We chose to cite just enough of the key pieces for a reader to have faith that the arguments we made had credibility. But there are a number of books that complement what has been written here and which deserve any discerning reader's attention. Some of these follow.

Berliner, D. C., & Biddle B. J. (1995).*The manufactured crisis: Myths, fraud, and the attack on America's public schools.* New York, NY: Addison-Wesley.

Carter, P. L., & Welner, K. G. (2013) (Eds.). *Closing the opportunity gap: What America must do to give every child an even chance.* New York, NY: Oxford University Press.

Cookson, P. W. Jr. (2013). *Class rules: Exposing inequality in American high schools.* New York, NY: Teachers College Press.

Darling-Hammond, L. (2013). *Getting teacher evaluation right: What really matters for effectiveness and improvement.* New York, NY: Teachers College Press.

Giroux, H. A. (2013). *America's education deficit and the war on youth: Reform beyond electoral politics.* New York, NY: Monthly Review Press.

Glass, G. V. (2008). *Fertilizers, pills, and magnetic strips: The fate of public education in America.* Charlotte, NC: Information Age Publishers.

Hargreaves, A., & Shirley, D. (2009) *The fourth way.* Thousand Oaks, CA: Corwin Press.

Horn, J., & Wilburn, D. (2013). *The mismeasure of education.* Charlotte, NC: Information Age Publishing.

Hursh, D. (2008). *High-stakes testing and the decline of teaching and learning: The real crisis in education.* Lanham, MD: Rowman & Littlefield.

Lubienski, C. A., & Lubienski, S. T. (2013). *The public school advantage: Why public schools outperform private schools.* Chicago, IL: University of Chicago Press.

Nichols, S. L., & Berliner, D. C. (2007). *Collateral damage: How high-stakes testing corrupts American education.* Cambridge, MA: Harvard Education Press.

Ravitch, D. (2010). *The death and life of the great American school system: How testing and choice are undermining education.* New York, NY: Basic Books.

Ravitch, D. (2013). *Reign of error: The hoax of the privatization movement and the danger to America's public schools.* New York, NY: Alfred A. Knopf.

Sahlberg, P. (2011). *Finnish lessons: What can the world learn from educational change in Finland?* New York: Teachers College Press.

Saltman, K., & Gabbard, D. A. (Eds.). *Education as enforcement: The militarization and corporatization of schools* (2nd ed.). New York, NY: Routledge.

Saltman, K. J. (2014). *The politics of education: A critical introduction.* Boulder, CO: Paradigm Publishers.

Timor, T. B., & Maxwell-Jolly, J. (Eds.). (2012). *Narrowing the achievement gap: Perspectives and strategies for challenging times.* Cambridge, MA: Harvard Education Press.

Welner, K. G. (2008). *Neovouchers: The emergence of tuition tax credits for private schooling.* Lanham, MD: Rowman & Littlefield.

Zhao, Y. (2009). *Catching up or leading the way: American education in the age of globalization.* Alexandria, VA: Association for Supervision and Curriculum Development.

Acknowledgments

Several persons and institutions have contributed to the writing of this work in ways not apparent, but that must be acknowledged.

Universities still provide an environment conducive to reflection and writing free from the heavy hand of ulterior motive. Ours do so: Arizona State University and the University of Colorado Boulder. The National Education Policy Center at the latter institution brings together scholars from around the country each September to discuss education policy and plan a series of publications addressed to the day's most pressing education issues. These discussions are most stimulating and we thank these scholars, whose names are too numerous to list here. Professor Kevin Welner and Emeritus Professor Alex Molnar deserve thanks for supporting and directing this annual meeting.

Jeanne M. Powers and Gustavo E. Fischman of the Mary Lou Fulton Teachers College identified the newly minted and soon-to-be-hooded PhD students from ASU who coauthored the present work. Michele S. Moses, Kenneth Howe, and Kevin Welner nominated the coauthors from the PhD program at University of Colorado Boulder.

About the Authors

David C. Berliner is an educational psychologist. He was professor and dean of the Mary Lou Fulton Teachers College at Arizona State University. Berliner received a PhD in educational psychology from Stanford University and was awarded the Doctorate of Humane Letters, Honoris Causa, from the University of Massachusetts, Amherst and from Manhattanville College, of Purchase, New York. Berliner has authored more than 200 articles, books, and chapters in the fields of educational psychology, teacher education, and educational policy, including the bestseller *The Manufactured Crisis*. He also coauthored *Putting Research to Work in Your School* with Ursula Casanova and *Collateral Damage: How High-Stakes Testing Corrupts American Education* with S. L. Nichols, and coedited the *Handbook of Educational Psychology*. Berliner is a past president of the American Educational Research Association (AERA) and of the Division of Educational Psychology of the American Psychological Association. Berliner is a Regents' Professor Emeritus of Education at Arizona State University. He is an elected member of the National Academy of Education and the International Academy of Education. He is winner of the E. L. Thorndike award in educational psychology, the distinguished contributions award of the AERA, the Friend of Education award of the NEA, and the Brock International Prize for distinguished contributions to education. David Berliner was the principal author for Myths 14, 16, 18, 24, 25, 29, 33, and 37.

Gene V Glass coined the term *meta-analysis* and illustrated its first use in his presidential address to AERA in San Francisco in April 1976. The most extensive illustration of the technique was in the literature on psychotherapy outcome studies, published in 1980 by Johns Hopkins University Press under the title *Benefits of Psychotherapy* by Mary Lee Smith, Gene V Glass, and Thomas I. Miller. He is a Regents' Professor Emeritus at Arizona State University in both the Educational Leadership and Policy Studies and the Psychology in Education divisions, having retired in 2010 from the Mary Lou Fulton Teachers College. Currently he is a senior researcher at the National Education Policy Center and a research professor in the School of Education at the University of Colorado Boulder. He is an elected member of the National Academy of Education. He is a recipient of the distinguished contributions award of the AERA. His personal website is at www.gvglass.info. Gene V Glass was the principal author for Myths 5, 8, 26, 39, 40, and 42.

Jesus Cisneros is a PhD student in the Education Policy and Evaluation program at Arizona State University. His background is in higher education administration, and his research focuses on campus climate surveys and the exclusion of systematically marginalized populations in higher education. Jesus Cisneros was the principal author for Myths 20 and 31.

Victor H. Diaz holds a PhD from Arizona State University and is currently director of design for Teach For America's Teacher Preparation, Support and Development team and an adjunct faculty member at Grand Canyon University. Over the past 10 years, he has taught 6th–12th grades as well as undergraduate and graduate courses in teacher education. His research focuses on using sociocultural theory to understand teacher education, critical pedagogy, and social justice education. Victor H. Diaz was the principal author for Myths 12 and 13.

Lenay Dunn is an educational researcher and evaluator. She has served as the Director of research and evaluation for a unit at Arizona State University, worked as a research analyst at the American Institutes for Research, served as a Teach For America teacher, and held leadership roles in various K–12 and higher educational programs. Dunn earned her PhD in the Educational Leadership and Policy Studies program at Arizona State University and her master of arts in Social Sciences in Education from Stanford University. Her interests include educational policy implementation, equity, educational opportunity, systemic reform, program evaluation, and research and evaluation methods. Lenay Dunn was the principal author for Myths 27 and 46.

Erica Nicole Griffin is a young scholar with a Black feminist research standpoint focusing on hyperghettoization, the U.S. dropout crisis, and adult education. Her most recent contribution to the literature was the "occupational shift," a mid-level theory explaining why Black American women drop out of high school and how leaving school without a diploma affects them over the course of their life. In 2012, Griffin started the Griffin Research Group, an effort in urban activist research. Current projects use the personal stories of Black Atlantans, from the retirees who constitute the Cascade Breakfast Club, to inmates in a downtown jail, to better understand race, politics, and the economics of urban education. Erica Nicole Griffin was the principal author for Myths 23 and 28.

Jarrod Hanson is a PhD candidate in Education Foundations, Policy and Practice at the University of Colorado Boulder and has a JD from the University of Chicago Law School. His research interests include civic education, deliberative democracy, and the role of education in citizenship formation. Jarrod Hanson was the principal author for Myths 9 and 19.

Melinda Hollis Thomas is in her 3rd year of PhD studies at Arizona State University. After a decade of teaching literature and composition in secondary and postsecondary schools, she now spends much of her time wandering the labyrinth of curriculum studies, exploring epistemologies of literacy, historical archives, and educational policies and practices. Her scholastic passions include working with preservice teachers, serving as executive editor of *Current Issues in Education*, and collaborating with interdisciplinary colleagues to cultivate the seeds for a Humanities Behind Walls project within the Arizona prison system. She has a bachelor's degree in English Education from the University of Georgia and a master's degree in English from the University of North Carolina, Wilmington. Melinda Hollis Thomas was principal author for Myths 6, 24, and 41.

Jessica Holloway-Libell is a PhD student in the Education Policy and Evaluation program at Arizona State University. She has 10 years' experience in the field of education, both in practice and in research. She earned her bachelor's degree in English Education from Florida State University and her master of education degree in Educational Leadership and Supervision from Arizona State University. She currently teaches Structured English Immersion courses for preservice teachers. Her research interests are in education policies involving teacher evaluation and value-added assessment models. Jessica Holloway-Libell was principal author for Myths 11 and 15.

Jamie Patrice Joanou is assistant professor of Qualitative Research Methods in the School of Education at Westminster College. She has a PhD in Educational Leadership and Policy Studies and an MA in the Social and Philosophical Foundations of Education, both from Arizona State University. Dr. Joanou's research focuses on adolescents in context, with particular emphasis on the relationship between space and identity development among marginalized youth. Her areas of specialization include qualitative research methods, the social foundations of education, multicultural education, and children living on the street in Latin America. Jamie Patrice Joanou was the principal author for Myths 17, 20, and 50.

Rucheeta Kulkarni is an adjunct faculty member and researcher in the School of Leadership and Educational Sciences at the University of San Diego. She earned her PhD in Educational Leadership and Policy Studies at Arizona State University. Her research interests include school choice, school finance, heritage language education, and multicultural education. Dr. Kulkarni's dissertation, which examined the experiences of low-income youth of color attending college-preparatory charter schools, was awarded the 2010 Dissertation Award by the Council on Anthropology and Education. Rucheeta Kulkarni was principal author of Myths 7, 35, and 36.

Rebecca Lish is a PhD student in the Education Policy and Evaluation program at Arizona State University. She holds an MEd in Educational Leadership and Policy from the University of Utah and a BA in Communication from Southern Utah University. Her research focuses on how higher education is portrayed in the media, the history of higher education, higher education policy, and the experiences of under-represented students in higher education. She is currently an academic advisor and has held positions in residence life, admissions, and student programming. Rebecca Lish was the principal author of Myth 45.

Bonnie Streff Mazza is a teacher, artist, and PhD student in the Educational Leadership and Policy program at Arizona State University. Over the past 7 years, she has taught HIV/AIDS education in rural Tanzania, 5th–8th grade in inner-city Atlanta and Phoenix, and undergraduate courses in teacher education. She has worked as a researcher for ASU's Sanford Inspire Program and as a section editor for *Current Issues in Education*. She holds a bachelor's degree in Psychology with minors in Spanish and Studio Art from the University of Arizona and a master's degree in Elementary Education from ASU. She lives in Phoenix with her husband, Danny. Bonnie Streff Mazza was the principal author of Myths 22 and 49.

David E. Meens is from Colorado's Western Slope, the son of school teachers. He holds master's degrees in Educational Psychology and Philosophy, and is currently working toward his PhD in Education Foundations, Policy, and Practice at the University of Colorado Boulder. He teaches in CU's Community Studies Program, and he has received several awards for his scholarship, teaching, and service, including the Stahl Prize in Ethics for developing service experiences throughout the U.S. Rocky Mountain West and his action research in Mexico. His current research focuses on democracy and education reforms, education for ecological citizenship, and methodological issues in philosophy and the social sciences. David E. Meens was principal author of Myths 30, 32, and 38.

Noelle A. Paufler received her MS in Education (Curriculum and Instruction) from Concordia University and BA (History and Political Science) from the University of Wisconsin–Milwaukee. She is a doctoral student studying Educational Policy and Evaluation in the Mary Lou Fulton Teachers College at Arizona State University. In addition, she conducts research and provides technical support for *Inside the Academy*, an online educational historiography created to honor distinguished educational researchers and scholars. Her research interests include the communication of research and educational policy, specifically the impact of value-added measures and systems on practitioners. Noelle A. Paufler was the principal author of Myths 2, 10, and 44.

Ryan Pfleger is broadly interested in using social scientific and philosophical lenses to shed light on inequities connected to education. His current inquiries focus on the economic contexts, both material and ideological, that influence educational and social inequity. Before returning to school, he unloaded tractor-trailers full of production gear for rock concerts, mixed audio for live television shows, and produced a documentary film. He is currently a PhD student in the School of Education, University of Colorado Boulder. Ryan Pfleger was principal author of Myths 43 and 48.

Jennifer D. Shea has more than 14 years of professional experience in postsecondary education, having held positions in student and academic affairs at the University of Alaska Fairbanks, Syracuse University, the University of Hartford, and Arizona State University. Her dissertation research, which resulted in a PhD in Educational Leadership and Policy Studies from the Mary Lou Fulton Teachers College at Arizona State University, examined the persistence of first-generation college students enrolled in online degree programs at a public university. She is engaged in research focusing on postsecondary education, educational equity, online education, qualitative methods, and comparative education. Jennifer D. Shay was the principal author of Myth 1.

Monica L. Stigler is a PhD student at Arizona State University. She is an accomplished public sector professional and has served as a neighborhood program coordinator, nonprofit development director, and policy analyst. Her research interests include democratic participation, community development, adult education, and policy studies. She is also interested in the changing relationship between schools, community, and the state. She has researched and published on charter schools, choice, and agency, and continues to study the potential for charter schools to be sites for progressive education and social change. Monica L. Stigler was principal author of Myth 3.

Sylvia Symonds is a PhD student in the Education Policy and Evaluation program at Arizona State University. She has more than 10 years' experience working in various leadership roles in educational outreach and student services, and is currently the director of a federal TRIO Student Support Services program at Arizona State University Downtown. Her research interests include college access, retention, and creating scalable student success programs for underserved students in higher education. Sylvia Symonds was the principal author of Myths 21 and 47.

Amelia Marcetti Topper is a teacher, researcher, and doctoral candidate in Arizona State University's Educational Policy and Evaluation program. Her work focuses on researching policies and practices that help individuals successfully navigate and complete higher education. She has published on a wide range of topics: low-income student outcomes, for-profit education, school choice, and English language learners. She is also a managing editor of *Education Policy Analysis Archives* (epaa. asu.edu), an open-access, peer-reviewed journal. She holds a bachelor's degree in Philosophy and the History of Math and Science from St. John's College and a master's degree in Teaching from the College of Notre Dame. Amelia Marcetti Topper was the principal author of Myth 4.

Kathryn Wiley is a PhD student at the University of Colorado Boulder, where she studies school discipline and teacher cultural competency. She is originally from Dayton, Ohio, where she completed her undergraduate degree in Psychology at Wright State University. She most recently coauthored a chapter entitled "Educational Opportunities in a Post-Desegregation District" in Gary Orfield and Erika Frankenberg's book *Stable Diversity or Resegregation in America's Suburbs* (Harvard Education Press, 2013). Kathryn Wiley was the principal author of Myth 34.

Index